Letters from
Marion

Copyright © 2015 by Joel Blaeser

Published by Big House Publishing Company Milwaukee, WI.

All rights reserved. No part of this publication may be reproduced, stored in a retrieval system, or transmitted, in any form or by any means, electronic, mechanical, photocopying, recording, or otherwise, without the prior written permission of the author.

ISBN 978-0-9864054-0-2

LCCN: 2015907522

1. United States Penitentiary Marion (Marion Illinois.)

2. Blaeser, Joel

3. War On Drugs prisoners - Federal prisoners.

4. Political uprising - Crack Law Riots

5. Solitary confinement Marion Illinois.

Original outline - Hiliary Martin & Joel Blaeser, created in 2005-2006.

Cover design - Dianne Murphy

Special consultant: Susan Dobra

Author website: joelblaeser.com

BIG HOUSE PUBLISHING
bighousepublishingco@gmail.com
917-743-6243

Printed in the United States of America

Letters from Marion

JOEL BLAESER

———

BIG HOUSE PUBLISHING COMPANY

Table of Contents

Copyright	*ii*
Preface	*v*
Chapter 1: Language of the Unheard - October 1995	1
Chapter 2: Con Air	19
Chapter 3: Guardian Angel - October 1995	28
Chapter 4: The Good Life - Summer 2005	38
Chapter 5: Not So Innocent	47
Chapter 6: Playing in the Sandbox - September 1992	59
Chapter 7: Dead Ahead	82
Chapter 8: The Green Duffel Bag - Autumn 1994	102
Chapter 9: Joy Riding	123
Chapter 10: Convict Code	140
Chapter 11: All in on a Draw	158
Chapter 12: He's Gone	178
Chapter 13: Poker and the Pop in the Housing Bubble	187
Chapter 14: Black Box	206
Chapter 15: Acceptance - November 1990	214
Chapter 16: Crime School and the Single Cell Organism - October 1995	238
Author Statement:	276

IN THE BEGINNING

THE IMPETUS FOR WRITING this book was the extreme nature of the Federal crack law riots on October 18th/19th 1995 in which 13 federal prisons near simultaneously rioted over the federal crack law not being changed and the wicked nature of the federal drug laws themselves. I witnessed and was a part of the federal prison riot in Talladega Alabama (the first one to riot), which was spurred by changes in these seemingly racial drug law interpretations.

This book is the eyewitness account of my day-to-day life, both inside and outside federal prison. I traveled the world with the Grateful Dead selling LSD, seeing them 101 times spanning 5 different countries from 1984 through 1992. In 1992 at 23 years of age I was sentenced for Federal LSD violations as a first time non-violent offender to 151 months of incarceration after losing my federal jury trial. Each chapter of this book opens with letter(s) written to a family member, most of which I wrote to my mother, Rosemary, or brother, Bradley, during my stay at United States Penitentiary Marion, (October 1995 arrival). USP Marion was the last and longest stop of the six federal prisons I did time at during my only ever incarceration. I was housed among wick-edly sophisticated and predacious criminals such as John Gotti, Bruce Pierce, James "Doc" Holliday, Big Mac-Michael McElhiney...

Each original letter and most of the accompanying envelopes are photocopied into this book. My family saved all of the letters and most of the envelopes that I sent them from prison. only a handful appears in the following pages.

I went to prison as a smooth-skinned, non-violent Grateful Dead following first-time offender. My crime had been consensual-victimless- as opposed to a non-consensual crime like murder, rape or armed robbery. Yet, I ended up in Marion. A man in a lower security prison could stab a prison guard and not get sent to Marion. A man could commit diabolical bank robberies or murder and not get sent to Marion. Those who ended up in Marion were to be feared and respected. It was designed for the worst of the worst.

Marion opened in 1962 as the highest-level U.S.P. ever built within the U.S. Federal Prison System (level 5.5). When Alcatraz closed at the end of 1962, all of Alcatraz's worst convicts were sent to Marion.

Built into a valley, USP Marion is a completely self-contained prison, fenced in by three walls of Constantine razor wire. Movement on the yard was heavily controlled and es-cape near impossible given the six gun towers that were manned twenty-four hours a day, plus a roving truck patrol that circled the prison on a special track. Adjacent to the prison was a picturesque mini subdivision of ranch style homes, which housed some of the prison staff.

Marion consisted of eight units, A through H, and the cells were designed to hold only one prisoner each. The first six units were reserved for "general population." G-Unit was for mentally disturbed criminals or those in protective custody. Finally, H-Unit— the first of its kind—was an ultra maximum-security unit deep within the penitentiary itself. Prisoners in H-Unit were only allowed out of their cells for one hour per day. Food was brought to them via cart and tray. In order to leave their cell, they first had to be handcuffed behind the back and then shackled at the ankles with leg irons connected by a short chain. This protocol was to be followed every time, even if they were leaving their cell for a shower or recreation. Furthermore H-Unit prisoners were mandated to be accompanied by two to three guards when out of their cell.

On October 22, 1983, the face of Marion changed forever and for the worse. On that fateful day, two prison guards were simultaneously murdered in two separate incidents on either side of H-Unit. Merle E. Clutts and Robert Hoffman were killed at the hands of a member and associate of the Aryan Brotherhood, Thomas Silverstein and Clayton Fountain. Allegedly both guards were known for routinely abusing and taunting convicts on the H-Unit Prison Range.

As the court records show, Silverstein broke away from the guards after a shower while still shackled and handcuffed, then stuck his hands through the slot of a fellow pris-oner's barred cell door. His comrade who had a homemade handcuff key quickly removed Silverstein's handcuffs and handed him a sharp homemade knife, or "shank." Silverstein went right for Clutts and repeatedly stabbed him to death. At almost the exact same time, far away on the other side of H-Unit, in similar form and fashion,

IN THE BEGINNING

Clayton Fountain a associate of the Aryan Brotherhood administered the very same fate to prison guard Hoffman.

This was not Silverstein's first in-prison murder. Eighteen months prior to this incident, Silverstein had taken the life of Cadillac Smith in the same manner in the very same unit. Smith was the head of the D.C. Blacks, a prison gang that started in Washington D.C. and spread throughout the country's prisons. Silverstein was given a life sentence for the murder of Smith.

Shortly after the two murders in H-Unit, the entire prison became designated a federal super-maximum lockdown penitentiary, (level 6) the first ever in the United States. At that point, each prisoner, not just those in H-Unit was put on twenty-three hour lock down status and allowed only two fifteen-minute phone calls per month, there were many other extreme restrictions. It now became known as the "Marion Model" and all other state or private supermax prisons would be based on this design. USP Marion stayed this way for the next 23 years.

In the ensuing lockdown, all of the prisoners were brutally beaten by staff in retaliation for the two murdered guards. President Reagan even issued awards to Marion prison staff for reestablishing control and locking the prison down. Marion's notorious reputation only grew larger and more ominous.

In 2006, twenty-three years after becoming the nation's first true Supermax, U.S.P. Marion was redesignated a medium security prison and "normal" yard movement was established. Florence Colorado's ADX became the new federal supermax though it is astoundingly safer than Marion due to the fact that inmates are not ever mixed with one another as all convicts have their very own separated recreation yards.

Ninety percent of this book is my experiences in federal prison as a first time non violent offender, the other ten percent is the rest of my life, childhood, family, after release, subjects like prison, poker, politics and the pop in the housing bubble as it relates to my journey. Also chronicled are the 101 Grateful Dead shows I saw spanning 5 countries.

THIS IS A TRUE STORY, THE EVENTS PORTRAYED ARE BASED ON MY EYEWITNESS TESTIMONY AND OFFICIAL COURT RECORDS, MOST OF THE NAMES HAVE NOT BEEN CHANGED.

Hilary Martin of Boulder Colorado was very instrumental with helping me come up with the entire outline for "LETTERS FROM MARION" and without her brilliance this book may have never come about, THANK YOU HILARY.

Letters from Marion

"There is no easy walk to freedom anywhere, and many of us will have to pass through the valley of the shadow of death again and again before we reach the mountaintop of our desires"
—Nelson Mandela

                Peace and Love
                joel blaeser

Joel Blaeser

Dear Rose   3/20/97

Hello, this may be a few days late as I waited 2 days to write it. I am getting tired of writing letters to everyone, its the same thing, same cell, same prison same changing of seasons, same everything. The stock market is up to 7000. Since I came to prison it has broke the 4, 5, 6 and 7000 mark. Maybe I will be out for 8,000. I finished Trouble Maker by Harry Wu about 6 or 8 weeks ago. Brad sent it to me for Christmas or Birthday. He spent 19 years in Chinese forced work camps. In his book he expresses how great a country it is we live in because we can rent a car or travel whenever we want or have any electronic appliance. What he failed to express in his book is that because this country has such a high demand for this type of living, that the balance of that is made up in prison camps in China and exploitation of other 3rd world economies. So you cannot have one without the other. So while he is in this country praising and living the good life all while criticizing his own country he is part of problem - simply because of his failed awareness of the situation and only to deal with the symptoms of the problem and not the cause. I liked the book at the end he was on the verge of exposing and directly linking the world bank to ~~the~~ some very big prison camps in china and that is when his name came to the international scene because he got caught. And he got caught because his assumptions about the world bank we're correct. The Yin Yang symbol comes to mind (which is from his country) which is the balance of opposites which applies to this whole democratic capitilist way. In order for Americans and other westerners to live the way that we do - other 3rd world economies, china and whoever need to be exploited. Its all part of the balance of this system under which we live. It was a decent book and I am glad I read it. There are never enough books around here. Have you read any good books lately? Why don't you wait to get a second job for as long as you can, if there is a favorable outcome with the appeal then there should be no need for you to get a second job. whether I get out this summer or in 4 years I have a plan of attack for my business. I want to start a operation in this country first somewhere in the west and that will be my stepping stone to Australia, then argentina, costa rica and then maybe china. I am going to try to get a firm hold in this country in 18-24 months then I plan to live in a foreign country somewhere. However I will travel to this country and others on a regular basis to check up on operations. Presently I know exactly what it is I want to do however I do not wish to discuss so other people can read it. Maybe you or larry could visit. If all goes well we can see each other as much as we want this summer,

3

If you want feel free to visit. To bring Larry all you have to do is call and arrange a special visit. Ask to talk to Mr Adlesburger — my unit manager or Bill Hedrick if Adlesburger is not here. Its a matter of formality. To put Larry or any other person on my visiting list would take many weeks and possibly months. Before I forget can you send me a picture of you taken within the last couple of years — one where you are all dressed up without glasses and with make up on. I want to compare it with the enhanced photo you sent me from playboy. Maybe one of you + dad at Jimmy's or something. Send it soon. Maybe one of you and Larry — no matter — No glasses though. When you visited the last time you looked just like you did in that playboy picture. Well enjoy yourself in that big city

Peace
Joel

Joel Blaeser
03491-089
U.S. PENITENTIARY
P.O. BOX 1000
MARION, IL 62959

Rosemary Blaeser
1730 N Clark #402
Chicago IL 62959

Dear Mom   12-31-96

   I just received your letter with the 50$ and the confirmation of the 2 book orders. Sometimes I think you could do more or should do more and I lash out frustration at you. You do not have to work on your worm ship. You have done more for me than anyone and everyone else combined. From the day I was conceived until now. It seems that some is never enough. There's a balance that every one needs to strike with themselves, others, Good/Bad etc etc. I apologize for saying that to you, And under stand that it not only comes from frustration but also the urgency of the situation and thus something that may or may not motivate you to do more.

   I finished that book by David Yallop - about Carlos The Jackal. It's a very long book and goes deeply into the Middle East history Israel, Palestine, Yasar Arafat, Quadaffi. It is a book that was 10 years in the making. It's main focus is all the disinformation used to propagate Carlos The Jackal and other figures and hence create artificial situations and War. It was one of the books you ordered for me from Strand. The second one on high pressure Alchemy is good but on a whole different level. - scientific discovery

2

is interesting to read about. This particular book concentrates on the synthetic diamond industry. Back in 1955 is the first time diamond was synthetically produced. Diamond has much more industrial uses and applications compared to the retail commercial market. Synthetic diamond properties are slightly better than organic ones making them more useable industrially. I am almost done with that book. The third book and final one of those 3 is a brief synapses about Jewish mysticism. That one was not quite what I thought it was but I am going to check it out anyway. Sometimes from the description in the catalog you can get the wrong notion of exactly where the book is going to go. If you would like to read any of these let me know. I was thinking you might like the first one I described about the Middle East + Carlos the Jackal.

Have you read any good books lately? You know our brains are muscles and need to be excercised daily. Reading/Learning is one of the best ways to keep everything sharp. "People don't grow old, when they stop taking care of themselves they become old." As someone famous has said before. Physically you do alot and from your letters it looks as though you still are sharp. It's always a good idea to stay on the top of it.

So larry doesn't even like to window shop? Sometimes theres more joy in anticipation of something than the actual experience. Window shoping sounds like alot of fun. I sit here many nights and question your relationship with him. My main problem is he cannot even pick you up from work. If you did have a car would you drive. Could you drive — In those busy rush hours. I suspect as I have said before that maybe its a relationship that is part Financial necessity, and therefore that it why you put up with that. I dont know maybe you guys are friends, then again wouldn't a friend feel the need (out of safety) to pick you up from work. Safety, courteous and to be plain nice. The comrades down in Peru have got World attention now that they have control of that diplomatic house with all those hostages Alot of rich Japanese business executives. The day after the Guerillas took control of the ccoumpound the Japenese stock market dropped 500 points. However The news broadcasters had a reason for the drop that I question, The drop sure seems to corralate to the hostage situation. For some reason though the news did not broadcast it that way, A clear indication of how the "Masses" are controlled and manipulated by the media. I often wonder what would happen if people (the "Masses") snapped out of their stupor and took control of their life and destiny the way nature designed it to be in the first place. This disinformation is part of the design, the design of balancing good/Bad opposites and dualities. The snapping out of the stupor comes from transcending the dualities + opposites and living with wholeness in wholeness. No struggle no

4

No fear, No Evil, No Good, No bad. The struggle and Reactions keep breeding the same cycle—And thus that is where the control is. Our free will allows us to break the cycle, And that is what is so ruthlessly controlled by all the bullshit out in the world (You all live in the Desire, Fear, Anger, good, Bad. Pay your taxes, or go to Jail, go to confession or go to hell, Be good or Santa will bring you coal etc etc. For whatever reason it came about may not matter, presently these and many other indoctrinations are being thrust upon you and everyone else out there, most of the time you are not aware of it. The effects manifest themselves in peoples every move. With as many medical uses as have been found for most psychedelics, the main reason these wretched Masonic pigs in the high government echelons dont like them and thus outlawed most of them in 1966 is because there power to let one become aware of ones enlightment which usually means radical social change. I never met a person who did psychedelics in a abusive way. Almost Everyone I met over did the Alcahol, caffine, nicotine and pot. So what does this mean—stay informed, more importantly though become aware of what you're not aware of and live with absolutely no fear, be loved, and have order, Balance, Evolution + Intelligence. No matter what never live in fear of anything never.

Well I am still waiting to hear from Brad hopefully we can get this going soon (Appeal). How is your job going? Is there any room for advancement where you are at!? Do you have any ~~entreprenour~~ entrepreneurial ideas, why not try one. Your in the stage of your life where its a good idea to start becoming self reliant. Some sort of business venture might be just the thing. Hemp stores are realy starting to take off. I get this Hemp Journal and I have been sending them to brad when I'm done with them. I'll send you the next one I get. Have you every seen that thing on TV — topsy turvy or something like that. It's a piece of plastic with a loop on the end, women use it to put different or pull there hair back in different ways. I read the article about the lady who invented it. She was in a movie theatre and was trying to figure out how this other lady at the theatre pulled here hair back the way she did. She went home, brainstormed and came up with what look's like a flexible toothbrush with a hard plastic loop at the end. That was 1992. The article did not say how much she profited, but she is a multi ~~millionare~~ millonare. What do you have to lose — go for it. Do you have any ideas you would like to discuss, I would be glad to help in any way I can. Well I am going to go. — What's up with your cold, Did you go to the hospital? What did they say? The playboy picture will be coming to you shortly. Peace and love

Joel

1

Language of the Unheard

OCTOBER 1995

THE DAY TALLADEGA BURNED started like any other day spent inside a Federal Correctional Institution (FCI). The buzzers hummed like an electric foghorn every sixty minutes, signaling to the inmates it was time to rotate. Just part of the daily routine for inmates in federal prison, occurring once every hour from 7 am until final count and lockdown at 10:00 pm.

It's similar to class periods back in high school. Inmates know where they are supposed to be, and just like a high schooler, they better damn well have a hall pass, because in a level 4 medium security federal prison, the guards perched in their gun towers are all cracker jack marksmen, can and will shoot you dead if you are wandering through the prison grounds without clearance.

It was 6:30 pm, and my unit was the last to eat dinner. I rose from the table with a stretched and full stomach. Food in prison isn't exactly gourmet, but there is plenty of it: all you can eat vegetables, rice, beans, potatoes, legumes, juice, milk, and one portion of meat per meal. Federal prison administrators were wise to allow prisoners back to the chow line for unlimited portions of all the sides, after all a hungry convict is a angrier convict. Each federal prison also has a commissary, or prison store, which offers food items and prisoners are allowed to shop there twice a month.

As I made my way out of the chow hall, I took the hard, dark blue colored plastic cafeteria tray to the dishwashers. My tray was licked clean so no need to empty it in the large trash bin before I put it on the conveyor belt leading into the steamy hot dish room. Like most systems in prison, the dish room and kitchen were operated by convicts. Paid nearly $35 a month, dishwashers earned a relatively generous wage compared to their fellow inmates.

I made my way through the chow hall and walked outside onto the compound. The sun blazed through the barbed wire fences surrounding the prison. Though it was mid-October 1995, it felt like a warm summer day.

Akin to most medium security federal prisons, FCI Talladega is built on over fifty acres of land dotted with various structures. Six housing units hold about 160 prisoners each, contained within fifty to sixty cells and common area. Scattered over the rolling southern landscape is a chapel, lieutenant's office, art center, the Hole (a jail within the prison), indoor recreation center, weight pile, chow hall, law library, and barber's office. All of the buildings are connected by a series of sidewalks, between which are perfectly manicured lawns and shrubs, creating an oddly suburban effect. A federal prison compound is a mini-city with 1,000 to 4,000 residents.

I stood 75 yards from the chow hall door at the junction where the sidewalks converge from the rec yard and other housing units when I was suddenly overcome with indecisiveness as to what direction to take. I remained motionless for nearly two minutes while trying to decide where to go and what to do, a long time considering you had only six minutes to move during rotation.

A calm hung over the prison. It wasn't right.

Two prisoners walked by silently on their way to the law library.

I then remembered making quasi-plans to meet up with my workout buddy, Dean, out on the yard. Dean was a pile of blonde hair stacked on a hardened and tattooed six foot one frame. He had a 20-year sentence, and a physique to match. Not only was he an ideal spotter but he also guaranteed no one would drop a dumbbell on my head during a lift. It happened on occasion. You can't be too careful in prison. After all this was my fifth federal prison that I lived in since losing my federal jury trial. As a recent transfer to Talladega, compounded with over one month spent in the Hole after a conflict with the prison lieutenant over my beloved green duffel bag, I was still learning the social dynamics of this particular prison yard.

I could see my housing unit and the chow hall from where I stood, but the yard was up over the hill and not in my line of direct sight. I had already done my regular 2:00 pm workout and decided to meet Dean out on the yard during the next move. I headed back to my quarters.

As I turned, out of the corner of my eye I could see conspicuous changes on nearby buildings. Extra bars had been welded over the glass windows on the chow hall, as well as on the entry door and window to the prison commissary. New solid steel doors had been put up on the front of the lieutenant's office that hadn't been there when I'd arrived.

I continued down the path toward my cellblock, intending to pass the time on my bunk. Having arrived in Talladega fifty-one days earlier from FCI Pekin, Illinois, I had not yet been assigned a cell due to slight overcrowding in the federal prison system. I was assigned a bunk in a common area in the cellblock, and my belongings were kept in a large steel locker at the foot of the bed. prisoners in my situation often waited six to twenty weeks for a cell.

I pulled open the heavy steel door to my cellblock and I stepped into a tremendous and raging battleground. To my right, convicts wildly smashed fire extinguishers into staff office windows, and to my left enraged men were ripping water pipes out of the laundry room while other inmates pulled exposed pipes down from the ceiling. Anything that was not welded down was ripped away from its mount. Even the vending machines in the unit were broken open and completely emptied out.

Prisoners screamed , swinging painted steel pipes and bars at doors, chairs, and windows, anything they could, taking years of frustration out on the cold prison. The din was deafening.

I stood watching. No one took notice of me. It was like I wasn't even there.

I was unaware of the violent racially inspired conflicts erupting elsewhere throughout the compound or other Federal prisons rioting as well, or that somewhere, a building was burning. However, I began to catch a faint smell of fire in the air.

To my left, two behemoth tattooed black prisoners cracked a large weight bar with heavy plates on it from the rec yard into the case manager's office. Bang. Bang. Bang. Every housing unit has a case manager whose office houses the records of every prisoner on the cellblock. Each record, or "jacket", contains original copies of court records, police transcripts, and further evidence of one's criminal history, in addition to highly subjective, and often false notes regarding the prisoner's behavior and activity while in prison. Like a bad shadow these jackets follow each prisoner around, throughout prison and out into the free world after.

I saw TJ trying to break the case managers door open. I had met him by happenstance a few days prior while watching TV in my unit. He was a soft-spoken African American with arms the size of my legs.

"TJ!" I exclaimed. "Is the door coming loose? Let me get in there!" Adrenaline flowing through my veins, I stepped over to assist.

"We've been at it for five straight minutes. Might take a while," he replied.

We were taking shifts, six hands on the bar all moving left to right in sync, crashing the weight bar into the door, over and over. It swung back and forth, one end of the steel bar hitting the door so hard sparks were flying. The brown steel door became more and more dented. I could smell ozone, and the scent of whatever was burning grew stronger. All of a sudden the fire alarms went off, adding to the melee of noise and chaos. Despite the best efforts of our maniacal pounding, we could not break the door down.

"The vending machine!" TJ yelled.

We moved on, hands aching to break something. At the end of the hall was an overlooked vending machine. We smashed the glass outward by breaking open the sides. Glass and candy flew all over like a mechanical piñata. I could hear the washers and dryers being ripped out of the wall in the laundry room behind me. There was not a prison guard to be seen anywhere. The entire prison was out-of-control. We would later learn that in other units prisoners had lit stacks of six or seven mattresses on fire. In the previously empty recreation yard madness reigned. Blood spattered as pipes cracked skulls in the ensuing racial rifts. The snitches and few remaining guards were beaten or raped.

I could see a division taking place in our unit. The housing units in Talladega are shaped in a triangle with two levels, stairs at each corner, and a common area in the center of the triangle, open to 18-foot ceilings. Cell doors ran along the edges of the triangle two tiers high, each tier or walkway about ten feet wide. A group of white inmates gathered on one side of the upper tier along the rail, armed with knives and pipes. I came up to the second tier and was handed a shank.

I ran down toward the vending machine to gather more of the candy bars that were strewn about the hallway.

"Get your ass back here," Burl shouted after me. He was an older, southern white inmate. "We gotta stick together up here," he said. "You can't be tempting the rugs like that."

He was referring to the black inmates gathering on the other side of the unit. In prison, races stick together. If there is a problem between two people of different races, both sides of the entire race are involved. Even in the midst of this riot, convict code would be upheld.

Ignoring his warning, I ran quickly across the lower tier towards the vending machine. I passed a black inmate, swinging a heavy metal mop wringer into a steel table bolted to the cement floor. His eyes followed me down the length of the tier. I reached the spilled candy, scooped up four or five candy bars, and ran back fast and steady. Two prisoners ran in from the front door of the unit.

"They're coming in with guns! Get down! Get down!" someone yelled.

It was now 10:00 pm, and dark outside. I scrambled up the steps to the upper tier and dove into a cell with Burl and his celly, Beaux. The cells in Talladega had steel self-locking doors, and we slammed it shut, locking ourselves in.

"Holy shit! What's going on? What just happened? Everything was fine in the chow hall and quiet on the upper compound. Why is this happening Burl?"

Facing me, he explained, "They're going off because of the crack law. Congress shot them down. You're damn lucky you did not go into the rec yard Joel," he paused. "I barely made it off the yard alive."

The alarm that went off through the loudspeakers was even louder than the fire alarm. Screeching sirens only added to the raucous cacophony. Hours passed and complete darkness set in. Burl and Beaux were sitting on the beds while I watched the activity outside the cell window. Armored vehicles with large racks of lights were starting to surround the entire prison. I heard a prisoner climbing the fence. Gunshots echoed outside, sending bullets whizzing by the cell window. Hot flashes from the tips of shotguns flashed just beyond the perimeter fence on the prison yard. I heard a prisoner scream off in the distance. "What the fuck!" Burl yelled. "This place is going to burn!"

The vehicles outside looked camouflaged, and were not anything like the normal security pickup trucks that rode around outside the prison fence. I heard a helicopter thunder above us. I knew the Bureau of Prisons did not own security helicopters. The presence of that chopper meant someone must have declared Posse Comitatus, allowing the federal government to utilize military weaponry against its own citizens.

Now that the military or national guard had arrived, the prison staff burst into the units. Guards in federal prisons never carry firearms outside of the gun towers or perimeter vehicle; it's not worth the risk of potentially being overcome by an inmate and placing a weapon in the hands of a prisoner. That didn't stop them from bringing in tear gas guns. They look like 12 gauge pump shotguns, but with a holster at the end the size of a 12 oz can of soda to shoot out the canisters. Prison guards were screaming "Lie down! Lie down!" as they came into our unit.

Prisoners scattered to nearby cells in response, or hit the deck if they were trapped in the middle of the common area. We were familiar with the command, as it's what the prison guards yell during a fight in order to gain control. Prisoners either compiled or were beaten and brought to the Hole. The guards were dressed in combat gear- Ninja Turtles as we referred to it, with full masks, padded dark blue jackets with shock plates, high-laced steel-toed black leather boots, oversized shin pads, black lead lined billy clubs and dark blue helmets. Ninja Turtles were reserved for extreme situations when a guard's safety was known to be compromised. In contrast to their normally authoritative and loud commands, the guards now seemed to tremble as they yelled, their words laced with trepidation and fear. This was a medium security federal prison, this was not supposed to happen here.

Outside the window you could now hear the snap-crackle of burning buildings and see the heavy smoke wafting around the prison yard. I watched through the window at the top of the solid steel cell door as guards fired the tear gas down the hallways while convicts lay motionless on the ground. The canisters were not designed to be shot at humans, but the guards used the opportunity to aim at prisoners lying on the ground. Bones shattered as one prisoner was shot in the leg. He screamed and rolled away in agony.

In spite of our attempts to stick a towel in the bottom of the cell door, tear gas began to seep through the seams. I started to viciously choke alongside Burl and Beaux.

Once the guards had everyone down in our unit, they dragged the remaining convicts into their respective cells, one by one, injured or not. After we were all caged, they stormed through, and yanked us out of our cells individually for final count.

"Name and number!" the guard spat as he pulled me out of the cell by my collar and slammed me up against the cement cellblock wall. "Blaeser 0****-089."

Two other guards stood on either side of me with what appeared to be stun guns poised and ready. I stated my number as calmly as I had every time it had been requested over the past thirty-six months. I was thrown violently back into the cell, landing on the floor. Burl and Beaux remained outside, explaining why I was in their cell. They were shoved in a little more gently. They were southern boys and had lived in this prison for their whole bit. I was new, and a "Northerner" because I was born in Chicago. The prison guard looked in and addressed me, "Blaeser, you can stay here for the time being," then slammed shut the steel door.

Six hours later, I was still awake, the prison was quiet. The searing smoke from the fires across the compound crept into our cell as the wind shifted, forcing us to shut our window. It was close to 4:00 am, but sleep wasn't coming easy for any of us, so Burl, Beaux, and I talked a lot about ourselves. I discovered they were also in prison for drug trafficking and were brothers who had been busted during the same sting. They fortunately wound up in the same prison, and petitioned to be cellmates, figuring it wouldn't be much different than the room they'd shared as boys.

It was just barely dawn and on an AM radio station, Paul Harvey mentioned something about Federal Correctional Institutions in Tennessee and Talladega. It sounded very innocuous, and was only a ten or fifteen second sound bite. However, by 6:00 am, the story had grown bigger. There was an interview by a young boy who said his father, an inmate named Langston Hughes, had started the riot in Talladega because of Congress's decision regarding the crack law. The story picked up momentum for a little while and then, within an hour and a half it was dropped altogether- not a peep about it on any radio station- as if it had never occurred. Right before the story's disappearance, one reference cited it as a "minor uprising."

"Minor my ass!" Beaux exclaimed.

Following the riot, all of Talladega was put on an official lockdown status, meaning that the inmates were to be locked up twenty-four hours a day and revoked of any rights previously held. All staff would receive triple time pay, the only time they could ever receive such a benefit. Our meals were cut down to only twice a day, the dreaded brown bag lunches consisting of two bologna and cheese sandwiches on dry white bread and an apple—a far cry from the chow hall food. We were not going anywhere: no shower, no recreation, no work, no phones, no chow hall, no commissary, no nothin'. For the next five days, I stayed locked in this eight by ten cement room with two beds, a toilet, sink, and a window. Still, this was a corner cell on the 2nd floor, the biggest one in the cellblock. Burl, Beaux and I passed the time by playing cards, doing push-ups, and sitting around speculating about the damage to the prison.

Prison riots are rare. History demonstrates that mass prison riots, like the one started in Talladega, happen almost nowhere else in history. One cause of a riots scarcity is that the social structure within the walls of a prison function by spreading discord between prisoners. Different gangs flock to each other, races are divided, the religious find like-minded prisons. Essentially it's a divide and conquer tactic and a full-scale prison-wide riot requires all prisoners to overcome their differences and rise against their captors and join forces to overcome the racial chains that bind them. In order for prisoners to abandon their prejudices against each other and ignore the consequences like any oppressed people, there must be a strong incentive. This is evident by the few prison riots that have made history: New York state's Attica rebellion of 1971 is well known as the granddaddy of all prison riots and occurred as retaliation for the racism, physical brutality and horrendous living conditions the inmates were subject to. Or the notorious Atlanta prison riot, an eleven-day long uprising initiated by Cuban detainees who were protesting repatriation to Cuba in the 1980's.

Both of these riots were born from a sense of outrage that stems from the core of our humanity: a need to be acknowledged as human beings with basic needs, the sense of powerlessness that accompanies the loss of autonomy and the frustration of being voiceless while your lives and fate are determined by others. So although the catalyst for our rage felt justified amongst us prisoners, the lack of news coverage seemed to invalidate our cause. I don't mean just the inmates of Talladega, but rather every inmate who rebelled in all of the 13 prisons across the United States that rioted simultaneously that day. You would think considering the news coverage of Attica, Atlanta and the like, that 13 prisons rioting at once would be newsworthy. Yet, the general public did not know about our outrage, much less the source of it.

The incentive that caused entire prisons full of men to decide they were done being unheard, was a decision made by the United States' Congress.

In 1995 the United States' African-American population was approximately 31 million people and total Caucasian population was approximately 210 million people. Of that population, 501,672 blacks were incarcerated in state and federal prison in comparison to 464,167 whites. That's only about 35,000 more prisoners, a number many used to dismiss the disparity, but when considered as a percentage of the population, it means the number of black Americans are incarcerated at a rate seven times that of whites.

According to the Bureau of Justice 106,536 people were incarcerated in federal prison at the time of our riot in 1995. Of those, 55,172, or 53%, were incarcerated for drugs. As of 2013, there are approximately 216,000 people in federal prison, and over 2.4 million total in federal, state and privately run prisons of which 51% are locked up for drug related offenses. Then and now, African Americans comprise almost 37% of the sentenced federal prison population.

Between 1991 and 1995, the U.S. Sentencing Commission had reviewed discrepancies in drug laws that federal defendants were sentenced under and recommended certain changes to Congress. The changes implemented resulted in more uniform sentence guidelines for the laws pertaining to LSD, marijuana, and L versus M methamphetamine.

At the very same time that the sentencing commission was created Congress also created statutory mandatory minimum sentences, a guideline for sentencing that formalized the relationship between the amount and type of drug and the length of a sentence.

For example, one of the proposed changes addresses that of marijuana cultivation. If arrested for 49 marijuana plants or less, the plants were simply weighed with the dirt removed from the roots. If arrested for cultivating fifty plants or more, even if the marijuana plants were two-inch seedlings, each plant is calculated as one kilogram (or 2.2 pounds). The penalty for that one extra plant can be as much as eight to twenty extra years in prison. Each weight corresponds to a number or level in the federal sentencing guideline manual which is referred to in order to determine the length of a sentence. In the eyes of many, the revisions to marijuana, LSD** and methamphetamines L & M, made the law more lenient, a much needed change made obvious by egregious discrepancies in sentencing such as the one mentioned above.

Once the Sentencing Commission votes on a change Congress can act to override the change. If they choose not to vote on the change the changes become law. These three changes mandated and approved by congress (LSD, L versus M methamphetamine, and marijuana cultivation) primarily affected white defendants. 93% of federal LSD defendants are white, whereas only 6.2% of federal marijuana offenders were black, and only 1.3% of federal methamphetamine offenders were black. Then in 1995 the Sentencing Commission proposed a reform for the powder cocaine and crack cocaine sentencing discrepancy.

Federal crack sentences at the time ranged from six years to 75 years. Bear in mind, these are non-violent consensual crimes, as opposed to violent and/or non-consensual crimes like rape, murder, bank robbery, or terrorism. The average crack sentence was 125 months, whereas average powder cocaine sentence was 82 months.

For years the mainstream media portrayed crack as a drug that contributes more violence against society. In reality and science they are the same drug. Crack is simply powder cocaine cooked down with water and baking powder. Same drug same addiction same crime against society, and yet vastly different sentencing guidelines. On average crack cocaine offenders receive five to eight times the amount of time as powder cocaine offenders for the very same weight of drugs.

After careful review the U.S. Sentencing Commission recommended that offenders convicted of crack cocaine charges receive the same mandatory minimum sentences as powder cocaine defendants. After all, the difference primarily lies not in the drug but in the drug dealer and user; powder cocaine impacts predominately white upper-middle class communities and crack cocaine impacts poor black communities. In 1997, 3,901 blacks were prosecuted under the crack law, which accounted for 84.4% of all federal crack prosecutions. This is mainly due to the socio-economic status of the user. Crack is much cheaper than its powder counterpart and African-Americans on average earn less than whites.

Congress, who had not shown any interest in intervening in the commission's recommendations for LSD, methamphetamine or marijuana awoke from their slumber over a change in crack cocaine sentencing. Congress was called into session and voted down the recommendation to lower the mandatory minimums for offenders caught with crack. FAMM, Families Against Mandatory Minimums founded by Julie Stewart fought vigorously for this as well as the other three changes mentioned earlier but to no avail. Congress erroneously cited that crack cocaine was substantially more damaging to society and therefore required significantly harsher sentencing guidelines.*

In mid-October of 1995, Congress's action was reported on television and radio news channels playing in America's prisons igniting a furious response from many black inmates. Upon hearing the news many convicted for crack cocaine went berserk. Riots broke out in 13 federal prisons across the country, first in FCI Talladega then immediately spreading to FCI Tennessee and beyond, causing almost 40 million dollars in property damage. The Bureau of Prisons' press office worked quickly to change the spin of the story to the American public. It was reported that there were only mild disruptions at three or four prisons around the country, very little damage occurred, guards weren't injured and the safety of the American public was never compromised. There were no reports of the need for the National Guard responding to regain control of the prisons. There were no reports of brutality, rape and public endangerment. There were no reports of attempted inmate escapes. These riots were a backlash of anger and frus-tration unleashed on guards and prison property nationwide, but the general public continued to remain oblivious to the changes, or lack thereof, of drug laws and sentencing in relation to crack.*

In retrospect It was pure luck I ventured to my unit rather than out into the yard. The yard was a battleground that far exceeded the violence in my unit. I might have been killed that night if I had turned left down the sidewalk. Miraculously not one fight or verbal altercation broke out inside my unit.

FCI Talladega remained on lockdown status for a long time. After the second day the guards removed all of the radios from our cells. We were locked away from the outside world and from news and information. We were cramped with three guys in the cell, my new cellmates had an extra mattress that they set up on the floor for me. Burl had a sinus problem and he salivated a lot, smoked cigarettes and continuously spit snot into a jar. The smoke aggravated his problem and lingering stench of burnt wood creeping in through our cell window. For the most part we sat around in semi-shock. We played poker and some checkers, and spent a lot of time waiting.

After the fourth day somber guards started rotating three to four inmates out of the cells at a time. They ushered us quickly to an ice-cold three-minute shower. We were afforded this privilege once more a couple of days later.

During the entire week the guards were quiet. Burl and Beaux were good ol' white boys who had been serving time in Talladega for years and knew most of the staff well. They asked questions about what was going on but received only silence in return.

On the fifth or sixth day of lock down three surly guards appeared in front of our cell. "Blaeser you are expected in the lieutenant's office."

The steel door of our cell had a small slot where bag lunches and mail were passed through. The guards ordered Burl and then Beaux to stick their hands through the slot to be handcuffed. Then they directed me to stick my hands through, behind my back, and they clasped the cold metal cuffs around my wrists. Once we were all fettered they unlocked the cell door. I stepped forward and a large mustachioed guard wrapped his hands around the cuffs behind my back.

"You understand that if you pull in any way, shape or form, that I will take that as an aggressive act and take action against you," he said.

I nodded and started the slow walk down the hall. As we walked down the gangplank in front of the other cells, I heard inmates muttering.

"No talking!" I heard one of the guards bellowing behind me, and he pounded his billy club on the cell door.

The cellblock became eerily quiet. The atmosphere grew even more ominous as we passed broken windows that had been boarded shut. Finally, we arrived at the temporary lieutenant's office where several guards in full Ninja Turtle gear awaited us. My heart rate skyrocketed.

The lieutenant was sitting behind his desk. I had only been in Talladega for a brief time, the lieutenant and I had failed to develop a warm bond. Our violent altercation was the reason for my month and seven days spent in the Hole.

The mustachioed guard who had escorted me to the office pressed me down into a chair in front of the lieutenant. Another guard built like a slab of raw beef towered over me with a can of mace, which he pressed up against my face. The black lieutenant sneered through over-sized clenched teeth. His eyes bulged out as he leaned forward across his desk, his voice confident but stern exclaimed, "I've got you now motherfucker."

The lieutenant's sneering face made me fear for the worst. I didn't say a word. I didn't want to get hit with the mace. Instead I got hit with a shot #105.

Following the riot, many inmates were interrogated at length and all were given a citation, better known as a "shot," for bad behavior. Each shot has a number depending on the charge being issued. When an inmate receives a shot, he may end up in the Hole and have days or months added to his sentence. For a more severe shot an inmate will likely end up back in federal court with an additional charge adding years to his sentence. The five worst shots are #100: murder, #102: assault, #103: possession of a deadly weapon, and my lucky number: inciting a riot 105.

With much less fanfare, the lieutenant continued, "Joel Blaeser, you are being charged with starting the riot."

I sat quietly and took my undeserved shot. I dared not say a word as the mace can was still being held less than two inches from my eyes by the Ninja Turtle standing next to me.

Twenty-two of us were escorted separately into the lieutenant's office and charged with starting the Talladega prison riot. I was the only white prisoner accused and the only one charged without interrogation. The lieutenant knew that I had nothing to do with the riot. He identified me as one of the instigators in a flagrant effort to get even with me for the violent confrontation we'd had over my beloved green duffel bag two months earlier.

I was escorted back to the cell and sat in lockdown with Burl and Beaux for another day. Plagued by a sinking feeling in my gut and the heavy, stagnant, soot-filled air filling my nostrils, it was one of the longest days of my life. Early the next morning several guards surfaced, cuffed me through the door and pulled me out of the cell I shared with Burl and Beaux. They slapped shackles on my ankles and walked me to the front of the building where there were a few other prisoners waiting with more guards. We were put into a lineup and instructed to each call out our name and prison number. The guards flanked us as we walked single file towards the front door. As we approached the door the smell of soot and smoke grew more intense. A guard opened the door, and we stepped out onto the compound for the first time in a week.

It was a dark and misty morning. The rising sun hid behind thick fog. We walked along the sidewalks and stopped periodically at different units to pick up additional prisoners. Each time we collected more inmates into our lineup, we went through the count again, shouting out our prison numbers on command. The guards wanted to ensure they wouldn't lose track of anyone. As we continued to cross the compound the damage became more evident. My mind began to slowly register the magnitude of what had happened. Piles of rubble lay where buildings once stood. The recreation facility was a crumbled heap of brick. There was a large charred outline on the ground where an entire building once stood. Enormous piles of concrete and steel were being hauled away. Windows were blown out in multiple buildings. A pungent burnt smell of charred wood permeated the compound. The sound of our jingling shackles was the only thing that broke the silence as we marched. We approached the chow hall and picked up even more prisoners, which meant stopping and yelling out our numbers yet again.

We passed a group of prisoners laying on the grass in handcuffs. They were attempting to sleep on the ground while guards hovered over them with stun guns. With buildings burnt to the ground, there were hundreds of prisoners displaced without cells; the prison compound could have been mistaken for a refugee camp. As extra punishment the inmates were being forced to stay outside on the ground during the day and sometimes during the night.

We arrived at the lieutenant's office headquarters and were held in a waiting room. They provided a sack lunch for each of us: a bologna special at six in the morning. We sat on low stainless steel benches bolted to the concrete floor. I recognized some of the faces. Rodney Davis was a black inmate whom I had never met but his case was notorious.

Down the line, I saw Jewboy sitting restlessly. He was a black Milwaukee gang member who sold weed and always demanded he get every last penny, earning him the nickname Jewboy.

"Fuck those punks," Jewboy said, loudly enough for the guards to hear. "We got 'em." I sat quietly eating my sandwich. Guards called names and prison numbers out to summon each inmate to a nearby stall that looked like an office cubicle. A very long uncomfortable silence hung in the air.........

"Blaeser," a guard yelled out.

I rose and shuffled over to the cubicle. They were calling out names alphabetically, so I was one of the first to go through check out. Two guards stood nearby with stun guns on hand in case I made a move while a third patted me down thoroughly before removing my ankle shackles. I removed my prison-issued tan pants, brown belt, and pale tan shirt. I knew the routine well. It was the same search for contraband that takes place any time an inmate enters or leaves a prison. Talladega was my fifth prison in 37 months. I had been through this process nearly 25 times due to the way federal prisoners are transferred from one prison to another.

I stripped naked and lifted each leg to show the guards the bottoms of my feet. I raised my hands high over my head and then twisted them back and forth with my fingers spread open widely. When directed, I stuck out my tongue and lifted it up and down, and then left to right. I tilted my head back so the guards could peer up my nose. I ran my fingers through my hair. Then I bent over and forced the mandatory cough as I spread my ass cheeks. The guards gave me a United States Marshal's traveling uniform, a cloth tan jumpsuit with snapping buttons in the front, which looked slightly different than the prison uniform. I put it on slowly knowing that once the cuffs were back in place I wouldn't even be able to reach down to scratch my balls.

A guard secured the handcuffs back onto my wrists and wrapped a chain around my waist. My handcuffs were then covered by a black box that restricted my arm movement back and forth. I had never been black-boxed before. That was reserved for extremely dangerous prisoners. My handcuffs were then clipped to the belly chain, fettering my hands to my torso, and finally my ankle shackles were locked in place. Movement from here to the next prison would be extremely limited.

Checkout usually requires going through property slips and other various checks but this time I wasn't taking any property. It had all been destroyed in the riot.

I scooted out of the cubicle back into the waiting area and parked my rear on a bench. Jewboy stood off to the side talking loudly to several other inmates.

"I had that bitch and man did I fuck her up!" he thundered proudly.

Apparently he had cornered a female guard in the law library, but I couldn't believe he was talking so openly about it. It was common knowledge that inmates that attacked guards would get serious time added to their sentences. Jewboy only had a few years left to serve and yet he was speaking loud and clear in front of guards who could hear him.

"I ripped off her clothes and beat that cunt with a motherfucking bat. I fucked that bitch so hard. Razer that pussy was trying to pull me off of her." He motioned to Razer, another black inmate sitting alone on the bench. Razer sat, face unreadable as eyes turned toward him. He made eye contact with no one and remained immobile. "Shit That lucky bitch had my cock rammed inside her," Jewboy continued.

I sat there in disbelief. His chest puffed with ego. Then a thought occurred to me: maybe the guards had put him up to this in order to lure other inmates into bragging about what they had done during the riot. In the chaos they would have limited knowledge of who caused what damage and though we were all charged with inciting the riot, if anyone was overheard copping to a particular offense it could mean a longer sentence.

No one jumped in. A nearby guard gave us a cold stare.

Outside an old prison bus squeaked as it pulled around to the front. The guards prepared us for departure. They put us back into a single file line and asked for our prison numbers. We filed outside through a gate and stopped for yet another count. The air still reeked of soot.

The prison bus was a big aluminum 1980's Greyhound-style bus. Inside a thick mesh steel screen ran along all of the walls and windows like an iron womb. The drivers and two United States Marshals stayed up front protected behind a metal cage and armed with sawed-off 12-gauge shot shotguns.

As we boarded the bus a Talladega guard yelled out for a final count. We each shouted out our number in order. We piled into the bus and I settled onto a window seat farthest to the back. The guard handed off the paperwork to one of the marshals and stepped off the bus, the doors creaking shut behind him. The driver pressed on the gas and released the temperamental clutch. We lurched forward and drove out of the prison gates.

Curiosity consumed all of us prisoners on the bus. We hadn't been told where we were being sent. For security reasons during a disciplinary move, prison staff always keeps the location of a transfer a secret until the arrival. But that didn't keep us from asking.

"Are we going to Terre Haute?" one inmate yelled.

"No. No. It's Oxford," suggested another.

"You guys have it wrong. We're going to Lewisburg," another chimed in.

"It must be USP Atlanta." Many chattered in agreement that Atlanta had been the first to cross their minds.

The marshals at the front of the bus remained stone faced. I watched out the window as the bus hummed along the highway passing exits to Atlanta and signs indicating we were heading north. Several hours into the drive horror began to creep slowly up my spine. Images from my argument with the lieutenant two months earlier flashed in my mind. I saw his angry face threatening me.

"Marion," I stammered before I could stop myself. "They're sending us to Marion."

In the huge oversized rectangular rear view mirror, I saw the bus driver's plastic face break into a sinister smirk. An immediate hush settled over the bus. My face went flush, my heart skipped a beat, I took a deep breath… Nobody said a word. Quiet and somber faces stared forward. A brother finally broke the silence.

"He's right. We're probably going to Marion."

*(Note, in 2010 Congress passed a measure that President Obama signed into law lowering the crack/powder cocaine sentencing disparity from 100 to 1 to 18 to 1. However, this was not applied retroactively).

**(Note, although the LSD paperweight provision did lower sentences across the board for those defendants, in some cases there can still be and has been a 1,000 to 1 sentencing disparity, extreme example: Timothy Tyler, 2 life sentences for LSD).

Joel Blaeser
03491-089
P.O. Box 1000
Marion, Il 62959

Rosemary Blaeser
1730 N Clark #4102
Chicago, Il 60614

Dear Mom   10-5-96

Hello I just got off the phone with you and now I am writing you. I have had second thoughts and am going to stick to my guns — I am not going to and don't <u>want</u> any visits. It does not matter how much money you or anyone put in the fund. I will see you all when I get out. You know it is best to live in non attachment anyway. As I was explaining to you on one of our visits here at Marion. Visiting is a form of attachment. Dad was a attachment, grandma, look for the seeds of opportunity in the ashes of disaster — Wei Nji (pronounced way gee) a <u>old</u> Chinese proverb. We talked about that when you visited with Jay. Anyway this is realy no disaster, it is a let down. I have been sewing the seeds of opportunity since this prison sentence — (disaster) started. Sooner or later one of us is not ever going to see the other in the same form, as we are use to seeing. Unless our hearts stop beating at the same time. As I said during the phone call I did get 2 issues of National Geo, a $20 check 2 weeks ago, The weightless workout came last week also. Thank you very much! If you could I would appreciate copy's of pictures (Florence with the spider) I will call on or around Christmas Eve. Will you still be at the same address and phone #? I think you should change the combination by which you live, you dont seem satified, very aware and you come off as living in fear, of what I dont know. You seem to have a decent amount of order, balance and intelligence but where is the evolution. Where do you want to go Physically, Religiously, Philosophically, Mentally, Financially etc. etc. Forget the dualities, opposites, attachments and judgement. try acceptance it can work wonders. <u>I love you</u> and hope to see you when I get out.   love Joe

I started to eat m and got sick so I am going back to no mea, no even fish I ate m on Thur, Fri Sat and Sun other than that it has been m I would give anything to read a National Geo every month. Its just not that way here. So now brad can enjoy it. This is a Prison not a country club. love you

2

Con Air

IN APRIL OF 1992, after nine days in the federal holding facility in Racine, Wisconsin, my family posted bail of $20,000. I was charged in a 19 count federal indictment for selling LSD and transferring money across state lines using Western Union. The bail would have been higher had my older brother not signed his business over as collateral in a chattel agreement at my mother's behest. This meant that if I skipped bail, or failed to appear in court, my brother would suffer the loss of his business.

Despite the nine days I had spent in jail, my life was the same as it had been for months: I was 23 years old, living and working with my older brother at his landscaping business, and generally going about my days as I had before my arrest. After all, the charges in the indictment were based on alleged illegal activity from almost two years prior. The whole process seemed a bit removed from me, until reality came crashing into my consciousness. Shortly, the realization that I might be spending the better part of my youth behind bars in federal prison would intrude on my every thought and fill me with a pervasive and paralyzing fear. Yes, bulking up and lifting weights behind bars had a dark appeal to me, but I was haunted by premonitions of my own rape and murder.

Yet I did not understand the enormity of what faced me. A sealed grand jury had been convened over 500 miles away on my behalf, a process that costs the government $50,000 to $1,000,000, and often is only reserved for the most high-level criminals, such as mafiosos and drug kingpins. Grand juries are cloaked in secrecy, not only to protect reluctant witnesses, but also to keep the suspect in question from knowing the stakes and perhaps fleeing the country. As if I, some hippie kid from the Midwest had access to finances or connections enough to start a new life outside of the US. This was obviously a case of mistaken identity. The prosecutor, an up and coming attorney from Kentucky, was building a case against me as if putting me behind bars was going to tumble the entire LSD manufacturing network. Her name was Laura Klein Voorhees, assistant US attorney for the Eastern District of Kentucky- 6th District. She was pregnant and by trial would be busting at the seams, helping her garner extra sympathy from the jury.

After my bail was posted, I was informed I'd have to get to Kentucky for the arraignment hearing in a few weeks. I had planned on driving my brothers vehicle to get there, but the night before I was to leave we got into a screaming match over a work issue. He told me there was no way he'd let me take his car, leaving me on the losing end. With court only one day away, I could not find an affordable flight, nor did I have a credit card to get a rental car.

When I realized I was not going to make my Kentucky court date, I called the Federal Marshals and the 6th district federal courthouse in Kentucky, but to no avail. The court date could not be rescheduled. My attorney was not going to be present because it was all just supposed to be a formality. Unfortunately, I was charged with failure to appear and promptly arrested.

In my naiveté, I did not realize the significance of missing my arraignment hearing in Kentucky. I was caught in a catch-22: I would not be assigned a new court date until I checked into the Covington Kentucky county jail, but without a new court date the United States Federal Marshal Service, who are responsible for the transportation of all federal criminals, had no reason to rush me to Kentucky.

After my phone call, I was picked up by the marshals in Milwaukee and taken back to the county jail in Racine, Wisconsin. The following morning I was awoken early to begin my lengthy trek to Kentucky, my first experience with the United States government's Con Air. I was taught the complicated pre-boarding dance of the prisoner: strip, bend down, cough, shower, paperwork, get shackled, belly chained, and dressed in beige thick cotton jumpsuit with tan canvas slip-on shoes.

The U.S. Marshal Service employ a combination of cars, buses, and jets for Federal prisoner transport, and I would experience all forms in the next month. I was taken by bus to Chicago, where I spent six days in the Metropolitan Correctional Center at 71 West Van Buren Street. It was a twenty-three story cement edifice with a rooftop rec yard for all the guests. I was put into general population on a very high floor. It housed lots of long-term federal prisoners and ones in transit such as myself.

Coincidentally my celly Ron D and I discovered that we had been born on the same day and same year in the same city, although one wouldn't guess it by looking at us. Ron looked aged and had clearly led a hard life, but he was much more street smart than I. Six feet tall with a muscular build topped with a light brown goatee and a collection of prison tattoos. He had been in jail before. Currently he was serving a seven-year sentence for armed bank robbery.

I, on the other hand, had no marks of hardship. With no tattoos, bright eyes and flawless skin, I didn't look a day over 18. Ron knew everyone on the floor and really took a liking to me. I took the top bunk, as I would learn all newcomers do. We became very close in a short amount of time killing time by playing lots of ping-pong. Ron was the floor champion and he won all sorts of food from the commissary. No one could beat him. He marveled at how I was indicted for something that happened two years prior. He concocted lots of ways for me to beat my trial and would share them late at night while everyone was asleep. He said I should start writing everything with my left hand and at trial have entirely different handwriting to discount any evidence that the prosecutor might use which involved my handwriting. I listened intently but it all seemed too much. I was on a wave for better or worse and wanted to ride it wherever it went. I was getting comfortable in my new digs, but on the sixth day I was hauled away to continue on my journey to Kentucky for federal arraignment.

It was 5:30 am when the guard approached our room. "Blaeser!" he yelled, "Name and number!" Ron rose out of bed to say goodbye. We shook hands, not saying much. Months later we wrote a few letters back and forth that went through my mother but it seemed like I would never see him again. I knew he was worried for me. I was facing 20 years and still very green.

"Keep in touch brother!" Ron exclaimed.

"Thank you for everything Ron. I love you."

"Love you too man."

"Blaeser let's go! Bus is leaving!" the guard yelled.

I was then prepped for transport and loaded into a van headed for O'Hare Airport. We pulled up to board the US Marshals' Con Air 727 jet around 11:00 am, and as I stepped out of the van, I immediately felt as if I was in a scene from an action movie. The jet engines were idling and never turned off. The plane was surrounded by eight to ten marshals standing guard with handguns and shotguns drawn, cocked, and ready. There were rooftop snipers on the nearby hanger with what appeared to be AR-15s. Another 10 to 12 armed marshals began checking prisoners' names and numbers, my sixth recitation since waking up that morning.

Each prisoner wore ankle shackles and handcuffs attached to a big thick steel chain wrapped around their belly. The restraints offered little mobility to look around the plane, and there wasn't much to see. The interior of the plane appeared like any other coach section of an airline, except there was no door on the bathroom, my first inkling at how little privacy we would be afforded in prison. One of the most interesting things about the trip was the flight pattern: at no point did we ever circle an airport. When the door was shut, we just took off immediately. For the next eight hours, the plane would land and take off six or seven times, picking up and dropping off convicts all over the country. Finally, we arrived at my destination: El Reno, Oklahoma, a full-scale medium FCI prison with a section for holdovers— people in transit to and from court or to their designated prison.

I spent some time speaking with the convict sitting next to me, Leo. He was a clean cut, incredibly articulate gentleman probably three times my age. He was also a seasoned career criminal, in for the third time on Federal counterfeiting charges. Leo explained that when charged with counterfeiting, the maximum sentence you can receive is five years, even if it was your third counterfeiting offense. It didn't make much sense to me at the time.

At one stop, I noticed three convicts board with unusual handcuffs. The handcuffs themselves appeared normal, but there were curious black boxes covering the chain between their wrists, and connecting to the belly chain as well. It was evident that these boxes not only restricted their movement even further but also were causing their handcuffs to carve deep red ridges into their wrists. I asked Leo about the purpose of the black boxes. He responded that these convicts were likely a big security risk and probably headed to Marion.

"Marion? What's Marion?" I asked.

He proceeded to tell me what I assumed at the time was an over-embellished story intended to scare a "fish," or new prisoner like me. He told me about this supermax prison designed to hold America's most hardened criminals. Leo explained that Marion opened as the highest-level United States Penitentiary (USP) ever built within the US. He even told me about Tommy Silverstein, an inmate so hardcore he ordered the murder of two prison guards. It sounded outrageous. Some lifer with a beef might shank a guard, but this Silverstein guy could get other inmates to do his bidding? It sounded like an urban myth, a campfire tale for prison, intended to scare me out of sleep and into shape. But Tommy Silverstein's story resonated throughout the corridors of every prison I would enter, each time told with the same medley of fear and respect I heard in Leo's voice during that conversation. Little did I know that, years later, I would be heading on a bus north to the infamous Marion to find out for myself if it was all just nonsense.

He also mentioned that in addition, the Marion "Camp" borders the outside of the USP itself.

"Camp?" I asked. A federal prison camp is where very low-level white-collar criminals, like Pete Rose or a government informant (also known as a snitch or rat according to convict code), serve out their sentences. Camps have no fences and inmates generally work around the grounds of the real prison doing jobs like laundry and grounds keeping. Serving time in a camp is considered a very posh sentence.

To my horror, the holdover stop in El Reno, Oklahoma, was not the dinky county jail I'd been expecting, but rather a full prison. I recalled every prison movie I had ever seen: prostitution, alcohol, extortion, the smell of marijuana permeating the cell block, the leering and scarred faces of men you'd never want to meet in a dark alley. Hollywood doesn't need to exaggerate prison life. It is shocking on its own.

There were nearly 300 inmates and only two prison guards in my housing unit. three tiers high, with block cement walls, cement floors and steel rails only four feet high After meals, the cell block echoed so heavily with other voices I could hardly hear myself think. Our cells were open from 6:00 am to nearly 10:00 pm every day and there were times when the two guards would disappear in their office for several hours at a time. While I wanted my "freedom," I was terrified at the prospect of an unsupervised open cell range and couldn't even begin to fathom the notion of open showers.

My celly was a bank-robbing murderer named Jim. During hours of recreation, only a chain link fence separated the general population of FCI El Reno from the holdover population. Jim used this to his advantage, talking to his connections on the "main yard" through the fence. Jim clearly knew his way around the prison and I paid attention to everything he said and did. He taught me a lot about "convict code" and the unwritten prison rules one must follow in order to survive. For instance, I quickly learned that when you urinated in your cell toilet you always wipe the seat with toilet paper. "No matter what," Jim growled at me the first time I failed to adhere. He taught me to never discuss your case, politics, or religion. His resounding motto, "Fuck, fight or hit the fence," was branded into my soul. Never wake a sleeping convict for that is when you're temporarily pardoned, don't associate with other races, never say "they can't do that" referring to the government and it's prosecutors. By this point, I knew I was facing a 20-year sentence and figured my life depended on this knowledge.

Each prison has a party system but rather than being characterized by political or regional affiliation, the parties are defined by race, though sometimes region too. Each party has a designated leader and abides by its own rules. You are always representing your color and confrontations with a member of the other race are never isolated instances. Much like a gang they promptly involve every convict of that race. Furthermore, if you are offended by someone of another color and do not retaliate you will be disowned by your own party be-cause it's seen as a sign of weakness. I had to develop a conscience of unity for my race only, a stark contrast to the Grateful Dead parking lot scene where it was unity with the entire human race. In this strange land of convicts and bars I was being told that my life depended on me being at one only with my race. What about the human race.

There were other informal rules. Never assist prison staff or talk to them unless necessary. Never reach over someone's food and if someone does it to you and does not instantly apologize, it's considered an act of aggression. Don't mess with the punks- a term for guys who are openly promiscuous- not for business, not as friends, not for any reason. I would later see people getting severely beaten for having sex with someone else's "bitch." Politics on a prison yard were serious business, especially in the higher security prisons. Never act weak because you always represent your race. Jim intoned these rules as if reciting scripture from a holy book.

It was a welcoming relief to finally leave for my bail hearing in Kentucky. The judge at the bail hearing took pity on me and believed me when I recounted the misunderstanding with my brother 35 days earlier. He dropped the "failure to appear" charge, reinstated the same bail, and released me on the spot.

I was numb. I was a free man until my trial in one hundred days but I was still on edge about facing 20 years. The least amount of time you serve on any federal sentence is 85% of the sentence? So on a federal 20-year sentence with good behavior the least you would serve is 17 years, If we lost at trial I would be 40 upon completion of my sentence.

After my release I met with the Kentucky attorney my mother had hired while I was in El Reno. Gatewood Gailbraith was well known and respected throughout the state. He even ran for governor in the state of Kentucky. Gatewood had tried cases in the US district court here in Covington, Kentucky and although he never won a trial, he did have a way of getting people lighter sentences if they pled guilty.

We discussed our defense strategy over a steak dinner and Heineken. As part of the rules of federal criminal procedure, the prosecution is required to hand over all the evidence and questions they intend to ask during a trial unless there is some very good extenuating circumstances. This process is called "discovery," and any evidence the defense thinks will be beneficial must be shared with the prosecution, whether they use it at trial or not. Therefore, my trial would fortunately be unlike the court television shows I was familiar with: no surprise questions and no last minute evidence. I was made well aware of the little amount of evidence the court had on me by the time we would actually get to trial.

Gatewood agreed to take my case all the way through trial. After all, my mother was paying his fees, I wondered if he thought I would plead out before we ever got to trial. He would have no reason to believe me when I said that I wouldn't surrender any LSD dealers much less manufacturers. Especially not when more than 90% of charged Federal defendants plead guilty, usually in fear of the full sentence the prosecutor threatens. Often, especially in federal cases, if one goes to trial and loses, the result can be life in prison. Faced with the ultimate gamble of your life, many convicts choose to plead guilty, sometimes regardless of actual innocence, because the specter of dying in prison supersedes the loss of five, fifteen or even twenty years of your life.

I knew the prosecution would offer a lower sentence in trade for information, but I couldn't let go of my stubborn middle-child mentality; it was beat into me by my dad, that there was no pride in telling on someone else. He acquainted with me the idea that you have to accept responsibility for your actions rather than shifting blame to someone else. I took it to heart and that notion solidified my definition of what it meant to be a narc and my resolve to never become one.

I knew it was rare for a case to be taken to trial, which gave me a false sense of security and confidence in our ability to win. In all of my years playing poker, I've never won a big hand on a naive, stubborn bluff. Yet, faced with my biggest gamble ever, I felt compelled to try once again, despite the fact that I was up against the toughest opponent I would ever face: the United States government.

Part of my incentive to take the case to trial and what inspired me to pursue my case, was that I had seen prison. I saw everything under the sun short of murder while I was in FCI El Reno, and I did not want to go back. If I wasn't going to cooperate with the prosecution's demands to name other LSD dealers, trial was my only choice.

"Expect to lose," Gatewood drove into my head. "We will fight the best we can. If anything else happens, it will be easy to deal with as long as you expect to lose. Prepare for prison, then you have all your bases covered."

Dear Mom   1-13-96

Happy Holidays, Thank you for
the Books. I received Diane's
Yesterday and the others will
soon follow. 2 weeks ago you sent money which
I received along with yesterdays. I was not
aware that Reading Genius was a course when I
heard it advertised on the radio it sounded like
it was a book. It's a little pricey and we
can't get tapes in here any way. I am
still very interested in something like that but
I will have to wait until I get out. Can
You send me the phone # for that course
if you still have it. Did you get my
letter requesting 2 statements
in regards to the visit last December. If so please follow instructions
I wrote. If not let me know and
I will send you another set of
instructions. Please don't forget, lately
I have been listening to a lot of classical
music, it's very relaxing. The in house
movie channel showed "Shadowlands" with
Anthony Hopkins. I watched it 5 times.
It is a love/tragedy. with some good
Philosophy. It still bugges me when people
see someone's Death as a tragedy.
It's as natural as birth. Part of the happiness
at birth is the pain of Death later on.

It is another one of
those movies that is not only entertaining but very educational in human
Philosophy/behaviour. Hopkins is such
a good actor which only brings the
point across much stronger.
Have you or are you guys
going skiing anytime soon.

Follow your dreams!

I am not going to ask
you about larry anymore, you
do not want to talk about it,
or you do not know yourself
what's happening, or maybe even
something else so I will leave it
alone. (relationship that is)
Who did you vote for?
Weed is legal in california for
medical purposes. Did you get
my letter in which I explained how
I fast. I wish larry could give
you a ride home everyday. Do
you share our conversations with
him I would not mind if you
do. Enjoy love Joel

3

Guardian Angel

OCTOBER 1995

THE PRISON BUS SLOWED down abruptly taking a hard left turn, instantly jarring me awake from my deep slumber. As my eyes opened and head popped up, I saw a green road sign, reading "Prison Road." Scared and curious, my attention was drawn out the windows. Bright sun forced it's way into the bus through the metal fencing encasing all the windows. Finally, I could see out of them.

We had traveled 350 miles over the last six hours. Strangely, Prison Road was lined with picturesque hills and rolling farmland. Oak trees were showing their fiery autumn colors as we rolled toward USP Marion.

Two minutes later the bus again slowed to a crawl, finally stopping at the front gate and booth. To the left of the booth was a big stone with metal sign reading "United States Penitentiary Marion." Two armed gate guards waived us through. Both had large automatic rifles and handguns in side-holsters with mean stairs to match. The diesel engine howled and vibrated as the stainless steel prison bus crept forward. The front view was blocked by the steel grate that separated the prisoner seating from the driver's cab area where the two marshals armed with shotguns and the driver sat. Looking forward I could only see the driver's face in the reflection from the oversized rectangular rear view mirror.

We drove forward about a quarter mile toward a tight left curve, which afforded me a view of a red tractor mowing a field. To the right of the curve was a tiny subdivision of brick and block ranch style homes on a pretty tree-lined street as if entering a small town.

This doesn't look so bad, I thought.

The bus veered to the left and turned slowly down the tight curvy road, then through a roundabout. We came to the bottom of the hill, our speed slowed again to a crawl. Two cement gun towers came into view. They had round bases with large square tops standing 25 feet tall. Rows of razor wire lined the ground between the three prison perimeter fences, each edge reflecting the sun like a mirror.

We drove up to the front door of USP Marion and to what looked like a battalion of soldiers.

I didn't think we were that important, but there waiting for us was a squad of Ninja Turtles dressed in full riot gear, twelve guards wide by ten guards deep. We were in some serious trouble. A single man dressed in a very nice suit with a video camera stood by to record our arrival.

They called each one of us off the bus individually. The first convict to get searched and patted down in front of us was effectively beaten in front of the camera. They proceeded to search us with brutal and direct force to every part of our bodies. The camera must have been a trick, and turned off to intimidate prisoners into believing the guards here at Marion had no fear of repercussions and were untouchable, or even worse, to watch later for entertainment.

We were called off one at a time and each beating was more severe than the prior, and I got to go last.

It was another warm October day in 1995, I squinted from the bright sun as I slowly stepped down off the bus.

"Name."

"Joel Blaeser."

"Number."

"0****-089."

I was not thrown around or humiliated like all the others. Obviously I was the only white guy, and they were trying to divide us. USP Marion is in the very southernmost part of Illinois, near the border of Kentucky, Missouri, and very close to Arkansas and Tennessee, these southern Illinois federal prison guards were good ol' boys. They knew if they could create a division, maybe in the following days I would have to fight, providing more free entertainment for them.

One hundred and twenty Ninja Turtles lined up behind us. As we were put in order, some of the guards came over and prodded us with their nightsticks.

A young very blond male guard said in a loud mean southern drawl " Your in Marion now. We do things differently around here. We will knock your teeth out so you suck dick better. Do not fuck with us. If you do, we will kill you. Welcome to the twilight zone. "

He then ordered us to march in single file toward the front door of USP Marion. The Ninja Turtles were in front of us, behind us and to the sides of us. The goose-stepped forward, their boots hitting the ground in unison, "Thud thud thud!

We entered the front door. The walls were painted a bright cream, and the floors were buffed so bright you could almost see your reflection on them. The clinking of our ankle chains against the hard tile floors coupled with marching Ninja Turtles made the whole experience surreal, as though we were taking part in some sort of postmodernist musical performance.

But we prisoners were silent. No one dared speak a word.

Whenever you come to a prison during your prison term, for whatever reason, there are a series of check in procedures you go through before you are released into general population.

You have a regular physical, fill out the necessary paperwork answering a lot of questions about whether you suffer from this or that ailment. A doctor interviews you. The interviewing doctor always asks whether you have "the package," the prison term for HIV or AIDS.

Next you see a case manager who asks you general questions about the time you've already served, your life outside and specifically gang affiliation or someone you may be afraid of such as someone you snitched on. I did not have to worry about any of these. I had no gang affiliations and had not pled guilty. I had not testified against anyone during my trial either. This was beneficial for me as the less you have to say during this process the less the staff remembers you and that means doing your time becomes a little easier. This was Marion though and with a total of only 383 prisoners staff kept a close eye on everyone.

You have your picture taken, get strip-searched, fingerprinted and receive new clothes and a bedroll before you are done. Halfway through the check-in process while unclothed we were individually led into a room directly after getting our picture taken. As we waited in the corridor we could hear each convict getting hit again and punched by the guards. When it was my turn to go into the room they joked and laughed, saying

"Hey Blaeser, you in prison for selling crack?"

My jacket was right in front of them they knew that wasn't the case. I stood silent.

"Blondie," a tall, bleach blond thin young male guard who gave us his little speech earlier said. "You really must have pissed someone off. You're white. What the fuck are you doing here because of the crack riots?" I stood silent and finally said, "No comment."

Rather than beat me they simply held me down and sprayed me. Whenever you arrive at a federal prison, you are sprayed with an odorless, tasteless mist out of a large aerosol can. The process takes about ten to fifteen seconds and occurs just after you get strip searched, but before you are allowed to put on your new prison duds. You are told to close your eyes and at this point in my sentence my body clenched in anticipation of the mist. There is no resisting it. If you did you would be beaten, held down and sprayed anyway. They say it is for lice and fleas, but I have always been nervous of the process.

After all, who better to test out a new virus or bacteria then convicted criminals?

I entered the final room to find my 21 other comrades sitting naked and bruised, awaiting instruction. Some had puffed up eyes already beginning to swell, but most had received rib shots or leg beatings with the baton. We were pretty shook up. We had never seen anything like this. We had all gone through the check-in process before but these guards seem to play by their own rulebook. The guards came in to inform us we were going through another strip search.

"Look forward, pull open your cheeks, lift your tongue up, pull your ears forward, look left, look right, raise your arms, turn around, bend over, spread your butt cheeks wide and hard, cough, raise each foot one at a time."

They asked what size I was, "Large" I said, then threw me a prison roll, consisting of a light beige khaki top with short sleeves, cotton socks, white undershirt, white boxer briefs, a large white towel and khaki pants with an elastic band. The clothing material feels like linen drapery with a mild odor of bleach and artificial floral soap smell. This procedure is standard everywhere, except for the beatings and 120 Ninja Turtles lined up to greet us before marching around like a musical number out of *Springtime for Hitler*.

It was clear to me that I was not as roughed up as the other 21 inmates were. Even in the haze of contempt for being in Marion and what we all went through checking-in, we found humor in it and began to laugh at something.

Blondie peered through the doorway and yelled, "Shut the fuck up!"

"Then take us to our cells," Rodney instantly retorted back in just as loud and stern of a tone.

Everyone except me had been beaten, we had gotten past the initial fear of Marion.

The real test was going to be in the following months and years out in the cell blocks in general population, with people like Ghetto, John Gotti, Bruce Pierce, James "Doc" Holliday, Michael Big Mac McElhiney and so many others. We would have to live with gangs like the Aryan Brotherhood, the Black Guerrilla Family, and La Eme.

In Marion you are never next to prison staff without being shackled at the ankles with leg irons and handcuffed behind the back. They started to handcuff and shackle us one at a time. There were slots in the large steel door that led out to the hallway. There was a slot at the bottom of the door, and one at waist height. They ordered everyone to face the wall then one at a time we were handcuffed and shackled as we stood at the door so the guards could reach through the slots of the bars to chain us. I was first. If anyone wanted to get me, now was the chance. Once I was shackled and handcuffed behind my back, there was no defending myself.

I received my shackles and turned to face the room, my comrades. No one moved. I let no emotion cross my face as I walked to the back of the room, but breathed an internal sigh of relief. I think the lieutenant from Talladega would have been pleased to discover I'd been murdered upon my arrival.

The day started seventeen hours earlier at 5:00 am under a thick early dawn fog and smell of burnt wood. It was now around 10:00 pm. The cellblock had windows open, as we slowly entered I could smell wet fresh-cut hay.

The sound of the steel bars rolling closed behind me as I stepped in my cell meant I would be sleeping alone for the first time in thirty five months and probably until I died or went home. The guard yelled "Clear for Blaeser number three!"

Gears groaned and my cell door closed. I have my own room I thought. I might have to prepare for battle one hour every day but for the other twenty-three nothing could touch me. Strangely, I fell asleep immediately.

This was a long ways away from following the Grateful Dead around the world. Now I was a first-time non-violent offender in the most notorious super max prison ever built, living among criminals who would undoubtedly see me as raw meat for the mill.

I had only 84 months left on my sentence because I'd won an appeal over a sentencing issue 18 months prior, giving back 31 months of my 151 month sentence. A change facilitated by a reinterpretation of the LSD paperweight law. That meant no less than 71 more months with good behavior until release.

We all were so tired upon arrival and check in. The big, prison-issued, down feather pillow with blue stripes certainly helped me fall asleep on the thin three inch "mat" bed on the thick cement slab. I had the first of what would become a recurring dream featuring my father. The context of the dream usually involved me trying to save him when he died, and then him coming to me afterward to make peace with me. These dreams occurred until I was released from prison. Eventually we made peace with each other. Throughout the time I was in Marion I would feel his presence with me, comforting me in death in a way he couldn't in life.

Bradley Blaeser
~~2504 N Oakland Ave~~ #8
Milwaukee, WI 53211

Dear Brad 3/5/77

Her is a page from a article from Details about Star wars. Check out the prices of the figures. IT also says a X-wing fighter goes for $35,000 That was the one you have or had. If you remember get the clerk of courts for Wauwatosa address, (76th + North avenue) whats happening anything new and exciting. See any new good local bands lately. If you come across a Shepards express and Milwaukee Journal I would love to read them. I realy need to get out in the free world. I am disapointed at your final result in helping me get money over the last 10 months. Out of all the family you have no mortgage car payments, kids, wife etc, you have the most energy and conntributed the least as compared to your ability, potential and liabilities. Are you battling a drug addiction or something. I cant understand why or how after 10 months you have done almost nothing to further this cause. life is a process and not a final result, however the process you have been involved in oder the last 10 months has produced a minimal final Result. Intentions are another way of saying Sorry. Effort has a direct relationship to the final product. Actions have spoken louder than words for whatever and however this less than acceptable final product from you came about. The last thing Dad would want to have seen is one of us having a battle with alcohol like he did. And if thats not the reason, what is you don't hate me do you. Are you subconciously getting back at me for our tumultous childhood relations. Whatever the reason the fact remains in my time of need (which obviously I put myself in) you failed me. Would you feel comfortable knowing that someone you counted on in your time of need, put forth the same effort and end result as you did for me. A time of need like this is once in a lifetime this isn't my 2, or 4th prison term. You are always so quick to defend yourself when I break things down to you like this - which is further realization that the statements are of a very valid nature. Being in prison has nothing to do with it, All of you think of me and my statements as something different than equal to yours because I am in prison. The truth hurts any way you slice it. Its unfortunate but this is/was a Litmus test as to how you overcome, conquer grow, entreprenuer etc. or you never realy intended to help me for whatever reason. OR you had other problems as I mentioned before, OR what? Its your life do with it what you will, when I get out we can hang out when

3

I'm in Millwaukee or when you come around were I live. As far as everything else is concerned, You have to come to terms with that yourself. You have a big ego and when you address those things, you address yourself and your way of living/philosophy and it probably frightens you to do so. Anyone seeking knowledge has fear The same as anyone going to war. So dont feel like you The only one who feels fear when you delve deep into The meaning of life — All men of knowledge or men seeking knowledge feel fear. Life is meant to be lived not described or is it. What is your philosphy. Maybe thats why people like to drown themselves out in alcahol and drugs because its keeps them a safe emotional distance away from the quest of knowledge. Peace be with you on your inquiry and journey of life Bradley

Power to the People

Joel

4

The Good Life

SUMMER 2005

I WAS ON MY way to closing my 36th property, my dream estate: a 6,000 square foot house in the middle of a secluded three acre peninsula, bordered by Eagle Spring Lake on one side and the 1600 acre Lake Lulu Nature Conservancy on the other. Water surrounded the house on all sides, but for the small strip of land connecting my half-mile long driveway to Jacks Bay Road. A 3,300 square foot deck that ensured its occupants could best enjoy the 1,300 feet of lake and conservancy frontage encompassed the two-story cedar-roofed structure.

The house itself was designed by the award-winning architect Eric Gnant, and boasted 120 floor-to-ceiling windows, none of which I could bear to cover with shades or drapes. Every room had six to eight sides and came equipped with its own separate entertainment zone; there were even weatherproof subwoofers and speakers mounted underneath each section of deck.

In total, there were three bedrooms, three bathrooms, a dining room, living room, library, bar, an in-home theatre, a large workout room featuring new workout equipment, an up-to-date kitchen, and an attached garage spanning forty feet.

The kitchen was my pride and joy. It had a double convection oven, a silent dishwasher, a sub-zero refrigerator, and a professional gas cook top with telescoping ventilating hood. There were 70 feet of solid butternut cabinets. I made sure that not an ounce of plywood could be found in any of the carpentry. The house was decorated with over 30 original oil paintings, 95 year-old Quaint Stickley furniture and Togo sofas from Ligne Roset. It would be featured in *The Week* magazine as "House of the Week" (12/1/2006), and the *Living on the Lake* magazine twice (5/1/2007, 2008).

My master bath was eight times bigger than my prison cell in Marion, except the bathroom had twelve-foot high ceilings. My master bedroom was twenty-three feet wide with a fifteen-foot three paneled floor-to-ceiling window overlooking the nature conservancy in front of the king size bed. Each morning you awoke to a breathtaking display of natural beauty. The water from the well—tested by a university and a private company—was declared to be some of the best and cleanest water they had ever seen. This would not turn the inside of my teeth green like the radioactive water in FCI Florence temporarily did.

It was an unobstructed view on Tom's Bay where there were no houses and no roads, just pure nature. Whippoorwills sounded the start of every autumn. Turtles, frogs, foxes, cranes, egrets, ducks, geese, beavers, deer, coyote, and over 56 varieties of fish were common visitors.

The neighbors were a far cry from those in USP Marion. There were only five other houses on all of Mary's Bay: one of the summer homes of the president of Siemens Corporation, an oral surgeon, a vice-president of Aurora Health Care, an agent for a Chicago professional sports team, and another doctor.

I was putting $320,000 in cash down on this $1.5 million estate. My plan was to buy, put in a few hundred thousand dollars' worth of enhancements, including adding a bedroom and bathroom among other improvements, then sell the property for around $3 million dollars. My monthly mortgage was over $8,000 per month for this house alone, not including the two other homes I owned in Milwaukee at the time. A year later my mortgage with taxes would be $9,800 per month as I would pull equity out of my "rising" property value. A little over two years later the property was listed for $2.9 million and during the first week of the listing there was a cash offer for $2 million from a Chicago philanthropist who owned 32 McDonalds in the Milwaukee area. Considering it was listed only a week and 33% less than asking price the offer seemed low.

It was eight years since I'd been released from Marion. Upon my release in 1997, I applied for twenty-one jobs in thirty days. I was eager to get my life back on track. Eventually, I was hired on as a stagehand at the Bradley Center in Milwaukee, the local arena where the Milwaukee Bucks play. I was doing menial labor, readying the stadium for home games and concerts, and making $5.85 per hour. I was grateful for the job.

I had initially applied to, and was rejected by, the catering department of the Bradley Center, but the Director of Catering, a woman named Kathy, heard about my past and came to learn more of my story. After talking at length, she said that if I were hoping to successfully reintegrate into society that someone would need to give me a chance. After our short talk she hired me on the spot. "Joel what you need is social interaction." "Working in the other department you will be used like a tool with very little human interaction." She was correct. We threw many large parties for corporations like US Bank and Manpower. The socializing was very stimulating to say the least.

I worked 50 to 70 hours per week, so that with each paycheck I was able to buy a specific landscaping tool with aspirations of restarting a landscaping company. I had started at the Bradley Center in September of 1997 and was hoping to save enough before springtime.

When summer finally arrived, I did a lot of raking, mowing, and patching of lawns. I was moderately successful, and managed to save a few thousand dollars of the money I'd made landscaping over the summer. I lived meagerly in a nice, albeit small, one-bedroom apartment in a three-family building in the Riverwest neighborhood of Milwaukee.

Winter came and I went back to the Bradley Center for a few weeks of work. I also helped my brother shovel snow throughout the winter. While working at the Bradley Center, I met the advertising director for a local community paper. I began thinking of ways to grow my business and decided to take a chance. I contracted $5,000.00 worth of advertising in the form of one-page inserts in the paper. The risk paid off in spades. I nearly doubled my landscaping designs and install gigs, including some brick decks and walks. When business was slow I had almost no overhead, and did the smaller jobs solo.

Twenty-two months after my release, I profited just over $37,000 from the business in one month. As a reward, I bought a used Ford F-150 pickup to improve my business transportation and cut down on travel costs.

My real estate career really began when I saw a drug bust while living at 818 East Wright Street Milwaukee, Wisconsin. I was leaving to walk the two miles to work at the Bradley Center when suddenly at least eight unmarked squad cars pulled up in front of my neighbor's house across the street at 827 E. Wright Street. A troop of officers shot out of the vehicles, adorned in dark blue jackets sporting DEA, FBI, or ATF in yellow on the back.

I was shocked. I had befriended my neighbor James and I never suspected him to be a drug dealer. Yet I was only one hundred steps from my front porch when one of the agents yelled. I watched as he pulled a plastic-wrapped white brick from a duffel bag.

My heart raced. I had learned the intimate details of federal criminal forfeiture laws while in federal prison, and knew with that kind of evidence the United States Marshals were certainly going to seize the house. The law libraries in federal prison are required by the Supreme Court to be very well stocked based on the Fourteenth Amendment to the United States Constitution, which reads, "[…] no person shall be deprived of due process of law." In the 1977 landmark case Bounds vs. Smith, 430 U.S. 817, the Supreme Court determined the interpretation of the amendment to mean that every incarcerated individual in federal prison must have access to legal resources or law libraries. I read a lot of law books in the prison law libraries and had many conversations with convicts who had their homes and property confiscated by the federal government, like my old friend Ferris Alexander the Patriarch of Porn. Therefore I knew James was going to lose his house unless he was not guilty, and that white brick in the agent's hand meant the evidence was strong.

While at work that day, my mind kept returning to that house, and the knowledge that I could get it for a song at auction. The process is slow and steady. It might be fifteen to eighteen months until the seized assets are sold at a public auction. While in prison I learned of an arcane and esoteric rule governing the sale of seized assets. If someone makes an unsolicited bid for an asset that is in the process of being forfeited the auction process can be forgone almost completely.

The very next day I went to the United States Marshal Office Asset Forfeiture Section and made plans with them for an unsolicited bid. Over the next 18 months I would call every two weeks. The marshals had to offer the property to the public, but not necessarily through an auction.

Finally, a tiny, three-line ad ran the following Tuesday, for one day, and if anyone was interested they had to make a sealed bid. If they outbid me, I had one final chance without anyone being able to bid after me.

There was one other bidder, but I'd built a relationship with the marshals in the office over the last eighteen months and they found my story compelling. I won the bid. I put up $26,000 of my landscaping money in cash from the previous summer, and launched what would become a successful real estate career buying, renovating, restoring, renting, and selling buildings and land.

During this time, I was also attending the University of Wisconsin-Milwaukee. I was working toward an educational goal that I had developed while in prison. I always had an affinity for water, the oceans, and all marine creatures, and I wanted to begin developing urban fish farms throughout the world. During the voluminous reading I had done in prison, I discovered that the US rate of consumption of seafood versus ocean capacity would create an economic need for alternative fish sources. My studies suggested that by 2010, in fifteen years, the demand for fish farms would be staggering compared to present levels in 1995.

One of the elective courses I chose during my freshman year was called Black Reality, taught by a professor Abo Ram Pá, a Ghanaian immigrant. As I read the course syllabus, I thought back to the six federal prisons where I did time.

The African diaspora of and to North America is something I became intimate with during my time behind bars through literature and conversation with other convicts and inmates. As I read the syllabus on the first day of class, I realized I was entirely familiar with the subject matter.

After a few classes I saw the professor outside of class and proceeded to tell him some of my story. I then asked if I could take the final exam and figuring if I passed that I could have some extra free time during the semester. The professor told me I would have to get at least a B to test out of the class. The first time I took the exam I received a B-. Because I was so close to testing out of the class, and I had exceeded his expectations, Abo Ram Pá allowed me to take the test for a second time and the following day I ended up with a high B in class.

He asked me to write a report on the riots and the crack law, insisting it was an important part of American history that needed to be told. Initially it was difficult for me to write about my experience. To me, the story was personal, and a story of my friends, comrades, and their struggle. I discovered however, once I began to write, I couldn't stop.

I completed the report in October of 1998 for extra-credit in the class. Before my final semester at UWM, I led a peace studies conference at Marquette University in Milwaukee (1999), during which I read and discussed my report. Professor Abo Ram Pá also proposed a possible honorary degree in Humanities from the University of Wisconsin-Milwaukee if I turned my story into a book. At the time however, my landscaping business and real estate investments were starting to take shape, satiating my material wants won out for the time being.

By the end of that summer and fall of 1999 I had grossed almost $140,000 from my landscaping business. After taxes and all other costs, I still had over $50,000 in cash. Even though I was one-third of the way to my bachelor's degree, I dropped out to focus on the business.

I had a passion for writing and reflecting on my memories of prison but at the same time it was something I wanted to forget forever. I vowed to come back to school sometime in the future.

Joel Blaeser #1035
Kenton County detention center
303 Court Street
Covington Kentucky 41011

Rosemary Blaeser
1150 North Lake Shore drive
Chicago Ill 60611

Hi mom   June 13, 1992

     Thought I would write you a letter. I know when I was little I caused you and dad Alot of Grief and I am Sorry. You & dad were always there for us when we needed you. Sometimes we weren't, like when you had your operation or teeth pulled, I Apoligize for myself & everyone else. You are the best mom Anyone could hope for. Presently I Appreciate everything you have done for me, I hope I can repay you some day. If I can ever help you in any way I will. don't Be Afraid to Ask It might Be some time though Before I get out

     How is your new Job Going, The Buns won last night, I think they will win the series. does Jen like her new Job, Are Jen and russ Getting Along. I am going to lift weights today I might as well make the best out of a poor Situation. well I am going to go now. Please Tell everyone I say High   love Always

                                       Joel

Joel Blaeser
03491-089
P.O. Box 1000
US Pen
Marion, IL 62959

Brad Blaeser
2304 North Oakland Ave #8
@ Milwaukee, WI 53211

Dear Brad   10-9-96

Hello, Mom sent me some pictures today of you, Emily, Becky, Mike and Cecilla. You look good, Becky and Mike look kind of discontented. Thats if you allow me to partake in words of judgement. 5 more years is real hard to swallow. The 5 year hallway is not a pretty view. It's past the point of can't. We need to do something, I have to get my physical freedom, or at least peace of mind knowing everything was done at the Judicial level to seek freedom. You say you're doing everything you can, I don't doubt that, unfortunetly that isnt enough. How about doing what it takes and just handle this affair with swiftness, wise action and power. I implore you to take evasive action now and pursue ruthlessly till we avail with the amount needed.

I sent you a letter yesterday with the latest Hemp world, last Sunday night. I sent out a letter to you along with 13 other letters for you to forward for me. thankyou I am low on stamps and want to make sure all my mail gets out. As Rod Serling has said when you enter the 4th Dimension it's not of site or sound it's The Twilight Zone, or whatever he says. They played a show I requested on the dead bar. Oct 16, 1989 - Brendan Byrne arena N.J. First dark star in 9 years. 1 year and 1 day after dads death. well Brother Enjoy

Did you get the other Mail

love Joel

5

Not So Innocent

M**y mother and father** met at Playboy. My mother, Rosemary, worked in the payroll department, and my father, Anthony, in collections. The summer of 1961 was the heyday of *Playboy*. Women were lining up to appear in the magazine, so it was quite the surprise when my mother received a call from Pompeo Posar, the staff photographer, to ask if she would pose for *Playboy*'s centerfold. An unsolicited proposal was incredibly unusual, and she was quite flattered so she sheepishly agreed.

Playboy Studios tested models with a first time photoshoot to determine if they were photogenic. My mother passed that test with flying colors, but as the date of her official shoot approached, she began to have some misgivings about how the publication might affect her as a young, unmarried woman. Just days before the final shoot she decided against it altogether, informing Pompeo and the staff that she would not pose for *Playboy*, and asked for all the negatives back. The entire staff was stunned. Apparently, this had never happened before.

Despite Pompeo's persuasive pleas, she was steadfast in her refusal, and eventually recovered all of the negatives from the picture shoot. She continued to work for Playboy until she married my father in November of 1963.

Both my mother and father highly regarded Hugh Hefner. He treated his employees well and during the course of their employment my parents attended many parties at the mansion on State Parkway in downtown Chicago, socializing with people like Shel Silverstein, among many other local and national celebrities.

My father quit Playboy to join his brother Jimmy Blaeser in real estate development, primarily throughout the Florida, Texas, and Chicago area. He worked with his brother into the mid 1960's, until they had a massive falling out and he was fired by my uncle. My uncle would continue the real estate development business achieving financial success in a few short years and officially becoming a millionaire by 1970, while my dad would struggle to keep us financially afloat for the rest his life.

Growing up we rarely saw Uncle Jimmy because of their rift. I believe some of the resentment for him that my dad harbored was rooted in pride, though I found out later that his business endeavor with Jimmy had caused him to miss out on some other opportunities as well, including becoming involved with McDonalds on the ground level. I have a feeling he blamed a lot of our misfortune on that single misstep.

My father would work in collections for various meat packing companies throughout the Chicago area for the rest of his life. Though he worked hard he gambled often. It was a love he shared with all of his children. By the time we were adolescents, we could all play most forms of poker — Five-Card Draw, Seven-Card Stud, Five-Card Stud, Texas Hold 'em, Jacks or Better — you name it, we knew the rules. But his skill couldn't compete with his passion for risk-taking and he never won enough to support his wife and five children at home. The result was a childhood peppered with financial stress and my parents often fought about money.

My mother had humble beginnings in Chicago. Her mother had come to America as a young girl in 1918 to escape the violence of the Ukrainian Revolution, and her father had immigrated from from Italy. They divorced when she was very young and she and her three sisters struggled to make ends meet and support themselves until her mother remarried years later.

My father came from a long line of German immigrants. His father started his career in the mailroom at Joslyn Steel in Chicago, and over the years worked his way up to become the vice-president of the company. I was later told it was his Catholicism that kept him from advancing to the role of president.

By World War II, my grandfather had acquired a degree in engineering and through Joslyn Steel's contract to supply steel for bombs was secretly invited to work on the Manhattan Project. My father once mentioned he remembered my grandfather disappearing for days at a time shortly before the bomb dropped and how somber my grandfather was the day it was deployed.

I have a distinct memory of my grandfather's downtown Chicago condo with its expansive balcony and floor-to-ceiling windows showcasing the view of Lake Michigan. It always smelled of fresh baked bread and pastries upon our arrival. He always kept china bowls filled with exotic silver and gold coins adorning the glass-top coffee table in his lush living room.

Despite that, or perhaps because he came from wealth my father never seemed to worry about money. But my mother, always the serious one of the two constantly fretted about it.

Often jovial, my father like many veterans had a darkness to him. I've often wished I could've known him before he went to Korea and wondered how he would be different then. He had a temper and my mother's unhappiness was just one of many triggers.

Some of my earliest childhood memories are of extreme and severe beatings from my dad, watching my parents argue through the seam in the door then during breakfast the sound of my mother slamming the kitchen cabinet doors so hard that my ears would ring until lunchtime at school.

When I was five years or six years-old, I did something wrong. I don't remember what the grievance was, but I do remember my father kneeling over me while I lay on my back next to the Christmas tree in our living room. His knees held my hands down, and he was taking full swings with his hand slapping and hitting me across the head and face. He only ceased when I wet myself, soaking my favorite yellow pajamas. He retrieved my mother to take care of the mess. I was dizzy and weak in the knees so she helped me clean up, and gently rubbed my back until I fell asleep.

My mother took a rather fatalistic approach to her marriage. After five kids together, and a very Catholic wedding there was no turning back. She had made her bet with my dad and was all in to the river. I would suffer through dozens more of my dad's violent rages until his death thirteen years later.

Still, my mother thrived in the position of beloved rescuer. There was no barrier that would have stopped her from trying to save any one of her children. She truly loved and cared for us and reveled in the adoration we doled on her, our heroine.

Our house was always spotless. The moment any one of my siblings or I arrived home, she would appear, wet washcloth in hand, prepared to tackle the dirt and grime of the day evident on our hands and faces. Shoes were not to be worn in the house. As a child, I assumed this was standard practice and always felt odd while wearing shoes in someone else's home.

My dad was always remorseful after the severe beatings. He would often round up my three brothers and I for a game of football, softball, or most likely golf. We had all been taught golf at a very young age because my dad had nearly become a pro-golfer in his youth. He was scouted and mentored as a young boy and on the path to become a national golf pro, until he was drafted at 21 in 1953.

After the war he only played for fun and relaxation, and in the occasional amateur golf tournament, but our house was decorated with his many trophies, sets of silver, and newspaper articles chronicling his first place wins at the Beverly Country Club in Chicago.

Often Dad would take us out for ice cream after a game. It was a real treat, especially after Mom had banned sugar from the house. I'd been diagnosed with ADHD/ADD and my diet was being changed as an alternative to current prescription drugs of the time.

Thus a new food regimen was enacted: no artificial flavors or colors, no partially hydrogenated oils, no BHT or BHA, no refined sugar, no high-fructose corn syrup, and no white flour.

Mom always enrolled us in all sorts of extra curricular activities in Oak Park Illinois. By age nine i was diving off the high dive at the Oak Park swimming pool, and going there alone by age eight.

When I was six I took official swimming lessons. My teacher was a blond woman named Debbie and I was smitten at first site. I asked her out on a date and she accepted. My body would become warm and tingly when I saw her. My mother packed us a wicker basket full of food for our date by the pool. It was the summer of 1975. She was tall and blond, always smiling talking with a smooth voice and never yelling at me. I looked up to her and trusted her emphatically. For one hour every morning she was all mine. There were about 12 kids in our class and we met every morning at 10 am in the Oak Park Illinois pool. When she would touch me it made me feel fuzzy and warm all over. We sat on the pools edge during our date eating cold cuts, lettuce and tomato on rye. The sun was out and I decided I wanted to marry her. I boldly asked, "Debbie, I like you. Will you marry me please?"

My feet were in the water at the pool's edge sitting next to her. I took a bite of the sandwich waiting for her to reply. In her sweet calming quiet loving tone she responded, "Yes, but we will have to wait until you're 13 Joel."

I turned red in the face. I was so in love. My mother and grandmother and 3 aunts assured me later that day that I would understand when I got older. Debbie was all I could think about. She dominated my conversations with everyone I knew. She rewarded me for all the good I did during class and never yelled at me fostering this implicit and immediate sense of trust in her. I had dreams about her in her bright red one piece bathing suite and long blond hair. She always smelled like coconuts. I would run to her and when we touched in my dreams my whole body would erupt and then I would awaken.

Each morning of the swimming lessons Debbie would toss me in the deep end because she knew I could handle it.

My mom did her best to pull me out of the pack and give me additional attention after my diagnosis. For my seventh birthday, she treated me to a weekend trip to Milwaukee, just the two of us. We boarded a train outside of our home in Chicago and zipped along the countryside for two hours. I stared gleefully out the window, mesmerized by the cows and farms whipping by us at seventy five miles per hour.

My mother then took me on a cultural tour of Milwaukee. She ensured all of her children were immersed in the arts at a young age. By the time I was nine I knew the story of van Gogh's ear, the painting *American Gothic*, had seen King Tut's tomb and countless plays, ballets, and symphonies. Needless to say I loved the Milwaukee Public Museum.

Next we visited the Mitchell Park Domes—an incredible plant conservatory that showcases foliage in enormous glass terrariums. It felt like we were walking through life-sized snow globes. My mother knew the names of dozens of plants and pointed out different leaf shapes colors and sizes. I had such trouble paying attention in school but her enthusiasm for nature was contagious and on that trip I caught the bug.

I cried when we left, sad to leave this magical retreat and Milwaukee with its cream city brick buildings and copper-domed downtown. My love for Milwaukee was implanted on that trip and I'd continue to foster it after we moved to the city a few years later for yet another one of my dad's job transfers.

Eventually my father's gambling would catch up with us and in an attempt to ease some of the financial burden my mother accepted a much-needed job working behind the deli counter at a local grocery store. She worked most afternoons and I spent more time under the supervision of my older siblings. My sister Jennifer three years my elder picked up some of the responsibility for childrearing. In the summer she took me to pick flowers in the park near our house where there was an incredible array of blooms in every color and size.

A petite gray-haired lady with a small dog teetered by and asked us where we lived.

"309 South Lombard," I answered honestly.

"No, no, we live at 1109," Jennifer said, while punching me in the arm. The woman scowled and moved on.

Jennifer scolded me for being too honest and trusting. "You can't give strangers our address, Bucky!"

My siblings teased and called me Bucky because I had a severe overbite. I was an easy punchline particularly when Michael and Jennifer teamed up on me.

For the most part I was the odd guy out. My three older siblings were very close in age and had a clique I could never really break into. My brother Bradley was three years younger than I and as the baby he got the lion's share of the attention from my mother. All of us had a natural entrepreneurial spirit. Even as tots we were all relatively sales savvy. My mother's parents owned a carpet store which served as a default daycare for us much of the time while she was working. While many of our peers were watching *Mr. Roger's Neighborhood* and *Sesame Street* we were exposed to pricing, inventory, and negotiations.

It may have been reinforced because from a young age I was aware that we struggled for money or perhaps it was simply in our DNA, but even as a child my brain was hardwired to earn money. I raked lawns, sold lemonade and had a paper route. My siblings and I also often played store. We would put our trinkets and belongings out on card tables in the front yard and attempted to sell our worldly possessions.

"Jesus Bucky you are never going to amount to anything. A sales guy can't have ketchup on his shirt." Michael flicked his finger under my nose as I looked down at the stain on my shirt.

I went back to building a Lincoln Log tower on the sales table.

"Bucky did you gnaw those logs with your front choppers?" Michael chided.

"Bucky quit fooling around," Jenny said. "Stop playing with the toys. You need to price those and get them ready for sale."

I sighed and searched for a pencil and paper.

Although we were always strapped for money my parents bought me a baby blue one-speed Schwinn bicycle for my eighth birthday in 1977. It had a matching blue speckled seat, a shiny chrome hanger covering the back wheel and chrome handlebars sporting glittering blue grips.

My incessant craving for the almighty dollar led me to believe that I wanted to sell the bike so I put it out in the front yard with a hand-drawn "For Sale" sign. My little brother Bradley watched from the front stoop as I stood in front of our house and waited for customers to approach. I'd watched people haggle in my grandparents' store and I was looking forward to the process feeling very grown-up and hoping the extra money would maybe mean a few days of peace around the house.

"Hi I like your bike," a small kid commented as he walked up to the porch. His friend who was on his own bike hung back by the curb.

"Thanks. Do you want to buy it?" I asked.

"Yes. Can I ride it first?" He touched the handlebars and admired the frame.

"Do you have enough money?" I asked.

"Yes."

"Okay." I lifted the kickstand with my foot and spun the bike around for him.

He slid onto the seat and grinned at his friend. They pedaled furiously down the road.

"Come back!" I screamed chasing after them as fast as my feet would fly. Bradley rode after them but he was only five and couldn't have done anything even if he had caught them. They disappeared over the hill and out of sight. My already skewed sense of trust for people eroded away.

After I graduated from high school I lacked direction. My grades weren't good enough for college and for the most part I thought school was a bore. I went to work for an auto repair department at a gas station. I was very handy and was able to diagnose and fix problems quickly. I learned a lot about repairing cars but still that entrepreneurial spirit pumped through my veins. So rather than continue to work for the shop I quit but worked out a deal to buy broken down jalopies from the shop. I fixed the cars myself, and then re-sold them for a profit. At any given time there were two or three different cars sitting in our driveway. This drove my father crazy.

"Joel, get those heaps of crap out of my driveway," he yelled at me one afternoon in the kitchen.

"Dad, I'm fixing those cars. I'll have them sold by the end of the month."

"My yard isn't a parking lot for trash dammit. You're nineteen-years old for Christ's sake. When are you going to grow up?"

"Dad I am making good money selling these cars, and I just got a job at the PDQ grocery store. I was trained yesterday and I am officially starting tomorrow."

My mother stood quietly at the kitchen table. She was icing her own birthday cake and didn't lift her head.

"You gonna be working a cash register when you're fifty? You need a plan to move your ass out of our house. You can't keep sucking off the tit, boy."

"I wish I were sucking a tit," I chuckled to myself.

"What did you just say?" He hollered and lunged at me. He grabbed me by the throat and pressed his thumbs into my larynx.

I struggled for breath. I rocked violently from side to side to loosen his grip. His face was bright red and veins popped out from his temples as he pressed down harder. My mother could no longer ignore the situation and screamed my father's name.

I punched him square in the chest. He released the stranglehold and fell backwards into the kitchen table. The table slammed into my mother's cake and it crashed to the ground.

"Fuck you! Don't you ever put your hands on me again!" It was the first time I had ever fought back.

My father scrambled to get back on his feet. His shoes slipped in the cake on the linoleum floor, and he fell back to the floor. My mother sobbed as she squatted down to help him.

"You disgust me! You think I want to grow up to be like you!?" I shouted at him as I ran out of the house.

I arrived home late that night and snuck up to my room. The next morning my dad left early to play golf. I got up late and putzed around the kitchen. I was still pretty shaken from the fight. I didn't have to check in for my shift at the PDQ until 2:00 pm.

In the late morning, I took my boom box out to the front yard and blasted some Grateful Dead while I went to work on one of the broken down cars. I had been to at least twenty Grateful Dead shows so far, and the music always took me to a peaceful place.

A few hours later I jumped on my BMX bike and pedaled to the shop. It was a warm summer day but I felt an unnerving chill on my neck as I rode. I arrived at the store and locked my bike to the rack out front. I had a sickening feeling that something was wrong and that I needed to go home.

Bells jingled to notify the staff of a customer's arrival as I entered the store. I immediately scanned the room for my manager Ben. I spotted his tall lanky form leaning against the counter while he read a newspaper. I headed straight for him an inexplicable sense of urgency hurrying my steps.

"Ben I know my shift on the cash register starts at two but I really need to go home." I said as I approached. He lifted his thin face and stared at me blankly through glasses as thick as coke bottles.

"What do you mean you have to go home? Your shift starts in two minutes and I don't have anyone else here to cover." His nose crinkled under his wire-rimmed frames.

"Something is wrong at home. I really have to go. I'm sorry to leave you in the lurch. I'll be back tomorrow."

"Like hell you will," he said, nostrils flaring. "If you leave here, don't bother coming back."

I ran out the front door quickly and unlocked my bike. My mouth was dry. I had this unbelievable sense of urgency to get home. As I turned the corner my house came into view. I pedaled full-throttle into the driveway and skidded out on the loose pebbles as I hit the brakes. I flung the screen door open. My mother and brother Brad were sitting in the kitchen.

"Where's Dad?" I asked frantically.

"He just got home from golf and was complaining of chest pain," my mother responded. "He's in the bathroom," she said pointing to our small lavatory just off the kitchen.

I ran over and banged on the door.

"Dad? Are you ok?"

There was no response. I opened the door and my father was slumped out onto the floor.

"Oh God, Tony!" my mother shrieked.

I knelt down and held him. Brad ran over and started CPR. We called 911. We kept pumping his chest and breathing into his mouth, over and over. Everything felt like it was moving in slow motion. It felt like hours before the paramedics arrived.

Finally an ambulance screamed into our driveway. The paramedics rushed in and relieved us. They jammed an adrenaline needle into his chest. His body let out a last gasp, but it was too late. He was pronounced dead on the way to the hospital.

He was 56 years-old. He smoked unfiltered Lucky Strike cigarettes for 43 years, and buttered his steak and french fries. He never believed in doctors. The last words I had ever spoken to him were so painfully disrespectful. He taught me how not to be a parent. But he was my dad and now he was gone. (October 15th 1988).

Dear Bradley,   10-31-96

Could you please forward this letter for me, I received the $ and went to the store this week. This is a very important letter and I have to be absolutely sure it does not get delayed. That is why I am having you send it out. If this letter gets delayed getting to you o-well. Rex has yet to respond to me either way. I wrote you 5 days ago with letters to forward to Jay, Mike, Jen and mom. I also asked if you could locate the address for Revolutionary Worker and call the 2 mags. (I included the phone #'s you gave me) I wrote one of the mags but they have not written back. I also asked about a loan for the lawyer.

Have you read any good books lately? Who are you and Lisa going to vote for in the presidential election? You are registered aren't you. Are you still doing pushups. I haven't lifted weights in over 12 months now and I can still do 100 pushups or 25 pull ups any style. I might crush you when I get out. I started to run the 2 days we go outside. I run 30 minutes and walk fast for the other hour and a half. When we have inside recreation I walk fast for those 2 hrs and when we go back in our cells I do the weightless work out. I do use some books in the routine though, as this is needed due to the advanced level of my strength and fitness. The exercise and food people eat today will either help or hinder them in years to come. Eating pure foods (no sugar, meat, etc) not smoking, or drinking more than I drink a day is the best health insurance. 350 years ago health insurance was non existent. 350 years ago the average age was probably no more than 45 years old, today the average age is almost 80. However the health industry (insurance, medicine etc) is almost a trillion dollar industry. For some reason that does not add up. Peoples bodies haven't been genetically engineered to last longer. Most of the Centurians (people who have lived to be 100) are not on any life saving medications. Studies have been done. Health insurance in one sense prays on people's insecurities and also capitalizes on these dietery and fitness flaws and ignorances.

        Well brother Peace be with you

Enclosed   love
2 page for Rex,   Sol
If you can handle it I would
be VERY appreciative if you could
type the rex letter for me (exactly as I wrote it)
and then send it. Even if it takes a extra day
or two, Maybe you or lisa could do it on
a computer. IT
is a important letter and needs to look professional.
Did you read the article in Sep 1996 GQ (P262)
about how these bitch prison guards murdered a inmate
I will try to get a copy of it and send it to you

6

Playing In The "Sandbox"

SEPTEMBER 1992

DIRECTLY AFTER THE VERDICT I was relegated to the county jail in Covington Kentucky, while I waited to be sentenced and subsequently transported to federal prison. I was not the only federal prisoner in this county jail but we were certainly the minority. We were mixed with state of Kentucky law-breakers. The difference between federal and state crimes is vast. To be put in federal prison meant your crime crossed state lines and fell under federal government jurisdiction. Crimes like interstate commerce, money laundering, smuggling, piracy, bank robbing, counterfeiting, hate crimes or other violations that fell under federal jurisdiction. The result in the population is that federal prisoners as compared to state prisoners are statistically older, better educated and come from a higher socioeconomic background. They are involved in more sophisticated crimes and often have ties to organized crime. These factors were all impacted by the war on drugs. According to the U.S. Department of Justice in 2013, 50 to 51% of federal inmates are drug war prisoners. Burglary, larceny, extortion, fraud, embezzlement, counterfeiting, and robbery, combined account for less than 15% of the current federal prisoner population.

This county jail housed murderers, rapists, child molesters, armed burglars, and drunks in for vehicular manslaughter. Needless to say this was a tough crowd of hoodlums and nefarious-looking characters.

The jail was a breeding ground for dandruff, viruses and all sorts of bacteria. Food was dismal at best and consisted of a plethora of high-carb cheese-laden dishes including beans, potatoes, rice, bread, green mushy vegetables, and some form of mystery meat. Breakfast was always cereal or oatmeal with one small carton of milk, one piece of thin white bread and two sugar packets. It would be seven months before I left this place as my lawyer continued to challenge the evidence at my jury trial to get a lighter sentence than the proposed 240 months the prosecutor was seeking.

My cellmate was a high level pot dealer from Mexico named E-Z. He talked a little about his case and explained that all three of his co-defendants were also in our pod. Each pod within the jail had a small communal room with a solid steel picnic table and one shower to share among the twelve inmates. The cell itself was enclosed by a steel door and featured two bunks, a toilet and a sink

Days after my arrival one of E-Z's co defendants Mario started to jokingly box with me. He was ten to fifteen years older than me, 2 inches taller and fifteen pounds heavier. His two front teeth had white gold highlights to them and showed as he was grinning and swinging. We barely knew each others name. I told him I didn't want to horseplay. "Mario I don't horseplay," I tried to say firmly and respectfully.

In response he took a real swing at me. I ducked. My heart started to race. I did not know anyone here. In El Reno Jim told me to always fight, "Even if you lose you will still be respected by your race." I didn't know where E-Z was or if he would jump into this fight. If he did would he be helping me or Mario? Mario swung again.

I couldn't duck forever. I had to make a move. The surroundings faded, my head emptied of all thought. suddenly I was full of energy. I hit him with three very quick consecutive jabs. First right then left, then right again. I grabbed his throat driving him back to the corner of the pod wall and delivered one more knee-buckling blow to his nose with all my might. Blood started to gush out of his nose onto my hands. His nose was badly bent to his right side and huge droplets of blood were spitting out of his mouth as he fought for breath.

It took all my strength to keep him propped up. I put my other hand on top of my left hand already on his throat, squeezing as hard as I possibly could, arms pushing forward locking him into the corner of the wall with nowhere for him to go, Mario tried to undo my hands and I just started to squeeze harder leaning forward with all my might driving more of my weight into his neck. His breathing stopped and his face darkened as fear permeated his eyes.

I looked into his eyes. He was dying.

No one in the cell said a word.

I looked up at his face and let go. He dropped to the ground, gasping for life and breath, his nose broken, bloody and bent.

Dismayed and distraught at the beating I was forced to administer to a man I barely knew, I exiled myself to my jail cell. Holding back tears and a nervous breakdown I tried to compose myself.

I was not a fighter and very rarely fought. The last time I remembered fighting was in the 8th grade.

E-Z walked in moments later and explained he thought his three co-defendants were going to testify against him. He said he wished I had killed Mario.

"Why didn't you fuckin finish him off? Fuck him! They would have ruled it self-defense!" he nearly yelled it at me. He then patted me on the back and exclaimed "Good job! I'm proud of you." E-Z was 225 lbs with a huge barrel chest and heavy thick black hair all over his body. He was at least twenty years my elder and I looked up to him.

I was speechless.

E-Z and his co-defendants had been caught with a U-Haul full of money and the truck had marijuana residue in it. They were arrested, held without bail and subsequently indicted on conspiracy, an easy charge to prove if just one of the four turned against the rest. He wanted to go to trial, but the other three wanted to plead guilty. He'd been busted twice before and got off at trial.

E-Z said he would send $100,000 in to whomever I wanted to in the free world if I agreed to testify at his trial on his behalf against the other co-defendants. "Joel take the money and do some good with it no one will ever know." he said with the sincere kindness of a father asking a son to please help him. I wanted EZ to win and hated people who became informants. "Joel just give me a address and a check will be sent by my lawyer." "I will have my lawyer visit you and tell you what to say so we can discount what I suspect my co-defendants are going to testify to." I had almost killed someone moments earlier. I was nearly numb.

I declined E-Z's offer. Eventually he was moved to another pod. Later, it was revealed in the local paper that all his co-defendants substantially assisted for a lesser sentence. This time he lost at trial.

My next cellmate was a real winner. He was a state offender. He brought his Sony Walkman with him into the county jail. I took a Styrofoam cup, punched the bottom out, and fastened it on the earphones to create a speaker effect amplifying the sound. The song "Under the Bridge," by Red Hot Chili Peppers came on. The lyrics are: "I don't ever want to feel that way/ like I did that day/ when I drew some blood." Carlos would sing on cue, except his words were a little different: "I don't ever want to feel that way like when I crushed her skull." Then he would laugh with a maniacal and crazy giggle that hinted at something very sinister and strange.

He was in for manslaughter. In a drunken rage he crushed his wife's skull. Because his wife was drunk as well he was only given 20 years on his guilty plea. This was a state of Kentucky crime and most likely he would only serve 11 years if he got marks for good behavior.

It was 1993, so "Under the Bridge" came on a lot during the short period we were cellmates. I couldn't have been more grateful the day the marshals finally came to get me to go to federal prison. Perhaps my cellmate in FCI Sandstone would be even crazier but I couldn't handle any more of Carlos's gruesome laughter or that god forsaken song.

After sentencing I was routed for FCI Sandstone in Sandstone Minnesota, and lucked out with a bus ride to Sandstone with only two stops and El Reno, Oklahoma, was not one of them. When the bus arrived at the county jail there were 30 prisoners on it already, heading west and then north, we were going to be picking up and dropping off federal prisoners on the way to Sandstone. The first stop was USP Terre Haute for an overnight layover. This was a high-security federal penitentiary with a huge 35 foot tall cement wall surrounding the entire prison. Built in 1940 on a 1100 acre property, it was pretty scary for a new fish like me to see. We were housed overnight in "The Hole," so some of the general population prisoners who got into trouble were on our tier. It was a one-floor tier about forty cells long (two hundred fifty feet long) with bars on the front of the cells. Each cell had a steel-framed bunk bed. Fortunately I was the odd man out and got my own cell, without a celly, which I was grateful for, albeit for one night. My cell was right in the middle of the cell block. We arrived late at night, it was past "lights out," but to the left was a tiny glimmer of light from the CO's office. To the right clear on the other end of the unit there must have been an open window because there was a nice breeze coming through that alleviated some of the tension and stuffiness from the air. Still we were restless and sleep wasn't coming easy to anyone. We began telling jokes to pass the time.

The jokes were predominantly racial. Hymie, wop, nigger, cracker, spic—all the slurs were used, but respectfully; everyone asked if they could say something before they made any joke with a racial epithet. The unit rang with laughter. We were all laughing at the string of jokes, including the correctional officers (CO's) down at the end of the tier. I recalled a terrible racist joke about Jeffrey Dahmer and without thought asked the tier if I could tell it. In all of my giddiness from the other jokes I failed to execute any kind of judg-ment on the impact this would have.

The majority of the inmates in this transfer were black so they yelled back and forth for about sixty seconds before it was decided I could go ahead.

"What does Jeffrey Dahmer have for breakfast?" I quipped.

Someone piped up, "Uh oh, here we go."

I paused another seven or eight seconds. The tension mounted.

"Coffee and bronuts."

Silence.

I yelled out the joke and punch line so I am certain everyone in the whole cellblock heard it. Another three or four seconds passed. Then the entire cell block erupted into absolutely hysterical laughter. It went on for at least two minutes straight.

All of a sudden sounds of marching boots coupled with the clicking of keys could be heard off in the distant it was getting louder as it came closer, the guards were walking very fast towards my cell, Fuck, shit, now what I thought, were they going to write me up? Both prison guards came to an abrupt stop right in front of my cell and looked in. "Wow dude, you got balls. Nice joke, we had to see who you were" then they turned around and walked back to their office.

The next morning we were all let out to shower and go on recreation for 50 minutes before we went back on the bus. A half-black, half-Puerto Rican inmate named Lie, approached me during recreation.

"Dude what's your name?"

"Blaeser," I responded.

"You going to Sandstone?"

"Yes," I replied.

"Yeah? Me too. My name is Lie. I am from the Bronx doing five years for a key." Key I came to learn meant a kilo of cocaine.

"I am from Milwaukee." Fortunately he came give me respect of all things, as did a lot of other minority inmates, for being crazy enough to say such a joke, permission or not.

My first federal prison destination turned out to be FCI Sandstone in Minnesota. It looked like a school built in the 1930's. Very innocuous looking with one fence and very little razor wire. In Sandstone there are two divided sections to the prison compound, an open low-security FCI with one gun tower that had been unmanned for the last 20 years and a housing area separated from the general population with a large wall, specifically designated for participants of the witness protection program. The housing units themselves were not at all what I expected. To my horror the housing units didn't feature cells. In fact it was far more reminiscent of a dorm room than a prison. The room featured ten foot high ceilings and two rows of 24 bunk beds. The beds were separated by six foot high walls effectively creating what looked like office cubicles with four bunks in each. The bunks were five feet high meaning if you were sitting up on your top bunk you were looking down at your neighbors bunk a few feet away -- there was no semblance of privacy.

One of my biggest shocks in prison was not the chow but the chow hall scene. The food itself wasn't bad and as in most federal prisons it was plentiful. We were fed three times a day. The chow hall in Sandstone was rectangular in shape, with food at one end of the hall and a beverage bar the middle of the room offering tea, coffee, water, milk and occasionally soda.

The shocking part of chow was the line. Visually, the chow line was very similar to a school cafeteria with one exception: In prison there are two lines, one for whites and one for blacks and other minorities. All the food in both lines was exactly the same. It seemed so bizarre to experience segregation in this day and age. The shock literally stopped me in my tracks upon entering.

This was a blatant divide and conquer tactic. Pitting races against each other in a subtle way to help control in-mates. Wardens, like the leaders of any ancient institution have had centuries to perfect their strategy. When the inmate to prison guard ratio is twenty five or thirty-five to one, there has to be something to keep prisoners divided in order to lessen the threat to prison staff, and history has proven that captive peoples who fight amongst themselves never lead successful revolts. Later I would come to further understand the full impact of a united prisoner front. For now my disbelief faded into horror and disgust, and I shuffled into the white food line to collect the exact same meal as my black and minority comrades.

There were ways to get unique food items in chow if you wanted a change of pace. In federal prison the law requires that prisoners are allowed to practice any religion. Generally you are allowed to change religion once every six months If you so choose. The specific designation is done through the prison chapel by the prisoner religious attache, employed by the Bureau of Prisons. Sometimes prisoners would change religions to take advantage of the unique meals offered in deference to religious freedom. For example, Jewish inmates had kosher meals prepared in advance and delivered at the chow line, and Muslims received special consideration during Ramadan. Later on during my incarceration I would change my religion to get better food or rather food that I found to be better for me.

Convicts could also buy food items from the commissary, or prison store. We were allowed to shop every two weeks by filling out a slip of paper the day before "store day" and putting the order in with our laundry bag. Though each prison had a few unique items in its commissary, the majority of the items were the same. Every federal prison including Marion, at the time of my incarceration sold raw garlic, shampoos, various toiletries, junk foods, protein powders, liquid amino, powdered carbs, sausages, cheeses, rice, ramen noodles, etc. During Christmas and Easter the commissary would carry holiday items like figs, dried mangoes, etc. You also purchased your phone cards from the commissary. They were sold in five dollar increments and could be used at night in the designated phone room on the prison yard. Friday and Saturday nights were especially busy nights for the phone. For the most part you could call every night for an hour or two if you had the money.

All commissary money was stored on an account. Your account was padded either by money you made at your in-house job or money your family or friends sent to the prison specifically for you to spend, which went onto your "books." At no point do you ever have physical cash. Instead, stamps or other unopened Commissary items acted as currency at low-level places like Sandstone.

At the age of two my Grandpa nicknamed me "Jolly" for good reason. I laughed every single day during my incarceration, starting back in the county jail the day after I lost my trial. Somehow despite my circumstances I maintained an innate happiness. Inmates and convicts were usually thrown off by my extremely positive attitude, but for the most part in prison it fostered respect because it showed I was genuine, a rare character trait on the inside and one that allowed me to socialize with ease among many of the higher-ups, or convict "shot callers" who "ran the yard" in nearly every prison I would spend time in no matter what their race was.

Much of my time in Sandstone was spent studying my case in the law library. While I was there I befriended some very interesting characters, including Ferris Alexander, the Patriarch of Porn. He had monopolized the porn industry in the Minneapolis area and at the time of his arrest owned over 38 porn stores and theaters. He was 71 years-old when he, his wife, and son were arrested on obscenity and racketeering charges. The prosecutor confiscated 10 pieces of commercial real estate, 31 current or former businesses, and $9 million in cash, because in all of the merchandise, four magazines and three videos were determined to be obscene. It was the equivalent of the FAA seizing every single one of United Airlines' planes because seven were missing a bolt.

His wife and son were acquitted, but he was sentenced to almost six years. He fought the charges. He was a stout old man who maintained the stance that he'd been railroaded by the government, all at the cost of his freedom of speech. He felt he was treated as if he were a kingpin of a mafia crime family, when in reality he was simply an industry tycoon closer to Rockefeller or Carnegie than Capone.

He appealed his case all the way to the Supreme Court. It was a close five to four decision, affirming the conviction and asset seizure. The dissension among the court was so strong that no prosecutor has launched an obscenity-predicated RICO case since. His case and appeal have since been re-examined by many first amendment rights groups and authors exploring the role of civil rights in our country (Alexander v. United States 1993, no. 91-1526 Supreme Court Of The United States: 509 U.S. 544). His obscenity convictions were based on titles like "Let's Have a Fuck Party," and "Leather Sleaze," common for porn movie goers today. He passed away in 2003, still actively assisting first amendment rights groups to argue for clarification of the term obscenity.

One of the more notorious criminals in Sandstone was Pistol Pete Lafroschia. He was part of the Gemini Lounge Crew, by far the most ruthless New York mafia crew of the time and probably ever. The crew's namesake came from the club where many of the members and leader Roy Demeo hung out and where many unfortunate victims were last seen alive. They coined the term "the Gemini method," a means for permanently getting rid of bodies via dismemberment. The authorities suspected the crew, and the Gambino crime family they were allegedly backed by, to be responsible for the disappearance of nearly 200 people, though very little evidence was ever found.

Pete was an expert car thief and could steal any car parked on the city streets of the five boroughs of NYC in less than 45 seconds. He also assisted in some of the crew's extortion tactics. He was sentenced to 13 years, and served the majority of his sentence at Lewisburg Penitentiary in Pennsylvania. Just before his sentence was up they sent him to FCI Sandstone. He only had about 12 months left on his sentence when I met him. He was featured in the book *Murder Machine*, by Gene Mustain and Jerry Capeci, published in July

1993, shortly before my arrival in Sandstone. I quickly bought a copy of the book and had Pete sign it.

However, it was rather unusual to find criminals with the notoriety of Pistol Pete and the Patriarch of Porn. The majority of people on the compound were low-level criminals with five to six year sentences or less. It turns out only one out of the thousand prisoners on the compound had more time than my prison sentence. Some of the prisoners were at the tail end of a long sentence and sent to Sandstone from a high security prison right before their release, like Lafroscia. Otherwise, most were low level criminals who had pled guilty and assisted the government in some way making them rats according to convict code. My time with the Grateful Dead conditioned me to crave a sense of community or father figure and here I was stuck in a prison full of rats and snitches, people who were self-serving and willing to turn in their friends in order to gain favor with the guards. I was uneasy.

Luckily, I met a kindred spirit in the law library at Sandstone. He was a big muscle-head named Hog Head, and I knew I liked him when he referred to Sandstone as "Sandbox" because it was a place with almost no "real" criminals. We became workout partners along with this guy named Chili, doing a power routine three days in a row and taking a day off before we started up again.

"Nobody's giving it away Blaeser! Push one more rep! You can do it!" Hog Head blasted at me as he spotted me on the bench press. Him and Chilli were two cocksure, hardened convicts in prison for cocaine trafficking. I could barely spot them as they were doing over 300 lbs on the bench for 10 reps. It was in Sandstone that I really began to be more conscious of my health, and form habits I would carry with me out of prison and into my daily life. I drank 25 to 35 ounces of water the minute I woke up and ate raw garlic every single day for my entire incarceration.

I was determined to better myself in more ways than simply health though. One of the first things I did upon arriving at Sandstone had been to apply for Pell Grants so that I might begin taking college courses. Post-secondary education used to be widely available in prisons in the United States, especially after 43 people were killed in the notorious Attica Rebellion of 1971. Attica is a state prison located in upstate New York, and was home to the granddaddy of all single-prison riots. These prisoners were too-long ignored. In Attica the prisoners rebelled with the hope their demands for improved prison conditions, including a better education program would be met. The result was that educational programming became available, not only to inmates at Attica, but also in prisons around the country.

Over the next 20 years, prison education flourished. Classes were often taught through mail correspondence and some were even held on prison grounds. To those inside it seemed an obvious union. The federal prison system and its inmates had access to Pell Grants because if you go to prison, you need an outlet to better yourself. After all you are surrounded by criminals and con men and if you aren't learning applicable job skills and schools of thought, what does that leave to learn but violence and criminal knowledge? There were over 100,000 people in the federal prison system and about 1.1 million total US prison population the year Congress voted to repeal prisoner access to Pell Grants. There was strong resistance from the Department of Education, the prison wardens and from Clai-borne Pell himself, the Rhode Island senator who was largely responsible for establishing the Basic Educational Opportunity Grants, as they were originally titled. Pell was vehemently opposed to Congress's ruling in 1994; "As I have often said, education is our primary hope for rehabilitating prisoners, without education I am afraid most inmates leave prison only to return to a life of crime," he stated. How could they expect prisoners to re-enter society as functioning and rehabilitated adults now that they had taken the tools from inmates that promoted self-improvement and change? The repeal of Pell grants indicated to inmates that the Bureau of Prisons and Congress had given up on the idea of rehabilitation and decided to simply house and feed instead. Congress had gotten it wrong again.

    When I found out Pell Grants were cancelled I was devastated. I was pre-approved during the preliminary screening process, then sent a letter and called into the counselor's office from my unit when Congress voted for the change. Upon arriving at Sandstone, I'd tried to think about preparing myself for life outside and improving myself, but with the loss of educational opportunity, resorted to what I knew: business. The irony was that I had not been selling drugs when I was charged and arrested. In fact, I'd quit for over a year at my family's behest in an effort to get my act together. I was still trying for that when I arrived in Sandstone, and then was shut down.

    I did not search out my first prison business venture, rather it found me. One day a fellow convict named Mark, came to me and asked if he could borrow some of my armor be-cause of a potential problem out on the yard that day, a very rare occurrence here in Sandbox. "Joel can I rent some of your armor?" Mark had a few prison tattoos on his arms and spoke with a very eloquent southern drawl. We met about a month before out on the yard. He was a hardcore Christian who did not believe races should mix when marrying or having children. He seemed to have been indoctrinated into that belief at a very young age and when speaking about it talked about it very matter of factly with no emotion in his voice or face.

    "Armor?" I was not quite sure what he was talking about. My mother would send me subscriptions to many magazines, including *National Geographic*. He went on to explain that *National Geographic* magazines act as the best protection against knife wounds during a battle when taped to your chest and belly under your clothes, hidden from the view of prison staff and opponents alike. It wasn't uncommon for inmates to receive magazines from loved ones but not many if any received *National Geographic*. It was an expensive subscription and did not appeal to most prisoners. However, the thickness of the magazine and paper stock would severely hinder a knife penetrating you if you were stabbed where one of these magazines was taped to your body. I had three or four of them saved up. The idea appealed to my natural entrepreneurial spirit. I was never one to turn down an opportunity to make money, so I let him borrow some of my "armor" for a fee. It turned out the fight he was preparing for was fair, meaning no other convicts jumped in and no weapons were pulled, so he didn't need it. But I had found my first business venture in prison. Of course there was a risk. If he had been searched or patted down while he had the magazines taped to his body, he would have been thrown into the Hole for 60 to 90 days "for investigation'", interrogated, and then probably transferred to a higher security prison. If he had named me as his source or they figured out they came from me, I would likely be subjected to the same treatment, but to me the risk was part of the appeal of dealing.

So I dealt in small things, such as magazines, specialty food items stolen from the chow hall, but I was craving more. I'd spoken with the few people I had come to trust inside Sandstone and had determined that it was not the kind of prison I wanted to serve out my full sentence at. There was no chance of having college classes and many of the prisoners here were snitches, so if I were to get involved in anything, I would likely get in trouble for and spend the majority of my time here in the Hole. My new friends who had been transferred to Sandstone from other prisons explained that there was plenty of marijuana and alcohol in other federal prison yards. Though I had quit selling drugs a years ago, I had not stopped doing them. It also meant that moving to another prison would be more lucrative for me. If I got into trouble I would probably get sent to either Englewood or Florence, both serious medium-security prisons in Colorado with drugs and alcohol, plenty of people with life sentences and guards with a different attitude.

After about eight months in the "Sand box" it finally happened. I got into trouble in Sandstone. I had started to buy broken radios for six or seven dollars, then pay a fellow prisoner in the electronic shop three or four dollars to fix them and then turn around and sell them for $18 to $25. The store sold them for $40, so I was undercutting the market price by quite a bit. I would get paid in stamps or commissary. Pretty soon the locker next to my bed swelled full of brand-new unopened commissary. A big blond kid named Aaron sold me a broken radio for five dollars. I paid my friend in the electronics shop three dollars to fix it. He found out I was selling it for $25 and threatened to "tell the lieutenants if I didn't give it back." I recognized my opportunity here, and refused, so that he would head to the CO's office and narc on me. In most other prisons he would have been beat half to death before he even finished his sentence. When the guards came to my cell and told me I was under investigation I was excited at the prospect of a new home for my long prison sentence. They charged me with illegal possession of a radio because I had two of them, one more than the allowance per inmate. A minor infraction yes, but one that would get me sent to the Hole nonetheless. I knew that if I continued to deny the charge they would transfer me out of the prison rather than put me back in the general population of Sandstone assuming I would hurt Aaron, who'd snitched on me.

It worked I got a first-class ticket to FCI Englewood, in Englewood Colorado, a suburb of Denver. I had to go through El Reno Oklahoma taking the marshal plane and holding over for about three weeks, and then back on the plane to Englewood. I had talked to people about Englewood. There was marijuana on the compound a lot of lifers or people with life sentences, meaning I could meet a high volume of real convicts, people I'd be in with for a good amount of time. Overall it was considered a good place to do a stretch at.

Halfway through our trip to Englewood via El Reno Oklahoma, something went wrong with the engine of the big diesel bus we were riding in. The Marshal pulled into a large garage and left the engine running. The smoke from the engine began filling the bus as the mechanics worked on it. Hog Head was on the bus too. He got into trouble right after I did and was heading to Florence Colorado. "Hog we got to do something. I can't handle the smoke," I said.

"Yeah. Let's rock this motherfucka."

A big black convict from the back of the bus yelled out. With our legs and hands shackled to our belly chains no one was able to avoid inhaling the smoke. Even though it was ice cold outside we began to make a ruckus to get the marshal to turn off the bus. Despite the racial division ingrained in us by the prison system there was always an underlying unity among prisoners when it came to convict code versus authority. In this instance it was certainly warranted. We all began to yell in unison to turn off the engine, causing the Marshals to board the bus and holler at us to knock it off, stating they couldn't shut the engine off due to protocol. Two more minutes passed. Then all thirty-five of us, Mexican, African, African-American, South American, Caucasian, and Native Americans/Indians, started rocking left to right. The whole bus was moving. As we rocked it, we yelled "Turn off the engine now!" "Turn off the engine now!" "Turn off the engine now!" Finally, they shut it off. They worked on it for twenty minutes longer, and though it rapidly became colder inside, the air was fresh and we considered it a worthy trade off.

On the way out as our lungs began to clear from the smoke and our bones were warming from the bus heater, the marshals turned the radio on, a sure sign they weren't too mad at us. I stared out the big metal bar-lined prison bus window at the snow-covered frozen landscapes passing us by, the violin of Paula Abdul's "Rush, Rush" lifting our spirits.

Joel Blaeser
03491-089
U.S. PENITENTIARY
P.O. BOX 1000
MARION, IL 62959

Brad Blaeser
2304 north Oakland Ave #8
Milwaukee, WI 53211

Dearest Bradley   10-19-96

    Hello dear brother. So where do we go from here? Let the words be yours I am done with mine — as Bobby would say or Jerry might say if you plant ice you're gonna harvest wind. Boy your letter seemed very windy. I am writing you this letter as I listen to my last Dead show (it says) in the free world. 6-20-92 Soilders field. Aint no time to hate. —Are you kind. Yes I doubted you, I don't like to, but I did. Nothing will take that away, since I came here things have been a little paranoid so to speak. Everyone here gets beat down once and continually fucked with by staff. knowone is realy singled out, it is just the Marion mind fuck game plan. "There Juvenile Game Of War." My energy around here does get misdirected from time to time. 22 hrs a day in a matchbox doesn't help. Things are getting better. By better I mean living and accepting things out of the context of dualities, (Good/Bad, Black/White, up/down) Reality is what it is. As far as you lashing out because of my insinuations is more of the same, I accept it and we will just let it go where it came from. We can define me doubting you and you putting yourself on the same level calling me names and getting indignant with me in your letter. I think the reason you got so mad was that I let you down in the sense that I second guessed our trust, thats what it looked like, and in a sense was. Obviously a misperception on my part. I took you non chalance as some sort of warning sign. Sketchy standards? what defines sketchy, I am in prison ~~oooo~~ with Honors, very rare around here and out there. Sketchy is obsolete bro. If anything I figured you borrowed it for bills or necessities in which case I really have no gripes if you did or do use it for that. What defines successful, it's all a matter of the perception of the perceiver. Amount of money? Physical mite?, Number of degrees, Religious convictions, Contentment?, Number of kids, Numbers of banks robed, Number of bodies? number of crimes gotten away with, Honor? The list goes on and on. It all comes down to the peace within that person doesn't it. Most or least is irrelevent, when you do see that your success will have gone another step further. What is, is nothing will change whats done, we can accept things with opposites or choose another path, renouncing the struggle against opposites or evil. Me, you, everyone. A mother who wipes a baby cheeks as he screams is seen as a loving act to most, A murder of a snitch may seem as a act of murder to most and punished accordingly. Seeing evil or my last letter of doubt we react with fear as I and you did. from this arises the struggle, and because we want it to go away the struggle seems legitimate. It looks like the fear and anger were the cause of evil. I feared and doubted myself and thus you, And our actions and reactions are or were breeding more of the same cycle. which can never end. But it doesn't have to be that way. There are no ~~got~~ guarantees in life, rite now today ~~a~~ I know I don't want to come back to prison - physical or otherwise. I cannot see into the future. People get sent back to prison for 3 and 4 years on a probation violation. Probations violations that I have seen range from a minor traffic violation or plain traffic stop to a dirty urine, I met a guy named Chuck who got a 47 month probation violation for suspicious behavior. No charges or even a violation. He appealed his case and was denied. Federal probation is 90-95% successful at returning people to prison within the first year of release. I don't think anybody wants to come back to prison. Alot of mistakes are made in expecting not to come back, and then partaking in questionable behaviour when you are released. If you completely ~~scrammed~~ absconded and left the country when you got released and did not come back you would probably be most successful. I am developing a specific and specialized plan for my release which will hopefully prevail against all the pitfalls that could beseech me. As far as me not getting the Hoss receipt I was just letting you know I did not receive it to let you know these clowns must have gotten it. As is the reason you are enjoying National Geo and not the Savages here. ~~[scribbled out]~~ Well I love you brother, Thankyou Lisa, feel free to let her read this letter if you care too. Lets leave this in the past were it belongs. Love you

Joel

P.S.
Please let me know you got this 3 page letter (10-19-96)

Letters from Marion

Blaeser
91-089
PENITENTIARY
BOX 1000
MARION, IL 62959

Rosemary Blaeser
1730 N Clark #4102
Chicago Il, 60614

Dear Mom   6-16-96
   Thankyou for the 1 magazine, all those cars are real nice. There are some good articles in there about all different kinds of cars. I saved all those stamps, 12 that seems like alot for 1 magazine. I got back a letter from the clerk of courts (Covington, ky) and it terns out I was only missing 1 page of the trial transcripts, she sent me the one missing page I will hold on to it until I need to send it to Alan Ellis if that ever happens. Thankyou for ordering those books, I am waiting eagerly for them. * You said you and larry may depart, it sands as though it's inevitable or is it? Same old stuff around here, I am voraciously devouring Secret Teachings of All Ages (The one from that Philisophical Society in LA) It will take me a while to finish, maybe 6 months or a year, the other books I read in between chapters of Secret teachings is to break it up. Did you finish were all doing time by bo Lozoff. O-yea Do you have terry Blaeser's address. I did receive Jimmy's Bobby's and Georgies. Has anyone sent you $75 for me in the last 6 months. Some one wrote me and said they were going to send it soon and that was 3 or 4 months ago I wasn't realy expecting them to send it but I could realy use it thats why I ask. The person has owed me the $ for 1 year now I guess I will write it off. The person is in another place otherwise I would have gotten it already.

2

Dont forget to see Bravehart! I want to see you again as soon as possible. I am working on my 6-Pack (stomach). I stopped eating all meat, Refined sugar and anything roasted in oil. I started my new diet June 1st. ever since I arrived in Marion I cut way down on my sugar intake but I was eating a lot of meat. On about June 6, 7, and 8th I went through heavy physical withdrawl from not eating meat. I am over it now and it is not even a consideration now. We shall see how long it lasts. I eat alot of fresh fruit, vegetables, whole wheat bread, milk and oatmeal. Rite now I have cut my intake to 1800 calories a day. I eat 6 small meals a day. When I get my meal I split it up and eat small meals throughout the day. It's more efficient that way. Your body assimilates protein every 2-3 hours anyway so by doing this you are more in tune with how your body naturally runs. Eating 3 big meals a day is a big fallacy. My body size along with the amount of excercise I do requires 2300-2800 calories a day. So there is a deficit there and thats when the fat comes off. Then when I get lean I can increase my intake level back up to maintain the new weight. But you have to be careful when doing this you want your daily intake to be 60-65% carbohydrates, 20-25% proteins and 10-15% fats. Otherwise you could end up losing muscle instead of fat. I am not really fat at all I have a tiny little bit around my waist which is covering my stomach muscles. In 6 weeks I should have a ripped up stomach (6-Pack). As far as no meat and healthy foods that is something that has nothing to do with wanting to look good, it's more like feel good

3

and I plan to eat like this for the rest of my life whether I am fat or skinny. It coincidently happens to be changed at the same time I am trimming a few pounds of my belly. It was nice growing up to your cooking and I am very thankful that you saw to it that we did not eat any bullshit foods. Most people would not but are ignorant of the facts. I don't smoke, drink coffee, sugar and now I don't eat meat of any kind. Whats next. Food is one of the few things we have any control over, as for as. If we want a special tray like I get or regular trays which have alot of fatty foods but no fresh fruits or vegetables like the tray I get. People don't even consciously realize it but it seems as though they eat all those fatty foods and buy and eat more from the store simply because it is one of the things they have control over. Unfortunately they are the ones who may have to pay the price later on in life. That old saying you are what you eat — for the most part is very true. Anyway I love you mom and miss you very much. Hello Larry.

love Joel

P.S.
Did that guy from that optical shop in Arizona ever pay you the money he owed you. Maybe you should tell him to send you a pair of <u>olypians</u> (Rayban) because he made you wait so long.

Dear Mom 9-18-96

I am in receipt of your Sep 10 letter, As usual I am in need of the 20 you sent, it was needed as much as it is appreciated. New England sands like I've imagined it, Very distinct and unique. Maine Lobster, crab and clams, I stopped eating all meat including fish (I started on 5-30-96) I think though, I would eat seafood if it was that fresh (daily). I would probably only do it if I was right there were it came from, As you were on the east coast, I bet the seafood is the wickedest (in a good way) of all. The water stays in Alaska freezing cold up there even throughout summer. It would be safe to say that that is probably some of the least tainted ocean around. But as I think about it the water up by Maine is pretty much the same, very cold and not much pollution at all. Yes Maine, I never did go any farther north than long island when my travels brought me to the east coast. I have always had a afinity for Maine even though I have never been there, I bet it was chilly there too. Exploration is wonderful isn't it. Traveling Physically (and now for me mentally) has always shown a sense of wonder to me. Mentally I mean in other exploratory ways (meditation etc). I did receive the other $10 check also (sep 3). Hello Larry Enjoy yourself

love
Joel

This is the only card I had, I dont like the cover

7

Dead Ahead

WITH A NAME LIKE Grateful Dead, I first assumed they were a heavy metal band. I'd never heard of them, but in 1984, the local Milwaukee radio station 93QFM had advertised $12 concert tickets with transportation to and from the show included in the price via yellow school bus. I had been looking for an opportunity to ask Melissa out, a cute girl from the neighborhood. A concert fit the bill perfectly.

As soon as the large yellow aluminum bus arrived at Alpine Valley, I understood why this was one of the band's favorite venues to play. The venue is an outdoor stage nestled among the lush, rolling green farmland of southeastern Wisconsin. The pavilion next to the stage boasts 9,500 seats covered by wooden awnings, but the real scene existed in the parking lot. As we exited the bus, we entered a sea of people, all ebbing and flowing in and out of tents, vehicles, and vendor carts. I would find out later the show had sold out, with over 50,000 tickets bought, and still more than 10,000 people wandered the grounds looking for tickets.

Laughter and happiness rang out, and people all around were hugging one another, singing and playing instruments. Some were even blowing bubbles. Women swathed in long, flowing dresses and skirts twirled through the crowd, the flowers in their hair bouncing as they cavorted like elusive forest sprites. It was safe to assume we were not at a heavy metal concert. At 15, I'd heard the word 'hippie' before, but this was my first experience meeting real hippies. We were in the midst of what seemed their spawning grounds. The smell of marijuana permeated the tree lined parking lots, as natural as the aroma of coffee in a cafe. Among the crowd, makeshift stages had sprung up, and a combination of jam band music, reggae and drum beats floated along the smoky wind. Apparently some of the bands had arrived with instruments intending to play, but others had just met in the parking lot and joined together in song through their mutual appreciation for the Dead and for music. There were guerrilla vendors everywhere. Tents and tables were set up every few feet, with wares varying from food to flutes. This section had come to be known as "Shakedown Street" and there was one in every parking lot at every Grateful Dead show. All of a sudden a flowery clothed long haired young girl was twirling through the crowd almost singing out "Kind peanut butter honey and banana sandwiches $2, or three for five!" A huge basket full of these amazing edible creations accompanied her. Then in a more masculine tone from the other direction you could hear "Kind bud! Kind bud!"

My date and I were both blown away with how genuine and kind everyone we met was. We were welcomed extensively when we shared it was our first show, and the enthusiasm was infectious. The atmosphere was one of joy; everyone was smiling and radiated warmth. I was overcome with a deep sense of calm, and a feeling I was unfamiliar with: belonging. We gallivanted about the parking lot for nearly two hours, meeting people and taking in the scene.

"I want to be a part of this," I confessed to my Melissa. In that moment I gave no thought to going home, only to how nice these people and this place was. I longed for this to be my new home and these people my new family.

As we ventured to the ticket collectors at the front gates, there were many people who had their hands in the air with their index finger extended. "I need a miracle," they were saying—the title of one of the Grateful Dead's songs had come to mean they were looking for a free ticket.

"I got five dollars for a ticket, help a brother out," others said.

After we'd passed the gauntlet of wishing hippies, we gave our bus tickets to the ticket collectors.

"What's this?" they said.

In all the excitement, Melissa and I had forgotten that we were supposed to trade our bus ticket for a concert ticket when we boarded our bus to Alpine Valley from Milwaukee. We relayed as much to the ticket attendant, explaining that we bought these tickets through the radio station and picked them up from the record store, like we were told to. The attendants seemed bewildered, but led us back through the crowd around the outside of the amphitheater to an office to speak to the ticket manager. After listening to our story the ticket office manager nodded and motioned for us to follow him out of the back door of the office into a forested area. He began to walk along a tall wooden fence, and so we followed, the foliage getting denser on the other side. I was beginning to question where we were head-ed when suddenly we entered backstage and walked in along stage right. The manager had acknowledged the non-validity of our tickets and taken pity on us. For a moment we were so shocked, it was at least 30 minutes after the debacle at the front gate and here we stood staring out at the crowd amassed before the stage. He smiled and told us to enjoy the show, gesturing to the reserved section of seats in the front row.

Soon after we sat down, an older hippie sporting a neatly trimmed goatee and long blond hair asked us if we wanted some mushrooms. I had taken them once before in Milwaukee about six months prior, so I accepted his kind offer for both me and my date. He refused to take any money from us. He simply held open the plastic bag in his hands and told us to help ourselves. He then hugged us and said "have a good show."

When the music began I was in awe of how peaceful and mellow it was especially compared to the heavy metal I'd been anticipating the whole bus ride over. I've heard it described as improvisational rock and roll with a touch of jazz, but in that time and place it was just music that made us want to dance. The lyrics were dense, with each song telling a story, and interspersed with complex guitar, piano, and drum solos.

During the intermission or "set break," as we were told it was called, we walked around and began talking with some of the other concertgoers. I noticed an area on the lawn where people were manning big tall stands with weird-looking directional microphones pointing towards the stage. At the bottom of the stands sat Sony and or Nakamichi Dragon High-Definition tape decks. I asked someone at the show how and why and we were informed that the Grateful Dead allowed people to record their shows at no charge. At this point, the Dead had been touring for twenty years, so they had about a 400 hundred song repertoire (approximately 150 of their very own) and expanding every year. They toured four times a year, split by the seasons and between tours various band members performed their solo work. No two shows were alike and often special guests would appear for a set: There was an entire network of people recording and trading shows on cassette tapes. If you were lucky enough to get to know Dan Healy or someone who did their sound you could get a first generation soundboard tape. Or if you were really well connected an original "Betty Board" (from a collection of reel-to-reel soundboard tapes of the Grateful Dead originally recorded by pioneering sound engineer Betty Cantor-Jackson between 1971 and 1980).

Now the entirety of their concerts can be found on the internet at archives.org, and thanks to modern innovation, Deadheads everywhere can revisit the experience or catch concerts they weren't able to attend.

The music in the second set was as transcendent as the the first set, perhaps even more so. Melissa and I swayed and swirled to the music as did the crowd. The entire audience, all 50,000 of us grooved and shimmied and spun and bopped. Seeing that many people all move at once, not necessarily in sync, but with the same rhythm, is an experience I have not seen replicated. It's as if you and everyone around you are on the same wavelength, let in to some secret of the universe and existing on a plane only those who know have been invited to. Ken Kesey said "The Dead are defenders of this space," and that night we were right there along with all of them.

As night came and skies darkened the band incorporated a unique lighting technique to make it appear as if certain band members disappeared from the stage while another was playing a solo. On stage the band often had the same presence: Jerry Garcia on guitar, stage left, Bob Weir on guitar center stage, shadowed by Mickey Hart or Bill Kreutzmann playing percussion, Phil Lesh on the bass, stage right, and next to Jerry, Brent Mydland on the keyboard (until 1990, when he died of a drug overdose, and was replaced by a combination of Vince Welnick and Bruce Hornsby).

Jerry Garcia and Bob Weir would alternate singing songs, or occasionally swap lines, singing back and forth to each other. Bob and Jerry each had their very own lyricist that they worked with over the years. Jerry Garcia's lyricist, Robert S. Hunter, was the only non-performing band member ever admitted into the Rock and Roll Hall of Fame when the Dead were admitted in 1994. Garcia always said "he's the band member that doesn't come out and play with us." Bob Weir's lyricist, John Perry Barlow, was his high school friend and a Wyoming rancher who went on to become one of the foremost Internet activists finding the Electronic Frontier Foundation.

All of these men would come to feel like family to me. A Grateful Dead show was a spiritually intimate affair between the band and us Deadheads, whether you knew them well or were just seeing them for the first time. It was as if everyone was your friend and loved you. The swell of anticipation, the butterflies in my stomach as we pulled into the parking lot for a show were always intense and uplifting, the music you would and could not help but dance to, the sharing of a hug, a smile, a joint or a drink with your neighbor; making and meeting new friends all over the country and world, but coming together to join in harmony over the communal love of the music, the band and humanity. There would be times Garcia would strum his guitar during a space jam right after Mickey and Billy's drum solo and it would sound like whales singing, or a saxophone wailing or a volcano erupting, the Grateful Dead's sound and synthesizing abilities are legendary.

After the show, the parking lot offered a similar scene as the one we had left when we had gone into the concert except now it was nightfall and there were thousands of Coleman lanterns lighting the tents, tarps and tables where at least a few hundred vendors were hawking their wares. Often they were simply Deadheads hoping to make up the cost of traveling to see the show by selling tie-dye shirts and pants in every color and size, crystals for any ailment you could think of, homemade jewelry and every imaginable variation of skeletons, lightning bolts and roses. I saw batik and silk screen shirts with these and other Grateful Dead symbols on them, intricate carnival glass pipes and another vendor who had a variety of sterling silver jewelry that looked to be imported from India.

Psychedelically painted school buses converted to campers adorned the lot, many selling food items. Again we passed another beautiful long-haired woman selling peanut butter, honey and banana sandwiches. Many were simply selling grilled cheese and bottled beer like Chimay Ale and Heineken out of the trunk of their car. Some were also selling and trading pot, or just offering it to one another.

My date and I were still so awed by how kind everyone we'd met had been. Even the vendors were incredibly nice and generous. Everyone took such pride in what they were doing. It was a traveling community of like-minded, free-thinking people who created an atmosphere of love and acceptance. The thought of going back to Milwaukee to live my melancholy existence did not sit well with me.

"Let's just go with them to the next show and never come back," I said to Melissa… We marveled at this scene for a little while longer before making our way back to the bus. We were the last to arrive back to the bus, and nearly missed our ride home as they were all waiting for our young tender 15 year old bodies.

On the ride home I was already thinking about ways I could come back. If I could sell the high-grade marijuana my friends were growing back in Milwaukee at the shows, It could finance traveling to see the Dead. I shared my experience with high school friends Chris and Aaron, and returned to all of the Dead's performances at Alpine Valley between 1984 and 1989. In high school the three of us piled into Chris's white two-door Cutlass and drove to upstate New York to see the Dead play in Rochester, then followed them to their next show at Wonderland Theme Park in Toronto, Canada. It was the first ti me we ventured that far from home to see them play. At each location we met fellow Deadheads who opened their home, pantries and hearts to us. We had money to pay but it wasn't accepted, though the pot we'd brought along was. It was an incredible experience to be subjected to such kindness, but then it was pretty standard practice among Deadheads.

Going to the shows felt like going to a family reunion with members of your family you hadn't met yet. It was a social feast with everyone greeting each other as if they were old friends whether they'd met once or fifty times. Many a friendship I have formed to the tune of the Dead, some that lasted the duration of a show or weekend, and others that stayed with me throughout most of my young adult life. Unfortunately, there is a stigma that all Deadheads are considered to be lazy, perma-stoned, out-of-touch hippies who are incapable of contributing to society. In reality the Dead appealed to more than the idealistic teen looking for a sense of community such as myself. Among the crowd were politicians, lawyers, members of well-regarded fraternities, and many who simply followed the Dead or caught the shows whenever possible, who had regular day to day lives. Not every Deadhead followed the group around the country. In fact, there are household names who are noted Deadheads, such as Bob Dylan, Dan Aykroyd, Whoopi Goldberg, Bill Clinton, and even Ann Coulter, who described Deadheads as "what liberals claim to be but aren't: unique, free-thinking, open, kind and interested in different ideas."

Still, first and foremost I absolutely adored and thrived on the musical rhythms of the Grateful Dead and so I made a point of being aware of the show. I never attended a Grateful Dead show drunk although I was often high on marijuana. I took LSD only a handful of times at Dead concerts or ever in my life. The notes and singing merged with the swaying and dancing of the crowd, melding together in the most beautiful array, creating a feeling of peace and harmony among all present.

Here's a list of all the Grateful Dead shows I saw, listed in chronological order, some with commentary:

1. July 7th 1984 Alpine Valley, Wisconsin, Very\ first Grateful Dead show.
2. June 21st 1985 Alpine Valley, Wisconsin
3. June 22nd 1985 Alpine Valley, Wisconsin
4. June 28th 1986 Alpine Valley, Wisconsin
5. une 29th 1986 Alpine Valley, Wisconsin
6. April 9th 1987 UIC Pavilion, Chicago, Illinois — My first experience with medical grade nitrous oxide. I was told to never stand up while doing this.

I was very interested in finding out how to sell it and in later shows would make small fortunes off of it. One tank cost around $250 and at $5 per large balloon you could net $2,000 in about two to three hours.

7. June 26th 1987 Alpine Valley, Wisconsin — Camped out at Bong Recreation Center, a state park about 20 miles from Milwaukee. Named for World War II ace Dick Bong, its name has taken on another meaning since the unfortunate death of Major Bong in 1945.
8. June 27th 1987 Alpine Valley, Wisconsin
9. June 28th 1987 Alpine Valley, Wisconsin
10. June 30th 1987 Wonderland Amusement Park-Kingswood Amphitheater, Ontario, Canada — Several hundred Deadheads are caught on the border with drugs. We were very naive and had 3 different kinds of drugs in the vehicle and didn't realize just how lucky we were being waived through until we saw our fellow Deadheads inside Canada at the 1st rest stop.
11. July 2nd 1987 Silver Stadium, Rochester, New York — Stayed at the homes of people we met at the show.
12. April 13th 1988 Rosemont Horizon, Chicago, Illinois
13. June 19th 1988 Alpine Valley, Wisconsin — There were two large stainless tanker semi-trailers filled with water for showers and water hoses attached for all people in the parking lot, provided by the band; one was always being changed out for the other so as to never run out of water. They called it "the dust bowl" that year.
14. June 20th 1988 Alpine Valley, Wisconsin
15. June 22nd 1988 Alpine Valley, Wisconsin — You were allowed to camp overnight but not during the day in the middle of the 4 dates.
16. June 23rd 1988 Alpine Valley, Wisconsin
17. April 15th 1989 The Mecca, Milwaukee, Wisconsin — While smoking a joint in the first row I was stink-eyed by the Mayor of Milwaukee, John Norquist, who was sitting one row behind me.
18. April 16th 1989 The Mecca, Milwaukee, Wisconsin
19. July 17th 1989 Alpine Valley, Wisconsin
20. July 18th 1989 Alpine Valley, Wisconsin
21. July 19th 1989 Alpine Valley, Wisconsin
22. October 11th 1989 Brendan Byrne, Meadowlands, New Jersey — I met Tim,

Lisa and Dan.

23. October 12th 1989 Brendan Byrne, Meadowlands, New Jersey
24. October 13th 1989 Brendan Byrne, Meadowlands, New Jersey
25. October 14th 1989 Brendan Byrne, Meadowlands, New Jersey
26. October 15th 1989 Brendan Byrne, Meadowlands, New Jersey — I had my first LSD Trip with Lisa.
27. October 16th 1989 Brendan Byrne, Meadowlands, New Jersey
28. October 18th 1989 The Spectrum, Philly PA
29. October 19th 1989 The Spectrum, Philly PA — Timmy and I had 75 cases of really good German beer confiscated by Philly police; no tickets were issued, leading us to believe they confiscated it for themselves.
30. October 22nd 1989 Charlotte Coliseum, Charlotte, NC — Timmy was known on tour as the "fried dough man." At this show it was so hot that eventually the rising dough starting overflowing out of his girlfriend's Toyota Celica.
31. October 23rd 1989 Charlotte Coliseum, Charlotte, NC
32. October 25th 1989 Miami Arena, Miami, Florida — These shows had amazing drums/space. Some of my all time favorites.
33. October 26th 1989 Miami Arena, Miami, Florida — After the shows Tim and I went down to Fantasy Fest in the Florida Keys. Afterward, I moved into Lisa's condo in Florida.
34. December 27th 1989 Oakland Coliseum, Oakland, California — My friend Dave and I drove my brand new 1989 Honda Civic from St Petersburg, Florida with 4 full size medical grade nitrous oxide tanks, 2 for us and 2 for Tim. We made a small fortune selling balloons full of nitrous for $5.
35. December 28th 1989 Oakland Coliseum, Oakland, California — I was arrested by very corrupt Oakland police on suspicion of marijuana possession in the parking lot of the Motel 6 while entering my motel room. I spent the next 5 days at Oakland County lock-up, until all charges were dropped and the $685 I was arrested with was returned to me in cash. Dave, Don and Timmy had a beautiful Deadhead girl for me and we made our way up to Cougar Hot Springs just outside of Eugene, Oregon.
36. December 9th Great Western Forum, Inglewood, California
37. December 10th Great Western Forum, Inglewood, California

38. January 25th 1990 Oakland Coliseum, Oakland, California — I loaned my first brand new car to Dan and Rainbow; they were rear-ended by a semi in a freak snowstorm. The driver of my car had to be cut out by the jaws of life. Eventually insurance paid off the car, and the driver made a miraculous and full recovery.

39. February 26th 1990 Oakland Coliseum, Oakland, California

40. March 14th 1990 Capitol Center, Landover, MD

41. March 15th 1990 Capitol Center, Landover MD

42. March 16th 1990 Capitol Center, Landover MD

43. March 18th 1990 Hartford Civic Center, Hartford, Connecticut

44. March 19th 1990 Hartford Civic Center, Hartford, Connecticut — This show was sold-out and Rick and I could not get a ticket to save our lives for any price; minutes before the show started he came to me and said "Take my hand," and we walked right in. We squeezed between the turnstiles as the ticket takers were distracted looking at people with tickets. Surreal is an understatement. If there were only scalper tickets available as a last resort I would always get them; at this show there were no tickets to be had anywhere. The show was added at the last minute because of the current continued demand for the Grateful Dead. After these shows the Dead played in Canada and I opted out as I knew of potential troubles at the border. I got lucky once before and was not willing to risk it again.

45. March 24 1990 Knickerbocker Arena, Albany, NY

46. March 25th 1990 Knickerbocker Arena, Albany, NY

47. March 26th 1990 Knickerbocker Arena, Albany, NY

48. March 28th 1990 Nassau County Coliseum — Jerry Garcia always complained about playing here because of all the "heads" that would get busted for drugs.

49. March 29th 1990 Nassau County Coliseum — This is the only show I was at and missed. I had a counterfeit ticket. The next day I was rewarded with a song the Grateful Dead hadn't ever sung in concert, "The Weight."

50. March 30th 1990 Nassau County Coliseum

51. April 1st 1990 The Omni, Atlanta, Georgia

52. April 2nd 1990 The Omni, Atlanta, Georgia

53. April 3rd 1990 The Omni, Atlanta, Georgia

54. May 5th 1990 Cal State Dominguez Hills, Carson, California — This show was followed by a big party at the Hotel Ibis.
55. May 6th 1990 Cal State Dominguez Hills, Carson California — Shortly after these I flew to Hawaii to see the Jerry Garcia shows; he played at the Hilo Civic Auditorium May 20th and the Waikiki Shell.
56. June 8th 1990 Cal Expo Center, Sacramento, California
57. June 9th 1990 Cal Expo Center, Sacramento, California
58. June 10th 1990 Cal Expo Center, Sacramento, California
59. June 15th 1990 Shoreline Amphitheater, Mountain View, California
60. June 16th 1990 Shoreline Amphitheater, Mountain View, California
61. June 17th 1990 Shoreline Amphitheater, Mountain View, California
62. June 23rd 1990 Autzen Stadium, Eugene, Oregon — Owsley was passing out purple barrels for a dollar or two. I sold 25 cases of beer and 300 grilled cheese sandwiches in 15 hours and then from the profits scored 2500 doses of LSD after the shows. Alan and I went to Boise, Idaho, to sell them to his connections for $5 per dose. I met a young voluptuous and beautiful guitar-playing woman named Tammy. She had 4 feet long fire engine red hair; we really hit it off.
63. June 24th 1990 Autzen Stadium, Eugene, Oregon
64. July 4th 1990 Sandstone Amphitheater, Bonner Springs, Kansas
65. July 6th 1990 Cardinal Stadium, Louisville, Kentucky — I sold some nitrous in the parking lot because the police or staff would only empty out the tanks if you were caught rather than ticket or arrest you. For the most part I never sold drugs other than nitrous in the parking lot of a Grateful Dead show because it was very risky proposition and generally not worth it.
66. July 18th 1990 Deer Creek, Indiana
67. July 19th 1990 Deer Creek, Indiana
68. July 21st 1990 World Music Theatre, Tinley Park, Illinois — Timothy Leary and some other significant people from the 1960's were all seen sitting on Brent Mydland's bench behind his keyboards during intermission and before the show. Soon after these shows on July 26th Brent would be found dead in California of an overdose.
69. July 22nd 1990 World Music Theatre, Tinley Park, Illinois — My first foray

selling Grateful Dead concert shirts. I illegally used the "Steal Your Face" logo on my shirts and after only selling 5 of them I had 110 confiscated by Brockman and Brockman, the copyright enforcement company hired by Grateful Dead lawyer Hal Kant to enforce copyright infringement both on tour and off tour.

70. July 23rd 1990 World Music Theatre, Tinley Park, Illinois
71. September 18th 1990 Madison Square Garden, Manhattan, New York — I attended these shows with my beloved friend Buffalo West.
72. September 19th 1990 Madison Square Garden, Manhattan, New York
73. September 20th 1990 Madison Square Garden, Manhattan, New York
74. October 19th 1990 Internationales Congress Centrum, Berlin, DE — I went to the Berlin Wall and smoked a special right at Checkpoint Charlie and rented a hammer from a local guy and chipped a piece of the Berlin Wall away. There were people blasting loud symphony music from old re-cord players in the square where Pink Floyd would later play. It was a very interesting place and amazing time in history. The mood around the wall was very upbeat. The Internationales Congress Centrum in Berlin is a very small, intimate opera house and a great venue to see the Grateful Dead at. In the States they would have never been able to play in a venue so small, just months prior they sold out all 9 consecutive shows at Madison Square Garden in under 30 minutes. I was 21 years old.
75. October 22nd 1990 Frankfurt Festhalle, Frankfurt DE.
76. October 24th 1990 Sporthalle, Hamburg DE.
77. October 27th 1990 The Zenith, Paris, France — Met a kind, blond American girl from Newport Beach. We went to Amsterdam together before the London Grateful Dead shows later in same tour. Amsterdam was nice- coffee shops, red lights and good company made for a very pleasant place to be.
78. October 28th 1990 The Zenith, Paris, France — I was given lots of hash from a local who could not speak English.
79. October 30th 1990 Wembley Arena, London, England — Free tickets were stuck on trees everywhere. You could not even give a free ticket away, especially for the Halloween show. I passed out free LSD, including to a Polish guy who could not speak English.
80. October 31st 1990 Wembley Arena, London, England

81. November 1st 1990 Wembley Arena, London, England
82. December 8th 1990 Compton Terrace Amphitheater, Tempe, Arizona
83. December 9th 1990 Compton Terrace Amphitheater, Tempe, Arizona
84. December 13th 1990 McNichols Sports Arena, Denver, Colorado
85. December 14th 1990 McNichols Sports Arena, Denver, Colorado
86. December 27th 1990 Oakland Coliseum, Oakland, California
87. December 28th 1990 Oakland Coliseum, Oakland, California
88. December 30th 1990 Oakland Coliseum, Oakland, California
89. December 31st 1990 Oakland Coliseum, Oakland, California — Hung out with Turtle and Neil Young during set break and smoked lots of nice marijuana.
90. April 27th 1991 Sam Boyd Silver Bowl, Las Vegas, NV
91. April 28th 1991 Sam Boyd Silver Bowl, Las Vegas, NV
92. May 10th 1991 Shoreline Amphitheater, Mountain View, California
93. May 11th 1991 Shoreline Amphitheater, Mountain View, California
94. May 12th 1991 Shoreline Amphitheater, Mountain View, California
95. June 6th 1991 Deer Creek, Indiana
96. June 7th 1991 Deer Creek, Indiana
97. June 22nd 1991 Soldiers Field Chicago— I saw this show with my mother and two of my brothers. We smoked a big fat joint of sticky indica marijuana. The floor was "Festival Seating" meaning you could sit in any seat on the floor (grass). We had 10th row center.
98. December 30th 1991 Oakland Coliseum, Oakland, California
99. December 31st 1991 Oakland Coliseum, Oakland California,
100. June 25th 1992 Soldier Field, Chicago, Illinois — I was out on federal bail when I saw this show and learned from Dave that Timmy and Don were in big trouble with the law as well.
101. June 26th 1992 Soldier Field, Chicago, Illinois — My last Grateful Dead show.

During this same period I also saw the Jerry Garcia Band around 25 times, mostly at the Warfield in downtown San Francisco, and other bands with the remaining members of the Grateful Dead in them another 20 times.

Joel Blaeser
03491-089
P.O. Box 1000
Marion, Il 62959

Rosemary Blaeser
1730 N Clark #4102
Chicago, Il 60614

5-16-96

Dear Mom

I have had the ruff draft for this letter for a few days now, but had to wait until today to send it because today is our store day. (I was out of stamps) I already new something wasn't rite from your last letter. First as far as Tim & Paul are concerned I will write them myself, if they happen to write you again let me know what they say, don't write them back though I will handle that. As far as the family tree I am giving up I have been trying for well over 30 months and at this point my efforts seem futile. Please Send me uncle Jimy's, Bobby's and grandma Terry's address. I have received the book from philisophical research society Thank-you for ordering it for me. I wrote you about 10-12 days back with a letter from a Strand book store with instructions to order 2 more books for me. If you haven't already, don't they were not that important anyway, if you have or have not let me know either way. Except for you sending me those addresses I asked for up above I don't want anything ever again from you but conversation. I was moved to another unit 5 days ago I get 3 phone calls in this unit per month and my hardcover books. last time we talked I said I was going to call you that Friday well I called Bradley it had been at least 3 or 4 months since I talked to him. I have 3

2

Calls coming for the month of may I will call soon. O-yea one more thing I forgot I got the legal papers thankyou but the trial transcripts only go to page 238. There were 260 or 270 so there's about 22 or 32 pages missing. They may have been taken out when I sent them. Check the copies you have please do it today or better yet rite now without these papers my appeal is being held up, if they are not there thats fine I will just get them from the court (they make a big deal though I would rather get them from you.) There is only one set of papers in there labeled <u>trial transcripts</u> Sep 8 1992 then at about half way through Sep 9. I only got up to P 238. [All the other papers besides those 238 (motions, etc) I got also.] Only those few remaining pages of <u>trial transcripts</u> were missing either way let me know rite away. As far as the box thats just the way it is it may have gotten through if you marked Approved paperwork. They recommended a box - thats too bad that you fell for it, you didn't get them in a box - fuck they. <u>except responsibily</u>, Adhere to the truth, balance and have a good map. Remember thats what Scott Peck said in the Road less traveled. You and dad are and were very straight laced and I am not trying to be like you. As far as living a <u>normal</u> type of life. I am a anarchist and will be to the day I die. Prison has done me a real big favor because I have become soo more times focused on who I am and what I am about. I don't plan to have guns and be involved in violence (unless to protect me or my family) but will live free - Absolutely

I got the check a while back, thank you!
You don't need any special arrangements to come.

<u>intelectualy</u>, spiritualy, physically, musically and every other way.

But enough about me. What about you. This is the way I see it and have for a while. You see being in a place as wicked as Marion you either go crazy or you start to see things clear, life, love, family, yourself, myself whatever I focus my attention on. I am living just like a buddhist monk it's totaly beautiful. I love it and I love myself, beleive that if I didn't I would not be able to write it ☺. Now I see you having some real feelings for Larry, but caught up in the material refuge living with him. Is he mean to you I have friends in Chicago, ~~━━━━━━~~ let me know has he been mean to you. I get a suspicion that he has not been mean to you, but I also see you too not getting along well lately and you hanging on because you are taking refuge in what you perceive as a safe haven. But that is one if not most of the contributing factor as to why you are feeling depressed. The drug you are taking for menopause may be having a effect also. The only way to check that aspect is to stop taking it. Your not a doctor and the people who are giving it to you don't know for sure thats why they are testing it on you. So if you think that you health is worth it (which it is) stop taking it for 6 or 12 months. Also I see you thinking about Dad alot lately ~~━━━━━~~ coupled with the fact that financialy you are not well off. It's weird how ~~westerners~~ equate lower, upper, middle classes with how much money you have. The way I see it upper class has to do with spiritual enlightment and intellectual knowledge. I have a sneaking suspicion you have 10 or 20 thousand put away which isn't much but its something. As soon as I am able I will be kicking you down handsomely. Of course it will be sometime soon after I get out of prison. Also I see you taking some of the blame for what you think of as a failure of me being in prison. The only thing that failed was that fucked up jury. There's nothing wrong with people doing what ever they want with there conscience. There is dignity in prison. Would you rather I turned into a rat and stayed freed. I am still appalled that all of you even sugested it. And all of you say you were just concerned for my well being. Thats the same god damed attitude of those fuckin jurors. So you see mother something seems to be rotten in denmark (as they say) isn't there. This government doesn't give a god dam about you or me. You are a slave intellectually and thus physically. There is no heaven or hell this is it. What are you going to do. I will tell you we are going to take stock in ourselves. It's time you start doing those things you have always wanted to do, paint, sculpture, what else do you like. If you can hold on until I get out of prison 12 months after I get out (at most) we can go on a trip around the world, climb a mountain or do whatever you want. But that will be then we need to concentrate on now. By the way that has been my plan since I have come to prison. I dont want kids and realy cant see getting married I am too free spirited. But I will on occassion have sex with a women. There's not such a big attraction any more there more trouble than there worth sometimes. As for as sex I masterbate once a day, I get myself off just fine and there's no mess. Ahhh haa! ☺

5

I am serious about everything I have said in this letter. On March 10 of this year I cut all my hair off. There's no air conditioning here and it was getting kind of ratty. It will grow back which is exactly what is going to be done. I have a book I am going to send you the same time I send this letter. Please read it then put it with my stuff. You have to take stock in your mind of your mind, spirit or whatever you want to call "it." There is no magical solution for the simple reason of the life and road you chose. (Thank you for bringing me and all my brothers and sister in this world.) There is a solution though. Your emotional state has always been on pins and needles. (The reason doesn't matter now concentrate on making it better) So maybe we should start there. Stretching the body especially the back/spine is very good for your mind, but if you have severe depression were your pleasure centers are totally out of whack you may need something like that new drug that came out a few years back, I can't remember the name of it, but it affects the Serotonin uptake receptors. Whatever course of action we decide you need to start somewhere and first and foremost with yourself. Shut everyone else and thing out and take a long hard look at yourself, not in the past or future but rite now at this very moment. And everyday would not be too much. Set aside 10, 15, 20 minutes to take a look at yourself in a quiet uninterrupted way again not the past or future but the rite <u>here</u> and <u>now</u>. As you will find you will have alot of stuff inside your head popping up. This is where things get interesting. This is meditation of sorts. Read the book and see what you think. We are all going to die one day it is as natural as being born. Enjoy it while you can. Before I go I would also note that you are feeling a sense of being cheated out of your

6

youthful goodlooks by not exploiting them to the best of your ability and also maybe thinking what would have if ---- ~~with~~ with another husband? We are all doing time of sorts, I am as happy ~~too~~ as anyone in this world and I am sitting in prison for nothing. I laugh everyday, do you. Maybe you should. I love you enjoy yourself

love Joel

Also included
1 article by timothy leary
Let me know if the book got there also. I did not bother to look up any misspelld words I feel lazy today. If you have sent strand book a check already dont cancel it, I realy needed those books, but if you didn't dont, you have enough to deal with now. Is there something you're not telling me if there is please let me know.

6 page letter
+ 1 article.

8
The Green Duffel Bag

AUTUMN 1994

I DID NOT EXPECT to make such a fast friend as quickly as my first day in FCI Englewood, Colorado. I recognized James "Sparky" Irving as a kindred spirit immediately. He was young and long-haired, like me. A few moments of conversation confirmed my suspicion that he was also a Dead Head; he'd travelled to nearly as many Grateful Dead shows as I had. I was shown my bunk by one of the guards after the check in dance, we finished just after dinner and by luck of the draw I was given a bunk rite next to Sparky. "I am in on a LSD charge," he said from a nearby bunk.

"What!" I exclaimed. "Me too!"

James smiled ear to ear as if I were a old friend he hadn't seen for years, then said, "Do you want to get high? How many shows have you been to?" And so our friendship started. At 20 lbs lighter with similar hair color and facial structure as mine he could have been mistaken for my younger brother or cousin minus his ten tattoos. I would soon find out how Sparky's demeanor was one that commanded respect on this prison yard. There were entire units in Englewood that had private cells, however I started in one of the "dual" units with cells and a common bunk area not unlike Sandstone except that my neighbors were real convicts with respectful attitudes and long prison terms to match. James had been in Englewood for 18 months, but just recently lost his private cell due to excess chow hall food being found in his possession.

Sparky had also taken his case to trial and had never pleaded guilty, a rarity in prison and an indication of a willpower to be respected; we trusted each other instantly. Sparky wasted no time and pulled out a plastic sandwich bag stuffed full of high-grade compressed light green and orange Mexican marijuana. My eyes wide open in disbelief.

What the fuck, I thought. "Dude, I have not seen a bag of weed like that since being out on the street."

"Yeah I know, kinda weird, right?" he grinned back at me.

I looked him straight in the eye, my voice wrung with excitement, "James, I am going to the case manager's office right now to get you a copy of my PSI." PSI stands for pre-sentencing investigation report and is essentially your life history. It is a document prepared before sentencing by a presentencing investigator who gathers information from many sources, including your crime and the outcome of your trial or your plea.

If you snitched on anyone or cooperated with the authorities in anyway it would say so in the PSI. At a real prison like this one, asking to read someone's PSI could easily be taken as a sign of disrespect because it can imply a concern of one's honor.

"Cool cool, I will go get mine after movement and you can read it then Joel," he said, already focusing on the task on hand. The fact that he obliged with getting his was a sign that he had nothing to hide either.

"James, be right back," I assured him as I hurriedly walked down the hall to the case manager offices.

"Please call me Sparky, but hurry, it's almost move time and we have got to get baked on this huge joint then," he smiled at me, both of us giddy at the prospect of getting ridiculously stoned. My case manager happened to be in the unit due to being on the check in crew for new prisoner arrivals, he gave it to me right away instead of making me submit a written request. I was back to Sparky in less than five minutes.

"Wow Blaze, yours is only seven pages long! Mine is pretty short too, since I have no priors like you,"

"Yeah tell me about it. Maybe we will get some action on the LSD law change," I said in a hopeful tone.

"We'll see Joel," His hair was longer than mine and he wasn't sure what to call me. "Come on," his face lightened, "I will show you how we smoke this monster joint in the joint without a trace." As we shared a mutual smile the loud buzzing noise of movement sounded off signaling it was time for getting stoned.

"During movement is the safest time to smoke pot on this yard," James said to me as we walked out the back door of our rectangular concrete 2 story prison unit toward the yard.

I followed James with anticipation and no hint of the horror that lie ahead. This corridor was out in the open air and surrounded by cement walls, totally out of sight of windows, gun towers or metal detectors, a blind spot about 100 yards long by 50 yards wide in between the outside yard and main compound of cell houses. A place to get stoned and where enemies could be beaten or stabbed. Sparky pulled the small baggy from its hiding place, the crack of his ass. He removed the joint we'd rolled moments earlier from its protective plastic casing, and lit it. The smell was like a homecoming for me. I followed Sparky like a hungry puppy following its mother.

You were allowed to smoke cigarettes any time you were on the yard, so the smoke itself wouldn't alarm anyone, We had to finish the joint before movement ended, and with each inhalation of the joint I held it longer and drew on it stronger. I tried to hold back the coughing but eventually could not.

"Easy Blaze, we don't want to draw too much attention," Sparky warned me.

Every 60 seconds or so 10 or 20 prisoners were making their way to and from the outside yard, causing us to be on high alert. "What about the guards, don't they ever walk through here Sparky?"

Sparky assured me, "No! Shift change isn't until next move so fat chance we will see any hacks now." We'd smoked the joint all the way down until we couldn't even hold on to it because it was too small, then buried all of the remaining evidence by quickly shoving the cigarette butt looking thing into the grass. "Joel here chew on this so we don't smell." Sparky handed me two pieces of Big Red chewing gum. I littered the paper and foil from them because that's what he did.

Sparky worked out but was not quite as big as me. His attitude was confident and humble, and he carried himself well. Lots of convicts nodded or said hello as we smoked our marijuana joint. Upon returning to the unit we both immediately requested to be put on a waiting list for a two-man cell. The cells had steel doors with small windows and therefore offered more privacy and safety.

Within minutes of being back into the cell block the marijuana high was unbelievably strong and getting more intense by the minute, reminding me of the first time I got stoned with my older brother at an AC/DC concert in 1982. I began to experience tunnel vision while hearing a sound similar to a freight train going through my head, getting louder and louder. My feet felt light and my eyelids were heavy. The middle of my forehead felt like it was melting into my nose. Could this joint have been laced and James not have known it?

In reality, I was simply very very stoned. Suddenly as I approached the gray steel prison bunk, the horror of what my life had become pronounced itself with a undeniable fury. I came into prison at the tender age of 23 and with the very best of behavior was going home at age 34, spending the best part of my life behind bars. My own voice echoed in my head, *What had I done to my life?*

I climbed up to my bunk incapacitated as feelings of rage, guilt, embarrassment, fear, and worthlessness began to wash over me in rapid succession. Nearly every other time I smoked marijuana in my life, I was either attending or on my way to attend a Grateful Dead concert in which case it was to celebrate life and the love I felt for the people surrounding me. It was always a ritual of peace, and so smoking today, during one of the darkest periods of my life clouded my positive attitude and plunged me into a deep depression about the situation. The combination of my situation and the fact that I had not smoked for nearly 15 months left me filled with extreme dread at the thought of my future prospects. Nasty pangs of physical pain crept deep into my belly forcing me into the fetal position in an effort to ease the discomfort of the belly pain and slow down all the spinning in my head. The high and mental horror only became more and more intense as the night wore on, keeping the peace of sleep from me for nearly three more hours until finally I fell asleep on my tear-soaked pillow.

In the morning I awoke and thanked God that I was in a corner bunk and able to turn to it in a semi-private state; I could have been targeted as weak if someone saw or heard me. I also took some solace in the fact that even faced with what seemed an insurmountable prison sentence, in comparison to many others -- including Sparky's 240 month sentence for a first time non-violent consensual crime, my 151 months was relatively shorter than most other federal drug sentences in this prison.

Still, the next day when he offered, I smoked again, slowly I regained my tolerance for marijuana and was getting high every day for the first month I was there. I finally asked Sparky how he managed to get his hands on so much weed.

In prison the prices are steep for everything not sold in the commissary, but especially pot and other drugs. A chapstick cap of marijuana cost $25 and yet Sparky and I were smoking joints with nearly six to ten caps in them on a near daily basis. He explained that he bought an entire ounce for $500 from two inmates who had an in through Unicor, the federal prison industry factory system. Started in 1934 Unicor now had 81 factories within federal prisons and produces about 175 types of products, ranging from clothing and textiles, electronics, and vehicular components to services including data entry and encoding. They mostly sell to other government agencies, often directly competing with free world businesses. In 2008 Unicor generated $765 million in sales and employed 21,836 inmates who made between $0.23 and $1.15 per hour, Just about every federal prison has one and typically one tenth to one sixth of the prison population is employed by Unicor.

Englewood's Unicor shop was a large print shop that printed all the forms needed for the Bureau of Prisons as well as forms for other federal agencies. Inmates run everything in the factory including clerking, ordering, payroll, and more. Prison staff oversee the prisoners but in the end there are ways around everything, Inmates do most of the ordering in the prison and the print shop was no different. FCI Englewood ordered palates of ink on a monthly basis from the same wholesale distributor. The clerk in the ink shop commissioned his wife to get a job at the ink distributor's warehouse. She secured a position within shipping and receiving so it was easy enough to find out when the order was coming in for FCI Englewood and begin the process: she would spread ounces of marijuana in balloons made from the fingertips of latex gloves, then place them inside empty ink bottles she'd retrieved, fill the bottles back up with the proper color ink and ship them to FCI Englewood within a large order.

The other mastermind in this scheme was an inmate whose Unicor duty was inventory and who could recognize the correct shipping by a secret marking on the box and bottle. Sixteen to twenty four ounces of marijuana were being smuggled in at a time and they would slowly release the goods over the course of few months; like any other economic system, prison operates off of a healthy supply and much stronger endless demand.

They were turning a pretty profit. On the outside even though they were purchasing high-grade Mexican marijuana it never cost them more than $800 per pound or $50 per ounce. Once inside prison walls however they would sell it for $500 an ounce to a few select inmates, Sparky included. They had a 1,000% profit margin. Once someone purchased an ounce they would divide the pot into chapstick caps purchased at the prison commissary and sell it in groups of five for $100—there were at least 70-100 caps in a ounce of marijuana so James was making a healthy profit off of what we didn't smoke up. The money the clerk made was sent to his wife from other inmates' family members on the outside as directed via calls from the prison telephone room.

Sometimes we were called to the lieutenant's office to take a UA or urine analysis for drugs. In the morning after my first breakfast in Englewood Sparky pulled me aside and proceeded to school me on the finer points of beating a prison drug test. "Joel sit down and let me explain this too you before we go to the yard and smoke another fatty" (referring to a huge sized marijuana joint). I had taken UA's at FCI Sandstone many times but there was never any worry of not passing them as there were no drugs on that prison yard. "Ok Blaze, once called to the lieutenants office you get two hours to pee in the cup, got it?" I did not "get it" and never heard such talk about beating a prison UA. He kept going on without waiting for a response from me, "Then they send you back to your unit for up to two hours or until you can pee. After two hours if you can't or won't they could give a fuck, you get a shot for refusing to pee, spend six months in the Hole and then a transfer to somewhere else. Drink this now," he said and shoved a gallon jug purchased from the commissary full of slightly warm water in my face. I obliged and starting to drink it. "We need to show you it works, no dirties for weed means they won't investigate us for all the weed on the compound and hopefully just focus on the heroin and coke. Those guys always get busted for dirties."

"Wow Sparky you have it all figured out."

"Shut up and drink that shit down now!" he yelled back in a stern convict tone. Sparky continued in between drinks of his own gallon of water, "The prescription is to drink the gallon in less than five minutes and no matter what even if you think you're clean, tell them you can't pee and they will send you back to the unit for up to two hours."

We each finished our gallon of water.

"Fuck I feel like i am going to puke."

"Don't do it Blaze, it will ruin the test if you get called."

Within 20 minutes we were peeing and after 45 minutes we had went six or seven times and it looked like clear water coming out of me. It works, I thought. My stomach felt stretched out and I was farting a lot but the water was clear and odorless. I urinated a total of 11 times within the two hours of our test run.

"Ok Blaze, let's walk the yard and smoke this out on the yard," he gestured, holding up a huge joint and then putting it to his nose closing his eyes and wiffing it with a smile, I obliged and followed my new friend who had the run of this prison yard.

With the current research and scientific advancement in drug testing, this may no longer be relevant but I was tested nearly twenty five times during my stay in six federal prisons and this technique never failed me. There were even times when I would be stoned out of my mind while I gave my sixth or seventh pee, but it always worked like a charm, having never tested positive for any substances while in prison.

I opted to stay out of the Unicor racket. I had a direct connection to the pot source, so I felt no need to get involved on that level. I'd figured out a system for dealing in commissary items. Anytime someone could get their hands on something unique that no one else had they would pay dearly for it. It was sort of a vanity ego thing. I brought two $4 dollar bandannas from Sandstone and sold each bandanna for $50 worth of commissary items in Englewood simply because bandanas weren't available from the commissary in Englewood or from the chaplain. Convicts who did not even know me would flock to me when I walked the yard with one of the bandanas trying to buy it from me any way they could. When a new prison bus came in, if someone had cool shoes on that were almost new, I would buy them, giving them money and a new pair of shoes from the commissary at Englewood. Within twenty-four hours I would sell them to a very wealthy inmate, usually a big drug dealer or a bank robber for at least triple the amount that I paid. Sizes 10-12 were the most popular. On one such occasion I sold a pair of like new used Nike Hi-top Airs for $450 that only cost $80 at another prison commissary. The currency was most often toiletries and stamps. With a good prison hustle you couldn't help but have 40 to 50 books of stamps, and a locker full of five of every toiletry item available from the commissary.

As a prisoner you are required to get a job though. Sparky introduced me to the two clerks who worked in the food warehouse. Tory managed and Sam did the ordering, and they were in need of a grunt to help stock the freezer and dry storage two or three days a week. Sparky had vouched to Tory and Sam for me and they would not hear of reading my PSI. The benefit of this job was that these guys had access to all the good food on the entire compound and I soon discovered there was an additional opportunity for me to make money here.

The staff in Englewood were using some of the inmates food budget money to stock their home freezers and throw lavish private parties. We would order food items that almost never made it out to the chow hall and in turn we were allowed to share in some of the booty. Every six or seven days I would come back into the unit with a big laundry bag full of steak, crab legs, Cornish game hens—stuff not available at the store and rarely, if ever, seen by any inmate in Englewood. After work you have to go back to the housing unit through the metal detector. The prison guard would turn a blind eye as long as the detector didn't go off. Despite that I had all I could carry in my laundry bag, it was nearly always sold within five to ten minutes of me being back into my quarters.

It was incredibly appealing for the prisoners because it was always great to be able to mix up the boring regimen of the chow hall food. After all there were limited cooking facilities in the housing units. There is a well-equipped commercial grade kitchen for the chow hall that prepares and serves three meals a day every day, but in the housing units there is only a hot water spigot with 180 degree water and a microwave. This meant we had to get

THE GREEN DUFFEL BAG

creative if we wanted to make anything ourselves.

I first learned about some of the unique prison recipes in FCI Sandstone. One night shortly after my arrival there I was asked if I wanted to participate in a nacho pot luck. I didn't have anything to contribute nor understand what a nacho potluck was so my cellmate threw me an onion and a couple of hot peppers from his stash and told me to follow along. Over the next 15 minutes we collected all the ingredients: bowls of ramen noodles, garlic, sausage and Doritos from the commissary, hot peppers, onions, garlic, cilantro, green pepper, and tomatoes. The ramen was then soaked until it was nearly gooey. Next, the fresh tomato and cilantro were placed on top of the seasoned ramen goo for flavor and we dipped the Doritos into the mix.

It tasted amazing and smelled even better. Compared to the colorless crap the chow hall poured out, mashed potatoes, fried chicken, white bread -- which were all varying shades of tan, the colorful collection of fresh vegetables was a sight for sore eyes.

I was intrigued with how this was prepared. It starts with a brand new plastic trash bag that comes from a friendly prison guard or is stolen by a convict on the maintenance crew. All the ingredients are collected from participating convicts much like your suburban pot luck. It usually takes place at night after dinner but before lockdown.

Once the ingredients are collected the initial preparation begins. Hands are washed, the top of the prison lockers act as a cutting board. Some prison staff will allow you to borrow a razor as long as you have a non-violent record and return it within a short time frame. This is used to chop up the vegetables such as tomatoes, onions, garlic, green pepper and cilantro. Only the garlic is available in the commissary, the rest have to be snuck out of the prison kitchen. Also any meat you're lucky enough to get your hands on is cut up at this time as well. Occasionally sausages are available in the commissary especially around holidays or sometimes scraps of what was served at dinner - chicken, pork chops, etc - are tucked into a waistband, but more often than not potlucks were without meat. Ramen noodles of all flavors were available at the store for 25 cents. Depending on how many items you acquired, you'd adjust the level of water with the hope of achieving a gooey but not runny consistency. The ideal finished product was creamy enough to dip a chip in without breaking it, or the sauce running off.

After all the ingredients were amassed you'd double a plastic bag, place the crushed ramen noodles in, then add in your cheese, spices, and very hot water. Top it with a few Doritos for a nice crust, and the bag is tied off to avoid leaking. Let it sit for five minutes, then gently roll the ingredients around to ensure an appropriate mixture of cheese and spices throughout the combination. After about two minutes of gyration, undo the bag and add in any meat and dried vegetables, then knead the bag for another 1-2 minutes. Afterward top with fresh tomato and viola! You have a delectable treat to be scooped out of the bag by Doritos, or dished onto a flour tortilla purchased from commissary.

My job in the Englewood kitchen warehouse allowed for quite a few pot lucks, thankfully only having to work a few hours a day at most. The rest of the day I was out on the yard working out, reading, playing softball and smoking lots of weed with Sparky. Everyone was getting high so I didn't have to fear being snitched on like I would have in the Sandbox. I had no enemies and the guards were nearly as corrupt as the criminals living here. The guards stole so much food designated for inmates and helped sneak in all the tar heroin on the yard. There was less petty violence because here if there was trouble it was more brutal. The violence was more personal and more deadly. The result was that we were often more respectful to each other in general, because a slight disrespect could mean you're dead or badly beaten. Also the relationships I formed on this yard were ones I'd have to deal with throughout the rest of my 151 month sentence, and that was another major difference between here and Sandbox. The pace of life was calmer and more institutionalized here in FCI Englewood. The landscape of FCIs had changed dramatically with the implementation of mandatory minimum sentencing, and the war on drugs. The prison sentence averages skyrocketed and in Englewood the average was around a 20 year sentence, a quarter of a persons life. Be that as it may, Compared to Sandstone I felt a stronger sense of belonging and community living in FCI Englewood, It was easier to relate to lifers and friends like Sparky as opposed to short timers in Sandstone. By most standards, even with 151 months, I was still a relative short timer to most others here in FCI Englewood and called "short timer" from time to time for I did not dare complain about the length of my current stretch in prison.

It was here that I learned the magazine tricks. I got a hold of some surfing magazine's bill me later postcards, and every three months I would send in another one, changing a few letters in my last name or prison number. All prisons had mail call right after 4:00 pm count. Prisoners huddled around the prison staff as they called names and passed out letters. It would become dead silent during mail call. It was like children lining up to see Santa on Christmas Eve, you did not dare say a word at mail call. Mail is the window to the outside free world, more than anything else in prison, even though all the mail was pre-opened and read it couldn't take the joy away from that connection. Yellow slips were the best and cause for most envy. They were slips with messages like "I love you," or "I care," and blue computer font showing how much money you were sent. Working for Unicor for an entire month might net you $50. The very best jobs netted $120 to $150 per month but were rare. So getting a yellow slip with $25 to $50 was sweet. If it was in the hundreds of dollars you were happy beyond words.

Sparky used most of his commissary money on art supplies. Each prison had an art center and Sparky was an exquisite graphic artist and tattoo artist. His specialties were pen and ink drawing, and since he was registered in the art center as a graphic artist, he could order ink from the prison art room. He was really using it to boost his tattoo skills; he had found a mentor in Slow, an old school tattoo artist willing to teach Sparky the finer points of tattoo art. He was so good that I almost got a tattoo, my virgin skin a prize canvas for such a good new artist to go crazy on, but I demurred. I refused to get a tattoo until I was free.

An older very wise convict told me of his regret getting one earlier in his stretch. "It is a permanent reminder that I was young and thought I would have a life outside these walls once." The thought was chilling. Sparky ordered India ink, a very traditional ink recipe dating back to around the fourth century B.C. Tattoo guns were made from a sharpened C-string guitar string from the music room, then powered from a motor stolen out of an adding machine from a random prison office. A ball point pen minus the ink cartridge acted as the barrel. After a few more modifications you had a reciprocating tattoo gun run by the batteries in your Walkman. Once broken down into parts the whole thing could be hidden very easily.

James got to be so proficient that soon he did not use a pattern, rather he free-handed the whole tattoo. A few more months into his training and his designs rivaled those lauded in tattoo magazines. He would become legendary throughout the federal prison system for his tattoo art.

Tattoos weren't the only reason I knew how to make a needle out of nothing. Englewood was flooded with tar heroin and I'd decided I wanted to try it. My first introduction to heroin was while I was traveling around with the Grateful Dead. I never did it, nor did most of the people I associated with in the Grateful Dead world. It wasn't a common drug of choice among the Deadheads while I was on the scene, although in the late 80's and early 90's it apparently gained momentum among the crowd and with Jerry Garcia the bands leader. I saw a few young pretty girls traveling with the few known heroin addicts, and by the end of the tour—like three weeks later—these same young women had become frail, sickly, with pale skin drawn tight, stringy hair, and sagging clothes. I was always fascinated with what drew people to heroin, thinking the high must be really, really good to get people to deal with being that strung out. I added it to my list of things I wanted to try even just once, before I died -- along with surfing and sushi and since those two things weren't going to happen while I was in federal prison I figured I would put some feelers out for heroin and a needle here in Englewood.

For days and days Sparky staunchly opposed me trying heroin and feared if he didn't introduce me to Roy I might get myself into trouble with someone who might try to take advantage of me.

Roy was the heroin connection in Englewood. He was a very mild-mannered, convict who was an associate of a notorious biker gang doing 25 years for a series of bank robberies. Roy was a seasoned convict already half way through his sentence. He had a full head of shoulder length gray hair and always pulled it back in a ponytail, with a perfectly manicured Fu Manchu goatee which made him look Chinese rather than Mexican. Roy had a talent for removing emotion from his voice. He could spit out a threat without a hint of anger; it was chilling to those on his bad side, but I found his cool demeanor calming and almost fatherly. He wore dark-tinted eyeglasses because of a medically approved light sensitivity. He never removed them, even at night out on the yard, lending to his mystique. He sure looked the part of the resident heroin connection.

"Blaze, you should always wear your hair in a tight ponytail," he said as he entered my cell, nodding towards my loose locks. My hair was at least 12 inches long and had not been cut since I lost my trial, well over a year ago. "If you are ever in a fight your hair can be a terrible weapon against you."

"Wow, I never thought of that Roy. Thanks."

"You're still pretty green Joel." He started preparing the shot. Sparky had vouched for me, and his word carried weight, so Roy trusted me.

"Here is a hair tie," he said, tossing one my way. "Keep it pulled back even in the showers. Do it now because we don't want to burn your hair."

Roy knew someone who worked in the prison infirmary and was able to get new and fresh needles through his connection. It was pretty easy to get someone to deliver them to him, since everyone who received medication went once in the morning and once in the afternoon. Besides even if someone wasn't willing to do it for him it wasn't too difficult to get prescribed medication.

Most prison doctors were liberal with their prescriptions, at least everywhere except USP Marion. When I first arrived in FCI Sandstone the doctor who gave me my initial physical said he would prescribe me anything I wanted within reason and further stated that the prescription would follow me wherever I went for my entire sentence.

"You're young, you have a lot of time. Don't you want something to take the edge off?" he said.

"Fuck no," I spewed back at him. "I need my edge. This is prison." I thanked him and was glad not to oblige the doctor his offer.

Roy provided me with a new needle for $50 in commissary. I still cleaned it with bleach and flushed it with tap water a couple of dozen times. There was always a fear of getting the "package." When Roy and I grew closer he shared the names of inmates he knew had the "package." It was important information to keep in mind just in case of a conflict. Roy's tar heroin was dark brown with a very gummy consistency and had a weird sort of harsh cleaning chemical odor to it, think paint thinner meets ammonia. We took a nice little pinch which cost roughly fifty dollars and is therefore called a fifty paper, put it in a spoon with a little water squirted out from the cleaned needle, then slowly heated it up. The smell of the heroin became magnified. I looked out the square window on the solid steel cell door. Sparky was on point and gave the nod. The coast was clear. Standing on point is prison jargon for watching for guards. If Sparky coughed loudly it was a signal to stash everything and talk as if nothing was happening. Roy continued heating the spoon with another match I lit and handed him. The concoction of black tar was bubbling up as it was heated and mixed with the water.

After about ten seconds, he took a tiny piece of a new cotton ball, put it in the liquid, and then drew up the light brown liquid into the needle through the tiny piece of cotton ensuring proper filtering of contaminants. My veins were all very visible and I did not need to tie my arm off to get the vein to bulge. I squeezed my fyst closed five or six times while I held my bicep muscle as instructed by Roy. He just barely inserted the needle into the big vein opposite my elbow on my right arm.

Slightly pulling back on the needle plunger. I was red in the face nervous with excitement. As he pulled back on the plunger some of my blood squirted into the needle showing itself in the clear glass cartridge. My deep red blood mixing with the brown water-heroin mixture reminded me a lava lamp; red goo blobbing around the clear liquid. At that point Roy knew he was in my vein. He pushed the plunger all the way in. Before he had even pushed it all the way in I was already starting to feel a warm buzzing and tingling sensation all the way down the back of my neck. My eyes saw and felt like warm snow. My breathing slowed. The tingling went all the way down my back out to my finger and toe tips, and up to the top of my forehead. My forehead felt so relaxed like it was sinking right off my face. I was sitting on the bunk. I laid back. Roy reminded me where the garbage can was—vomiting was almost inevitable. I lay there for about 25 minutes. Roy fixed himself a shot.

Afterward, Sparky came into the cell to talk to us. I thanked Roy and paid him.

Sparky and I walked out to the yard to get some fresh air. I never vomited. We hid the needle in a secret spot out in a common area of the prison. That is where you hide most everything because if the staff found it no one would get blamed. If you really wanted to keep something from being found you keistered it. You acquired a latex glove from the hospital or kitchen cut off a finger, put your item in that, rewrapped it with another one tying it closed air tight, greased it up with Vaseline and inserted it into your rectum, or swallowing minus the vaseline. This was the only way you could carry drugs from one prison to another while getting transferred.

Days later I thought about my first experience with heroin. It was expensive. It was dangerous. After using heroin consecutively for three to seven days your body automatically becomes physically addicted to it and if you can't get any more you go through extreme and brutal withdraw. I thought back to the young junkies I'd seen on the Grateful Dead's east coast spring tour of 1990, how beautiful those girls had been at the first show and how hollow their eyes were at the end of the tour.

With that mental image in mind I decided that I would just stick to smoking pot; however with all the people on the yard who wanted heroin I could potentially make a lot of money. I had a good prison job with great fringe benefits, so why not I thought.

Roy sold me a gram of tar heroin for $500 and in one day I turned it into $1,250. I never fronted the drugs. This was tricky because $1,250 represents way more commissary than one can fit into the standard issue prison locker.

After the first gram of heroin that I bought and sold, I wanted more but could not get it, Roy was out. I sold the entire gram in $50 papers. I had no urge to use heroin anymore. I went back to selling weed and doing time.

Besides, there was another appeal Kurt Phillips my appellate attorney, and I were working on.

"This one might take a few years, but the issues are good," he assured me while on one of my legal phone calls to him via the counselors office approved days earlier from a letter he sent me.

We were fighting the calculations of the Sentencing Commission versus the mandatory minimums. Sparky had the same issues and was appealing the very same thing. I still spent a lot of time in the law library at Englewood. I had a lot of faith in Kurt Phillips; he encouraged me to remain realistic about my appeals but worked to find grounds for appeal. The Sentencing Commission made changes in regards to the way LSD sentences were determined. It affected the sentencing guidelines but not mandatory minimum sentences. Anyone sentenced in federal prison for LSD would automatically get their sentences recalculated under the new guidelines which at the time was about 300 to 400 inmates for the entire 1994 federal prison population.

It should have been good news but it was unclear as to whether these recalculations would affect the mandatory minimum. My six thousand hits of LSD was just over a half-gram of pure LSD which under the law was a level eight or nine in the Federal Sentencing Guideline Manual—a 27 to 33 month sentence. Since I did not assist the government in any way I was sentenced under the 10 year mandatory minimums to 151 months. It was a vote by Congress that implemented mandatory minimums, although the Sentencing Commission was created by the Sentencing Reform Act provisions of the Comprehensive Crime Control Act of 1984, which was the same act that created mandatory minimums. The confusion was a bit of a chicken versus egg conundrum in that mandatory minimums and the Sentencing Commission were both born from the same congressional act. However, the commission was not congress and it was very unclear if they could in fact have the power to reduce sentences below the mandatory minimums through this new directive.

Remember, there are 12 federal judicial circuits, some of which disagree on interpretations of the law, civil, criminal etc and when that happens it is considered an "inter-circuit conflict." This can only be resolved through the U.S. Supreme court. There ended up being a massive inter-circuit conflict over this LSD law change. Because of the law change promulgated by the sentencing commission my sentence was reduced from 151 months to 120 months. People in California were luckier, and most defendants in the ninth judicial circuit (California, Oregon, Washington, Idaho, Montana, Nevada and Arizona) had their sentences lowered to whatever the new guidelines were even if below the mandatory minimum sentence. Same law with two very distinct interpretations among different federal district courts.

Still, overall I gained back 31 months while I was in Englewood. Sparky's sentence was reduced from twenty years (240 months) to 151 months. Our letters came the same day from the courts informing us of our sentencing changes and we smoked a big fat joint in celebration. It was kind of funny; here we were happy having to serve ten years and twelve years, seven months, respectively. We were not disillusioned though. It was still a long way to go and we were not done fighting.

After seven and a half months of time at Englewood I was in trouble once again. I found myself under investigation, this time for a big batch of hooch that was found in a common area of our living unit. We had perfected a technique using tomato puree and brown sugar: ten pounds of brown sugar and ten pounds of tomato puree to five or ten gallons of water. We found that the brown sugar cooked off faster than the white processed sugar. Tomato puree has tons of acid and made for a quicker cooking time and slightly better taste than citrus hooch. The only other thing you needed was a little yeast. Yeast was locked up in a special lock box in the prison kitchen. The bakers always capitalized off of this. They were always in for some of the bounty as payment for the yeast. One sixteen-ounce cup of this stuff would knock you on your ass. It was risky to make because batches were always getting found and once drunk you were subject to a random breathalyzer test. Every Friday night the lieutenants would round up 50 random inmates and perform breathalyzers.

I was never officially charged with the hooch they found in our unit, but was getting transferred anyway under the guise of investigation. I was headed to FCI Florence a medium security FCI located a mere few hours south of Englewood in Florence, Colorado. Florence had the FCI compound with two fences because of its medium security status, as well as a high-security penitentiary with an additional wall, and the ADX, which was just coming about as the new glorified super-maximum prison based on the "Marion Model," with added security technology, though prisoners there were all sent to separate recreation yards and never mixed with one another making it astoundingly safer than USP Marion ever was or would be. Florence also had a camp just outside the prison walls and fences where the bitches and snitches lived and took care of the grounds. But I was excited nonetheless, it boasted a newer facility bigger cells newer weights and a 270-degree view of mountains. Also when I'd left Sandstone Hog Head thought he would be going to FCI Florence. I wondered if he was there, it was all the rage amongst convicts and supposedly a good prison to do lots of time at.

At that time Englewood had a pretty even mix of whites to other races; the racial breakdown plays a large role in determining the yard dynamics. FCI Florence on the other hand had the occurrence of being a predominantly white prison yard, which meant that I would have even less worries than in Englewood. Still if I had my druthers I would have stayed in Englewood.

I was going to miss James "Sparky" Irving. I had never expected to find a friend like Sparky in prison of all places. He had started teaching me guitar and in exchange I showed him how to lift weights like I learned in Sandstone from Hog and Chili.

THE GREEN DUFFEL BAG

Within two weeks of my arrival James handcrafted a duffel bag for me as a gift. It was fashioned out of a large thick dark green 100% wool army blanket with a big chrome zipper and a double-thick shoulder strap. It looked like it could have been bought from a store in the free world, making it a rare commodity. Very few people had a workout bag at all much less one so unique. If you wanted to carry something it would have to be in a prison issue laundry bag. Repeatedly I would get offered lots of money and drugs for my green duffel bag when I went to workout in Englewood, I would not hear of it; it was too sentimental an object. James had risked so much just making it for me, it was a symbol of our bonding and friendship.

I valued owning anything that would set me apart from the masses. You couldn't put a cost on a chance at true individuality in prison. It was invaluable to me, like a baby with its baby's blanket, It was highly functional and I used it every time I worked out.

When you leave a federal prison for another prison or for any other reason whatsoever all your property is inventoried before you leave as it was when you arrived and you get a copy of what is called a "property slip" signed by prison staff. This slip is the only physical thing you are allowed to travel with while in transit in the federal prison system except medications which are held by the transferring marshal staff. During this process of inventorying your property, some property may be thrown away because you have too much of something or an item may be deemed contraband. I was nervous about the bag during the exit inventory process, but my beloved green duffel bag made it through and was logged in on my official Bureau of Prisons property form. This would ensure that legally I would be able to have it on any prison yard. The drama of the future implications in this simple twist of fate still affects me in positive ways today. However getting to that point meant going through the crucible of USP Marion.

Joel Blaeser
03491-089
U. S. PENITENTIARY
P. O. BOX 1000
MARION, IL. 62959

Rosemary Blaeser
1730 N Clark #4102
Chicago, IL 60614

Dear Rosemary   3/29/97

Hello, Thankyou for the money it was right on time. I was informed of the miscarriage. It seems as though it is not as tragic as say if she were 7 months pregnant. Being deformed as it was I think it was all for the better. Glen Biggus wrote me for the 2nd time last week and sent me a 2nd book. The first book he sent me was a compilation of short stories by Thom Jones. The 2nd book is called The Civilization of the Renaissance in Italy By Birckhardt. It covers the 1400 - 1850s, Art, poetry, Government, Man, religion, Morality, Science and it also has 100 prints in the back from artwork from that time period. I am only on p 3 though. Glen is moving from Washington to Boulder and he does website programing. The book I had about the Jackal By David Yallop was lost when the person I borrowed it to went to the hole. In that book David Yallop addresses the book that you reccomended to me about the middle East. I have only read one book on the subject, And David Yallop makes a strong argument and backs it up with alot of facts to support his claim. He also shows have alot of those other books are based on false/misinformation.

    I am a little befuddled to hear about all this dental work you need. Ever since I have been in prison you have had alot of stuff done. Is all this necessary? Lets estimate you live 25 more years in that time how many more of these things will need to be done. Having ones teeth one was born with is a big thing for me as it is for you. I brush after every meal and gargle with salt water at night. However is there a alternative to all of this for you. If your teeth will last another 25 years then no amount of money should stop you from attempting to keep them. However if in the future it proves to be futile then maybe you need to try something else. How can we assess this — I don't know — a unbiased dentist maybe. Dentures are my worst nightmare — If I ever get them I think I would go with permanent ones — as I understand it it is the same maintinence as regular teeth. It would be nice if I don't ever need them — but I cannot predict the future and one day I might. Once someone gets these permanent plates I don't see what other problems could occur. It is something to consider. If your teeth can be saved and its not futile then go with it.

    I will keep you updated on the appeal I talked to Marcia yesterday and we may get a extra month to file the appeal she said she needed me to call again soon to let me know for sure and to discuss relevant points of the case. I will keep you informed. Since so many people are trying to make the deadline it will take longer than usual to hear a answer back. If there is a evidentiary hearing then we will be looking real good.

3

The weather is starting to warm up around here, yesterday there was a violent rain/hail storm. It was actually kind of nice - there was alot of fresh in the unit.

You know Aunt Iris wrote a while back and she was mentioning some stuff about the family tree. I remember when I was little and you guys (the sisters) told us kids about that castle in Italy that we could get if we paid the back taxes on. We could use that as a starting point with all of the other info we got and go to that Mormon warehouse in Utah. I saw a show on T.V. about that place - basically they are the authority, they're even hooked up with the feds in their computer system. They did not say how much they charge, from the looks of it, it didn't seem like they charged outragous prices. Being the authority they are there are not many disputes with the info they put out. It would be nice to see who was grandmas (Brown) mothers mother and where they lived and see if in fact we have claim on a castle in italy. I also have the same sense of wonderment on Dads side.

I am glad to hear Jen is content at her new job. That is great if her main problem with not being content is where you work. Actually though that is the place where most find discontentment and over time it can and does permeate discontentment in all that persons life. Alot of people dont have the choice or luxury of & switching jobs at a whim because there not happy. Most people work out of immediate necessity and don't have the option to switch jobs unless or until they are forced to. So it sounds like she is in a nice situation to live as she has been living.

Did you send me a picture yet. I am working on a drawing right now based on the playboy picture, however I need a recent one one where you have make up on like when you visited me – a close up preferably – I need it soon so I can complete the drawing – Please send one soon. TODAY! If you have to go to a store where they have a machine you sit in and it takes your picture for a 1$ or whatever. Make your self look like you do when you go out on the town with larry I am concerned only with the face. Enjoy yourself Mother, Hello Larry.

Peace

Joel

P.S.
I need you to call Marcia today, keep her on her toes, don't tell her I told you to call. Act concerned and be firm with your inquiries. Don't forget
404-653-3797
If she is not there when you call find out when she'll be in next and try then

9
Joy Riding

I DON'T KNOW IF I was born an alcoholic or not. The first time I tried beer was In 1981, I was eleven years-old at a back yard party my older brother had thrown for his friends. My dad had provided a quarter barrel of beer for them, and I began sneaking cups of beer when no one was looking. The first sip felt like flames burning the back of my throat. Still, I went back to get more, I just wanted to feel part of it all. My sister noticed me heading for the keg and nodded her head to acknowledge that I could have more.

Every time I managed to slam four or five gulps of beer I would end up in a coughing fit and spit out what I couldn't manage to choke down. Though I'd grabbed 4 cups I probably only drank the equivalent of 3 beers.

I had a similar experience about two years later when I scored my first bag of weed. It was an eighth of an ounce that I bought for five dollars. Two friends and I sat behind Hawthorne Elementary School on the Honey Creek Parkway in Wauwatosa, Wisconsin, and smoked almost all of it but did not really feel anything.

I didn't smoke again until my oldest brother bought me tickets to an AC/DC concert for my thirteenth birthday. Though I appreciated the tickets, the real gift was that he wanted to hang out with me. He was coming with me even though he was seventeen and probably had much cooler things to do than take his thirteen year old brother to the "For Those About To Rock We Salute You" AC/DC tour.

Before the concert we met up with some people in an alley near the Mecca Arena in Milwaukee. The ground was wet the sky misty and the street nearby hummed with the excitement of concertgoers. There was a fierce wind which toyed with the end of one of the girl's skirt. Someone pulled out a pipe in the shape of a skull and packed it full of sweet-smelling Columbian weed. On my first hit I noticed the red crystal eyes embedded in the skull. By the sixth or seventh hit I was feeling light-headed and more than a little fuzzy, yet details were clear such as the way the skull pipe's red eyes glowed with the reflection of the streetlight.

Night fell and we all hopped into someone's green four-door Ford LTD and headed to the concert. As we were walking towards the door of the arena the full effect of marijuana hit me. All of a sudden I began to weep and tugged at the sleeve of my brother.

"What's going on? I can't handle this. I can't handle this! Take me home. What's going on? MY HEAD IS SPINNING AND WON'T STOP!... Why do I feel like this?" My sentences were tempered with sporadic whimpering as I attempted to cling to his sleeve all the way into the concert and the crowd.

"JOEL!" my brother shouted, "It's going to be ok, just hold on."

For the next fifteen or twenty minutes was mentally chaotic. We soon met up with a friend of Jason's who shared his Jack Daniels mixed with Coca-Cola. I sputtered when I sipped it, the taste reminiscent of what I perceived sweet gasoline to taste like.

After that night I began smoking pot regularly but struggled with the guilt of having to hide it from my family. I would go through phases where I would flush my bag of marijuana down the toilet vowing to never smoke again. Then I would find myself gravitating toward smoking it more and more frequently and finally selling it to smoke for free. I had a strained relationship with my parents already, and feared talking to them about my drug use would increase the tension that already dominated my home life. I considered going to a school counselor to talk about my emotional instability; I think on at least some level I was aware that I was getting high as a form of escape from my exceptional sensitivity to outside factors. In the end, my inability to trust won out and I kept the struggle to myself.

By the time I was fifteen I was already selling. My friend Adam's parents had taught him how to grow marijuana. He would order seeds from "Neville" a renowned seed cultivator based in Amsterdam. In 1984 we paid $50 to $100 per ten seeds for high-end strains such as Big Bud, S.K.1, Hash Plant and Northern Lights. We typically grew a very hardy Indica that could survive the harsh Wisconsin fall weather some harvested as late as mid-October.

In the summer of 1985 I bought seeds from Adam and grew three plants on my own. I tended them rigorously, loved them, watered them, weeded the garden around them and watched as they thrived. Right before harvest they were stolen. I'd planted them in a very heavily populated area, but in the white upper-middle-class neighborhood where we rented a house, I doubted anyone casually passing by would have recognized them for what they were. I was obviously wrong, and heartbroken as a result. After that, I never bothered growing again. Instead, I would buy a quarter pound from Adam for $250 and sell it for $500. As a teenager I often rode my Redline BMX bike around with five or six hundred dollars on me.

Most of the time I would have "the kind" (slang for very high quality home grown pot) sold before I even bought it, so I rarely had to worry about being caught with weed physically on my person. On the few occasions it wasn't sold before the harvest had even come in, I had a spot to keep it in. I refused to bring drugs into my parents' house; it seemed an unnecessary risk. We lived close to a park and so instead I kept it buried until it sold, at which point I would go dig it up with gloves on. I never owned a pipe or any paraphernalia and if I ever had a rolling paper it was crunched up like a piece of trash jammed in the corner of my pocket.

I was discreet because of my parents, but caution soon transitioned to an active and constant wariness after my freshman year at Wauwatosa East High School, when I witnessed first-hand the consequences of getting caught using drugs: Once when smoking a huge bowl of marijuana in the bathroom in between classes, I passed the bowl to my friend, Craig DeSmith. A hall guard came into the mens room at the very same time Craig took a huge hit.

"Pipe is in your mouth, DeSmith. You're coming with me. You're getting suspended," he said. "All the rest of you Blaeser, Bainbridge its your lucky day. Get out of here."

It was a wake-up call for me. I was a varsity wrestler in the 98-105 lb. weight class and risked being kicked off the wrestling team if any of my actions warranted disciplinary sanction. After realizing how severe the consequences could be for me, I was much more careful about my drug use and distribution, I vowed to myself to never to get caught.

Later that year at a big Friday night party my friend Ted suggested taking his parents' car out for a joy ride. It was Saturday night and four of us had been sitting around his house drinking for hours. We clumsily piled into his parents new Pontiac and took turns driving.

"Hey, I should drive first," I suggested. I had my permit and considered myself a decent driver. I plopped into the driver's seat while Ted settled in next to me and Kurt and Chris jumped in the back.

"Turn up the tunes!" Chris leaned forward over the bench seat and grabbed at the radio knobs.

"I got it! I got it!" Ed said pushing the heel of his palm against Chris's forehead, shoving him into the backseat again.

David Lee Roth wailed over the speakers. Chris and Kurt grabbed the front seats and wildly rocked their heads back and forth. Ted pounded on the dashboard in time with the beat. I put the car into reverse and rolled out of the driveway.

"Go down Vliet Street," Kurt yelled. "Let's go by the Scherwanka's house!"

The Scherwankas were drop-dead gorgeous identical twins in our freshman class. With a whoop of consent I accelerated the car and we whizzed by manicured lawns in the quiet town of Wauwatosa, a western, middle-upper class suburb of Milwaukee. We pulled up to the twins' house, and the car idled as Chris jumped from the back into the driver's seat and took his turn.

"Let's head over to Gilles Frozen Custard and check things out," Kurt suggested.

Chris gunned it heading toward the local custard stand and popular high school hangout and we were off again. The tree lined picturesque suburban streets were dark and quiet. We hauled down the road, peeling around sharp turns.

"Chinese fire drill!" Ted yelled as we approached a stop sign.

All four car doors flew open. We jumped out and ran around the car in search for another door. I flew around to the front passenger seat in time to see Chris and Ted collide in front of the car. Chris fell backwards onto the street. Ted laughed helped him up, and jumped behind the wheel. The car doors slammed shut and we were tearing down the road again.

Boy George began to belt out Lyrics through the speakers. "Oh, puke! Turn the station!" Chris complained.

Ted turned the dial and landed on "Owner of a Lonely Something." We jammed along to the music feeling young, free and invincible.

"OK, Kurt, your turn," Ted said as he pulled the car to a stop.

We switched places again. I joined Chris in the back. Ted took the co-pilot seat up front and Kurt pressed on the gas.

"C'mon, Kurt! You're driving like a grandma. Pick it up!" I yelled from behind him.

"Alright! I've never driven before. Chill!" he responded, aggravated.

"Punch it Kurt!" Chris encouraged. We cackled with laughter.

Kurt pressed the gas pedal all the way to the floor. The car had a surprising pickup. It was equipped with a 455 cubic inch motor, which was impressive for a wood-paneled Pontiac station wagon. The wagon zipped along the street, Kurt swerving outside of the lines. We were rapidly heading towards a small bridge that crossed a ravine in the Washington Highlands neighborhood, a very upscale part of Wauwatosa. The car veered a little to the right.

"Watch it Kurt!" I yelled.

"Slow down, dude!" Ted screamed from up front.

The car bumped up against the curb on the right and Kurt cut the wheel sharply to correct his error.

"Shit!" I yelled as the car barreled across to the other side of the street.

The car jumped the opposite curb shot up a hill and slammed directly into a tree head on. My face bounced off the back of the driver's seat. Kurt and Ed flew forward into the windshield. The glass splintered into two enormous spider-web cracks where their heads hit.

"Oooh fuck," Ted groaned grabbing his forehead.

"Holy shit are you guys ok?" I asked. A hot sting started to spread from my nose across my cheeks.

Four doors opened again and we stumbled out to inspect the damage.

"Dude this doesn't look bad at all," I said. I walked around the front of the car. "Start it up. We should be able to drive it home."

That I thought the car looked fine was a testament to how incredibly drunk I was. The front of the car looked like the tree had grown into it. There was no way it was coming loose without a tow.

"I'm so fucked" Ted said still rubbing his bloody forehead.

"We have to get out of here," Chris said.

"What do we do?" Ted said.

"We need to get out of here," Chris repeated.

We took off on foot. We just left the car wedged into that tree. The police came across the wreck and a tow truck pulled the wagon out.

There was a football game at the high school that night at Hart Park. I heard from the student spectators that the tow truck drove the battered car right by the field. The car was crushed to the point that people in the bleachers buzzed about how there couldn't possibly be any survivors.

My parents got a call from Ted's parents later that night. Although Ted kept his mouth shut about his accomplices his parents pieced together the scenario pretty well. Two days later my parents got a call from the school outlining their disciplinary action. Both Chris and I were kicked off the varsity wrestling team for our alleged participation in the car accident. Although it was Ted's family car he remained on the basketball team. His father was pretty influential in the community and was able to make a plea to the school principal on his behalf.

I never confessed, a hallmark trait that I'd learned during my youth and would play a role in events for years to come. My father was furious but didn't lift a hand to me which was odd considering he beat me as a child for tiny infractions or yelled furiously for something as small as spilling juice.

It wasn't long before both Chris and I fell out of the jock crowd and connected with the druggie clique. My attention focused even more on drugs.

The first time I bought LSD with intent to sell was at my second Grateful Dead show. After the first show I'd realized what a financial opportunity the parking lot scene was. There was ample access to LSD but not necessarily to good marijuana, something I could easily get my hands on in Milwaukee. So before I headed out to Alpine Valley for the second time the following year in 1985 I made sure to bring a stash of Adam's fine homegrown Indica weed. Upon arrival I would find one of the older hippies who had obviously come on tour with the Dead and offer them a joint. After we smoked they'd usually offer me a deal on LSD out of respect for the quality of the weed I'd shared with them. Though the price was usually around $100 per sheet I typically bought them for $30. I'd then head to the parking lot where cars were coming in.

If you've ever been to a professional sports arena with open parking lots like Milwaukee's Miller Park Stadium, the parking lot system was very similarly set up; rows of vehicles would pull in one after another often with every seat full of young concert goers. I would walk from car to car and sell the sheets hit by hit, typically for $5 per hit or I would offer a five for $20 deal. I ended up with 15-20 hits sold per car because most of the buyers bought 3 or 4 hits each. I managed to sell all the sheets after just a few cars and was walking away with hundreds of dollars of pure profit.

At my third show (June 22nd, 1985 Alpine Valley Ampitheatre, Wisconsin), I witnessed a big drug bust go down in the parking lot. I asked an older Deadhead what was going on and specifically how they got caught. I discovered there were groups of undercover DEA agents roving the parking lots talking up strangers for LSD connections. I was even told that they'd often smoke a joint or even offer a joint to people in the parking lots in an effort to build trust and to glean information about the big game LSD players. Many years later in federal prison I learned first-hand that in the very late 1980's the DEA (drug enforcement agency) even went so far as to set up marijuana grow houses as fronts to try to catch LSD dealers and manufacturers. I discovered certain venues were more notorious than others for drug busts at Dead shows. I was warned to be particularly wary of a few places such as Nassau County Coliseum on Long Island, New York. Even the Grateful Dead especially Jerry Garcia complained to the promoters about the number of concertgoers who were hassled at Nassau; at least four hundred to six hundred Deadheads would get arrested on drug charges every time the Dead played on Long Island. The Grateful Dead bucked the system in every way not just by building a dedicated fan base through touring, always detesting the studio and it's business representatives, but also in caring about their fans who took long treks to see them, to the tune of trying to get police in certain venues to agree not to arrest anyone unless it involved violence.

I began to take more notice of the Deadhead activists out in the parking lots. They handed out newsletters chronicling people who were locked up and warned newcomers to beware of these venues. "Safety first," was the motto of the crowd in regards to any sort of drug activity.

I realized any one of the cars I had been approaching in the parking lot at my second Dead show could have been chock full of undercover agents and decided this was far too risky. My attraction to the shows was for the music and the social scene first and foremost. Besides I would actually make far more money buying LSD from "the family" at the show then selling it for five times the price in Milwaukee or other large cities.

Despite that I was still smoking and selling I still managed to make it to class every day and graduated high school in 1987. I would sell high-grade marijuana during the school year and during the summers I would score LSD at the Alpine Valley Grateful Dead shows and sell it back in Milwaukee.

Morally I felt that all drugs should be legal, yet I took comfort in the fact that I was not selling alcohol, cocaine, heroin, or crack. All of those substances are highly addictive and I did not like the idea of selling them. I felt it gave the drugs a negative karmic value and therefore I did not want to any part of that. I believed and found LSD mushrooms and marijuana were different if used in a ritualistic way, and felt somewhat removed from the evil associated with the label "drug dealer." After all, for the most part I was only buying from and selling to friends of mine or friends of theirs. At the shows I always met new and wonderful people and occasionally they'd ask to be hooked up. It helped too that as long as I was selling I was making enough money to travel as I pleased and attend pretty much any Dead show I wanted. It was the family code not to sell drugs in a parking lot at the shows.

A year after my father had died in my arms on October 15th, 1988 I finally had an opportunity to follow the Dead on tour. I'd saved enough money from my Hi-Ranger factory job assembling cherry pickers, a job that I hated but viewed as a means to an end. With the money I'd saved I bought my first brand new car a 1989 Honda Civic and felt I was ready to face the world. Or at least my first full-on Dead tour. They were starting in Hampton, Virginia for two shows then headed to Brendan Byrne Arena in New Jersey for five shows, three shows at the Spectrum in Philadelphia then continuing south to Charlotte, North Carolina for two more shows finally ending at the new Miami Arena in Florida.

My girlfriend at the time and I seemed to be getting serious or at least had been dating for almost three and a half years. But before I entertained ideas of getting married I wanted to travel. I begged and pleaded with her to come with me on the tour and see the world before we settled down. She adamantly refused and couldn't understand my desire to travel. We had a massive fight over it and couldn't reconcile our differences. When I left town I had about $1,500, a half a pound of extremely potent cannabis indica and no reason to return especially after she slept with my younger brother Bradley and older brother Michael to spite me.

The marijuana gave me instant carte blanche to some of the more exclusive circles in the Dead community. Super high-grade marijuana was in high demand as it was more tradable than any other currency. Dan was a older red haired hippy from Maine I met at my first dead show and saw at most every show I ever went to. He liked my marijuana and took a liking to me so we began meeting up regularly at shows. After the first show of this tour, Dan introduced me to Tim and his friend Lisa. Blonde, tan, and buxom she was a total knockout and I was in love at first sight. We traveled together frequently and over the course of the tour the four of us became a family unit.

Tim Tyler is well-known among the Deadhead family because of the controversy surrounding his prison sentence. When I met him he was simply known among the crowd as "the fried dough man." Every show he would set up and fry dough in hot oil and then roll them in powdered sugar. They were the size of a large plate and 2 inches thick, fluffy, light and coated with powder sugar selling faster than he could make them at $2 each. Timmy would sometimes sell 500 per show. He had two Coleman four-burner stoves topped by deep pans to heat the vegetable oil in. Eventually I started joining him at the grill making grilled cheese to sell alongside the dough. At the end of the Grateful Dead show we would line up by the door inside the venue, listen to the encore song and then run out to set up. We'd fire up the grills get the beer coolers set up and get ready to start selling to all the people coming out of the show. You could easily make $500-$800 profit in an hour or two.

We always tried to pick up the dough from a local bakery rather than a well-known chain store where it would be available.

So much like any other town we'd been in, when Tim, Lisa, Dan and I hit Charlotte, North Carolina for the next show we stopped at a local bakery to buy the dough which Tim loaded into his girlfriend's borrowed new Toyota Celica. We were selling some of the dough in the parking lot before the show, but it was so warm that the remaining dough in the car began to rise. It rose so rapidly that by the time we realized what was happening it had already started to ooze out of the windows in the front seat and the hatchback. That car never was the same, even after the $100 interior detail job Tim bought to help clean it up.

I'd sold LSD on and off for four years and still never taken it. During the fourth show of the 1989 fall east coast tour Lisa convinced me we should take a couple of her hits together. The LSD she had was patterned with small blue unicorns, but the design was so simple it could easily be replicated. It wasn't unheard of for people to go around and sell "blanks," sheets of blotter paper printed with popular LSD designs, such as dancing bears, dolphins or snowflakes that weren't laced with LSD. I had no idea what the timeline would be for it to go into effect. The show had opened up with "Let the Good Times Roll," and we waited the entire song and then ate two more each, and neither of us felt any change. We assumed that the blue unicorns were not good and continued to eat them. By the time we had started to feel it we each had eaten about ten hits, about eight hits more than we'd intended to.

An LSD trip lasts about ten to twelve hours whether its 3 or 10 hits, and the majority of the stimuli is internal. Intellectually it acts as an organizer succinctly allowing you to articulate whatever it is you want to say. But your experience of the external world is altered. I remember feeling as if I could see the life in everything as if the seats and lights themselves were breathing just as I was. I could see the aura of everything and everyone; all the colors of the world were bigger, bolder, more vibrant, and I knew the names of more shades of color than I'd known existed. I was sure I was experiencing all of my organs working and could feel the movement of my blood as it circulated through my body. I could see sound, hear colors, taste an object. Everything looked and felt beautiful and I felt pure love and gratitude for everyone around me, and was sure the power of my happiness was shining forth in a beam of light shooting straight from my solar plexus.

We laughed, danced, and sang with the Grateful Dead riding the wave of enlightenment. After the show we stopped for dinner at a Chinese restaurant. I remember ordering the pu pu platter and Lisa convinced me the hot mustard was a sweet sauce. I took a big bite of it, the hot spicy flavor exploded over my tongue and I felt a little betrayed. Then we laughed uncontrollably for minutes on end.

Later that night we had sex on and off for nearly six hours. You don't necessarily want to have sex on LSD, but if you do the experience is heightened. Everything you feel and touch is suddenly experienced in a multitude of ways. All of your senses are triggered. In the morning when I awoke and attempted to get out of the bed I fell to the floor because my knees and thighs were still so fatigued.

We never abused LSD taking it only a couple of times a year at most. It is a powerful substance which warrants a level of respect but rarely inviting abuse. Unlike most other street drugs it is not addictive. Anyone using LSD frequently will build up a tolerance to the drug and therefore the appeal of taking it often lessens. In comparison a heavy heroin user might use four or five times a day, whereas a heavy LSD use is extremely rare. In my circles it was not taken lightly; it was revered as a spiritual experience intended to pave the way for the mind to encounter the world in a new magical and blissful way most assuredly always reducing your ego.

LSD originated in a Swiss pharmaceutical lab called Sandoz on November 16th, 1938 thanks to a scientist named Albert Hoffman who was synthesizing a naturally occurring fungus to determine what medicinal uses it could have. Over the course of his studies he created medicines that lowered blood pressure and improved brain function in the elderly and on his twenty-fifth attempt he extracted lysergic acid diethylamide, more commonly know as LSD-25. When he accidentally absorbed some of the substance he began to feel euphoria, experience heightened visual stimuli and synesthesia, or the confusion of senses. Hoffman introduced LSD to the world of professional psychology as an aid in guided repression therapy and as a treatment for alcoholism. Prior to the late 1960s when it was criminalized and classified as a "hippie drug," its medicinal use was praised by celebrities such as Cary Grant and Henry Luce, the founder of *Time*, *Life* and *Sports Illustrated* magazines. Even one of the founders of the twelve step program Alcoholics Anonymous, Bill Wilson, experimented with LSD for five straight years while deep in his sobriety. After his first LSD trip, at the Veterans Administration (VA) hospital in Los Angeles on August 29th, 1956, Wilson began to believe it was "insight from the experience" that could help alcoholics recover.

It was still legal when Sandoz stopped distribution, so in order to continue its use as a therapeutic aid, labs began to pop up around the country. In today's day and age with the popularity of methamphetamines among American youth, the term lab might bring to mind steel Airstream trailers and toothless hillbillies with sunken eyes and shaky hands. But real LSD-25 requires an extensive knowledge of chemistry and professional lab equipment.

Unlike the media's portrayal of a drug concoction, it is not something you make in your bathtub or basement but rather, requires proper equipment and technique. The chemical compounds cannot be bought at your local corner store and are rare, high-grade materials that are expensive and hard to come by. Nowadays most of the ingredients for making LSD must be bought industrially and are closely monitored by the DEA.

Despite its villainous reputation, there were and are very few LSD manufacturers throughout the country. It is not a particularly lucrative drug because the costs of ingredients and equipment to process the drug are so expensive, and unlike many other more marketable drugs you do not build up an unhealthy, dependent clientele due to its non-addictive nature. It doesn't appeal to the average street corner dealer's low-risk/high reward mentality. Realistically the risk is incredibly high because the government keeps tabs on all major ingredients which means huge prison sentences if caught and demand is not endless like with narcotics.

Very few LSD labs have ever been busted in the United States, Augustus Owsley Stanleys Richmond, California lab was the first in 1967, very few have been found since.

Contrary to the belief of the prosecutor in my case, I was not one of the elite few master LSD manufacturers in the country. I did however, know a few of them.

The people I met who made LSD were truly some of the kindest, most loving idealists I've ever encountered. They did not like hard drugs or authorities and truly believed LSD should be utilized as an agent to bring about radical social change, a commodity in the fight against ignorance, not a drug to be abused or taken for granted. It was the vehicle for a sacred journey of self-analysis and self-betterment that instilled a sense of camaraderie within all involved.

Over the course of my time travelling with the Dead, I met some of the major players in the LSD scene. One of whom I came to know was Augustus Owsley Stanley III, the original sound man for the Grateful Dead. Aside from the high quality LSD he produced and distributed (sometimes called Blue Cheer), Owsley was most notably known for many patents and a number of electrical recording devices as well as for creating the "Steal Your Face" skull, a symbol now synonymous with the Grateful Dead. It was originally conceived as a mark for their amps, speakers, and instrument cases to keep them from getting mixed up at venues where multiple bands were playing.

But he was also a staple at the shows. He set up at the "Save the Rainforest" table at most every Dead show. I would meet him by the table during set breaks where we would discuss a variety of topics; we talked about everything from the rise in the Earth's temperature, which he believed was causing the polar ice caps to melt, to making gold alchemically, which he claimed could be done. He was also an artist who specialized in brass, gold and silver paired with enamel, his belt buckles with the skull on them were especially popular. Owsley made a pretty penny off the buckles as well. I bought one from him at the 1990 Paris Dead shows for $250. He perpetually wore and was selling a gold ring in the shape of a serpent wrapped around an enormous old single-cut ruby. I admired it often, and he let me wear it even though it got stuck on my finger almost every time I tried it on. He explained that rubies could be made synthetically, and he had been learning how to make his own synthetic rubies and diamonds.

I also ran into Jack Herer at the same show who authored the book titled *The Emperor Wears No Clothes* about the value of hemp as a renewable resource during a time when it was certainly not popular opinion. By the end of 2014, *The Emperor Wears No Clothes* will be released in it's eleventh edition and thus injected once again into the national conversation about drug law reform that is changing marijuana laws throughout the country, fueled at least in part by his ideas about the ban on marijuana by petrochemical industry tycoons and backed by celebrities such as Willie Nelson. I first read it in 1985 when i was 16 in high school.

Going on the 1990 European Grateful Dead tour was an impromptu decision as most of them were then, and I had to get a "rush" passport, meaning I had to pay an extra fee and provide a printed itinerary of my trip. All the shows except the London England show were at smaller venues. I'd made friends with an older Deadhead in Florida named Mike and we traveled to Paris together for the show. We were enjoying the night hanging out before the concert when he began weaving a tale about the Grateful Dead's legendary original sound man presumed dead. I proceeded to take him out back behind the concession stand and introduce him to "Bear," a well-known nickname for Owsley who was very much alive, and in rare form was very happy to share a joint of kind bud with us.

Still as easy-going and peaceful as we all were the threat of prison and of cops was very real. Dan and Rainbow taught me that safety was of paramount importance. They would tell me that if I thought I was being followed by police I should ditch the product or money because I could always get more to buy from them. Freedom and safety were the first order of business it was almost a motto and one they never let me forget. When I first met Dan he often spoke in allegory: He would present a scenario, then gauge my decision or reaction. Dan and Rainbow had a reputation for cherry-picking the best dealers and this was Dan's way of vetting my trustworthiness. They were also conscious of risk factors. If they ever suspected you of having a drinking or harder drug problem, one where you might potentially compromise yourself or others within the community you would be cut off forever from their LSD. You could also be cut off for associating with suspect characters who were alcoholics, heroine or cocaine users anyone who might potentially be a narc or threaten the community at large.

I only met and socialized with Rainbow three times. His LSD was equal to Owlseys or Sandoz's. Rainbow was renowned for having the most beautiful and intricate designs as his brand on the blotter paper which acted as a carrier for the LSD. He commissioned a female artist in San Francisco to create the sheets and had two signature designs: One print was of a rubenesque woman surfing a very steep wave, and the other featured Da Vinci's *Vitruvian Man* with the words "So you say" printed below the design. Sometimes both designs were used on either side of the paper as well. Rainbow used an antique white perforated 100% organic cotton bond paper and each sheet was batiked with the design. Very edible low toxic colored ink was used.

Rainbow got his name from of the array of colors used on his designs; the entire sheet would blend from one color the next, giving the appearance of a seamless rainbow starting from one corner of the page and flowing outward. Often the designs were batiked on eight pages of 8" x 10" paper all at once, which were attached, perforated, and folded at the top in the fashion of continuous stationery computer paper from the 1980s. Each stack (8,000-10,000 hits) of paper was impregnated with one gram of pure LSD-25. Each 100 hits of LSD was referred to as a "sheet" and had a single *Vitruvian Man* or surfing lady on it; a full "page" was 1,000 hits. The complexity of his designs also served as quality assurance because they were more complicated and therefore more difficult to replicate, meaning that Rainbow preserved his reputation for having a quality product in a way that others could not.

In 1990 while at a Jerry Garcia show in Hawaii I met a local grower on the island of Oahu who had some high-grade locally grown marijuana. I convinced her to give me four ounces with the promise that when I got back to Berkeley in two days I would send ten sheets of LSD. In total it cost me $300. That exotic breed of pot was rarely seen on Dead tours and was therefore worth over $1,000.

The day after that transaction at the Oahu Hawaii airport I bought a ticket to Oakland California with cash and no ID, and sent a letter to my mother. Every time I flew I would send a letter to my mom from the airport (which isn't allowed anymore) that documented the flight I was on, the fake name I was flying under and what I was wearing that day. Otherwise if the plane crashed no one would ever know who I was. I would call her the moment I landed to tell her to disregard and destroy the letter that was coming. I would always follow up to make sure she destroyed the evidence. My mother received about 25 letters over the course of four years. Years later while sitting in my cell at the supermax prison in Marion Illinois, I would contemplate the stress and worry they must have caused her.

While on the Grateful Dead tour there was a system we used. I would give prospective customers a sample of the LSD and explain how I would deliver the LSD and receive payment. I would get a contact phone number for them, then days or weeks later call from a pay phone. We never spoke of drugs or paraphernalia, instead we would discuss front row Grateful Dead tickets for an upcoming show; the price $125 to $150 for each "ticket," and the minimum order was ten tickets. I paid 30 cents per hit of LSD or $3,000 per gram. My customers would send me the money via Western Union. Front Row tickets to rich yuppie Deadheads could conceivably be sold for $125-$150 each. At this time in the 1980s and early 1990s, you could send money through Western Union with or without an ID and pick it up without an ID. The sender would fill out a special form at their local Western Union office with a physical description and secret test question with a fictitious name. I or the person picking up the money would fill out the form exactly as the person who sent it answering the question exactly as written and answered by the sender. You would then get a check sign it and Western Union would cash it on the spot.

Once I received the money I would send the LSD to them via the US Postal Service in overnight envelopes. Stamps were $8.95. I had a stack of overnight envelopes and stamps with me at all times. I never carried LSD with me. People ordered and paid me before I would send it. When I sent it I never licked the stamp, used rubber gloves whenever I touched the envelopes and wrote the names with my opposite writing hand. No traces of me were ever left anywhere. I signed the checks at the Western Union with the opposite hand as well, and usually simply signed a straight line. The LSD would be delivered to them overnight and I always checked the box for the postal delivery person to leave the package if the person was not there to sign for it. None of my LSD ever got intercepted by any of the authorities. The minute I bought it it went into the large envelope and stamped using a wet towel. All communication was done via pay phones only. Dan and Rainbow taught me to always use quarters. At the time calling cards were a new modern item and they warned me about those being a danger because of possible tracing. Calls were usually long distance costing $2.75 to $3.25 a call. It was imperative to always have at least two rolls of quarters in the car at all times. Every week or two no matter where I was in the world I would make a call to my customers to see what was needed. I would drive to the post office in a clean car, meaning a car without a Grateful Dead sticker on it, insured and of course with up-to-date registration and license plates. I never travelled in a car with a Grateful Dead sticker on it because police on the east coast had started to target cars with any mention of the Grateful Dead. At the point of the overnight envelope being stamped and addressed, the only way for anyone to intercept it besides the person it was addressed to was with a warrant from the Postmaster General. Most of the time I would drop it off at the overnight mail drop box at the airport of the town I was in.

Once after a Dead show around San Francisco I went to a Western Union and filled out three different money pick-up slips, got checks with three different names on them, signed with three different names and left fifteen minutes later with about $5,500 in my pocket, $3,800 of which was profit. Up until that point that was the most money at one time I ever had in my possession and was the most I ever had until after being released from prison. Just prior I made calls to Milwaukee Wisconsin, Tampa Bay Florida, and Westchester New York. That money would last me months while touring with the Dead. I was rich. I had $3,800, a car I owned, I was twenty-one years old had ten fingers ten toes and a girlfriend named Tammy with long fire-engine red hair. Life was good.

J Blaeser
03491-089
U.S. PENITENTIARY
P.O. BOX 1000
MARION, IL 62959

Rosemary Blaeser
1730 N Clark #4/02
Chicago, IL 60614

12-31-95

Dear Mom
Hi, I love you, I love you, I love you! I was so happy to see you, you looked good. I am ok, please don't worry. I want you to come here as soon as you can so we can have a nice talk again. I am sorry that they turned you away, that they are not allowed to do, so when you come back keep tryin to get in. Please take it easy and relax I will be fine. Who knows at the rate I am going I will be able to say hi to AJB for you. I was wondering about that lady you met who gave you the rides, I can't remember where it is you said you met her. I talked to Mr Enise today he had let me know of your concern. It looks as though I might be here for a few years Lets hope the Supreme court rules in favor of my case. They heard the oral arguments the last week of November. Who knows maybe they already made a decision. Bradley is keeping me up to date on that decision. I gave him a # in washington and some people there are going to let him know when the decision comes down. After that decision is when I can start my last appeal The 2255 I was telling you about on the visit Gatewood made alot of errors AT the trial so one of my strong points would be ineffective assistance of counsel. Anyway enough of that have a good ski trip the next time you go. You said Montana right? Well say hi to larry and the family for me I love you and miss you more than you know

love
Joel

P.S.
I have decided that I want to cut my

10
Convict Code

PRISONS ARE ALWAYS IN a state of flux. Inmates are stabbed, raped, intimidated, threatened, extorted, and caught with drugs on them or in their system on a daily basis inside the walls of federal prison. Any of these as well as many more other infractions are grounds for a transfer. On average 5,500 to 15,000 Federal prisoners are transported per week across the nation. The logistics involved with transferring all of these prisoners is staggering, and however chaotic it seemed, the system worked. By this time I had been on that damned 707 six times. Still, I always got where I needed to go. I was shackled and handcuffed en route via plane, bus or car nearly 18 hours a day. It was our own "criminalized" version of *Planes, Trains, and Automobiles*.

There were certain convicts who were on what was called Diesel Therapy, a state of perpetual travel issued as a punishment. Not for the violent or big time offenders, not those who killed guards or were caught with ounces of heroin in federal prison. No, this was reserved for the legal eagles that would use the law libraries to sue prison staff and ruin their credit rating often by using the Uniform Commercial Code to put a lien on a member of the federal prison staff or prosecutor. There were also other lawsuits filed in the guise of not enough food or discrimination against a certain religion. Some frivolous and some not.

Diesel Therapy was heinous at best. The Marshal Service has buses all over the country going to many different prisons and county jails on any given day. Whenever I would get transferred to another prison with the marshals, I was always run through the outpost in El

Reno, Oklahoma. The transfer day started at 6:00 am and ended between 8 and 10:00 pm. At best you were in handcuffs and shackled for 12 hours and on long transfer days it was closer to 18 hours. I had heard of people on Diesel Therapy being shipped out on a perpetual bus ride for weeks, months, and in extreme cases years— never even going to or through El Reno Oklahoma. This keeps that convict from filing more paperwork and or being able to respond to lawsuits already filed thus rendering them on hold indefinitely. It also keeps them from using the phone eating and sleeping properly by forcing them to remain shackled and handcuffed for over half their day while riding a bus 200 to 600 miles day in and day out.

We went from Englewood Colorado to the Denver airport then to Oklahoma, and finally we landed back in Denver to board a bus en route to FCI Florence. Although it is a mere two to three hour drive from Englewood to Florence, it would be forty-five days before I set foot in my new home.

Florence was one of the newer prisons which meant the mood on the bus had a jovial tone. As we were getting closer you could see amazing views of the mountain ranges. When we arrived at Florence I was last to be logged in and interviewed. We were paraded out to the yard in groups of three or four, each group going to their respective units. The lower compound was massive, 300 yards by 250 yards. All the living units faced the lower compound. As we walked out onto the compound looking right you could see the housing units, to the left the law library, chow hall, chapel, lieutenant's office and the visiting room as well as a large outside brick corridor leading to the inside recreation area and outside rec yard. Florence's rec room was one of the best I'd ever experienced. It offered a large full-size gym, weight room, aerobic room, and band room, complete with a set of drums.

There would soon be a war waged in Washington D.C. over the BOP's budget with regards to the weights. The Pryce-Stupak amendment was being proposed to be added to the Violent Crime Control and Law Enforcement Act of 1994. Everyone on the yard knew about it and it was a hot topic among certain prison staff and inmates. It sought to vastly limit and stop all weight lifting monies for federal and state prisoners. Most of the wardens banded together and went to Washington D.C. to fight this, for they knew that bored prisoners are dangerous and that ultimately most prison weights were used constructively and kept large numbers of federal inmates busy at one time with relatively low costs and low risk.

The air was warm as the sun began to set on the prison yard. This FCI looked more like a college campus than a prison; all the buildings were made of new red, gray, blue and brown brick, the grounds were meticulously maintained— not one blade of grass was out of order. The chow hall, law library, and lieutenant's office all featured separate metal roofs like the new high-end strip malls I'd seen being built in Boulder Colorado years earlier while traveling after a Dead Tour.

The rooms were Cadillacs by prison standards originally built as single cells then converted to doubles and yet they were still bigger than any cell I had ever seen. Both bunks were lower side-by-side bunks with a space between them where prison lockers were stacked for each cell mate. Cells were about eight and a half feet wide and eleven feet long, with a stainless steel toilet-sink combo at the foot of the bed and each featured its own solid wooden door with small rectangular window. Each unit had 16 private showers with medium water pressure and huge hot water tanks, an everyday amenity in the free world that I came to be very grateful for inside the walls of prison.

To my astonishment upon arrival in my assigned housing unit I ran into a old close acquaintance named Kurt. Kurt was ten years my elder. His skin was extremely fair but he sported a huge afro that was a deep reddish brown and a biker style handlebar mustache. He looked like an outlaw biker with bad attitude but Kurt was anything but that, a true peace-loving Dead Head through and through. I knew Kurt from the outside; he and I went to many Dead shows together and had partied a lot up in the mountains above Boulder in Nederland Colorado. We also scored LSD from the same person. We talked about our cases. He'd refused to reveal his sources as well, and ended up with a 17 year sentence because of it. He seemed to be holding up ok and was in surprisingly good spirits. "Brother Joel!" Kurt shouted as I entered the unit for the first time.

"Oh my God Kurt!".

He ran up to me, shook my hand and gave a half hug.

I said, "Fancy seeing you here Kurt."

"Yeah, I heard you went down bro."

"No shit?" I said. "Who the fuck would have thought, three Dead Heads all busted for LSD, two went to trial and no one told."

"How long you been down?"

"About 20 months."

"I remember when you got busted Kurt. You must have 5 years in?"

"66 months bro, with 151 months to go. I am a three time loser and lucky I didn't get more."

He continued…."Some motherfucker ratted me out and they intercepted the overnight envelope with 10,000 hits in it."

"You took it like a man bro." I retorted.

"Fuck it. I don't know what I took it like, stuck in this motherfucker for another 13 years."

Unfortunately, we were unable to be cellmates, but were lucky to be housed in the same unit.

As you move through higher-security institutions, more and more of the prison politics are controlled and run by convicts and inmates. I'd been in the game for a while now. If I truly didn't get along with my new cellmate I could pull some strings or scratch some backs and other arrangements would be made.

Kurt mentioned there was a new fish named Eric in from the street who was in need of a celly.

"Eric is new and needs someone experienced. He is a good solid straight white dude. There he is, hey Eric!" Kurt shouted across the unit. He seemed like a good match. I was almost five years his elder and he had only been in prison a couple of months. Both bunks were bottom bunks so no need to play dominant. He was serving seven years on a marijuana growing charge. Only 21 years-old with red hair, 5'11," 180 pounds, mustache and looked older than he was but now once in prison he had a brand new look about him. We hit it off instantly.

There was a large carpeted common area in each unit in FCI Florence. The inside of the units were built in the shape of a triangle two tiers high. There were three TV rooms one for blacks one for whites and one for Mexicans. There were also two rooms with tables. There was the CO's office, stairs to the second tier and a phone bank where you could make unlimited calls as long as you had the money. The walls were painted very soothing colors; a light misty creamy white with darker blue-gray trim. Clusters of private showers were located in each corner of the unit. If I could not find a cell that I felt comfortable in I could always sleep in the common area where there were three or four bunks for overflow when the prison was extra-crowded. Short of telling the guards what to do we were awarded many freedoms here.

Walking out to the yard you could not help but take in the majestic 270 degree view of the mountains. The next day at recreation I found Hog Head on the yard with his workout partner Paul Perez, a massive muscle head with absolutely no facial hair on his baby-faced mug. He was technically Mexican but had lightening bolts tattooed on his arm and identified with the whites as he did not speak Spanish. Hog Head and Paul gave me the breakdown. This prison was predominantly white with a 75% caucasian population. "We run this yard Joel and now that you're with us as a workout partner no one will fuck with you". Paul assured me. Although getting a weight dropped on your head was rare, it was still a perfect way to settle a beef with someone. Paul reminded me that Having him and Hog Head as workout partners coupled with my good convict attitude would help keep me insulated from such an attack.

Paul had a job in the Unicor factory assembling office chairs. One day I was asked to stand at a specific time and place on the outside rec yard to act as a lookout. Exactly at the negotiated time Paul threw two pieces of steel onto the recreation yard from the Unicor factory back door. These rods were used to adjust the seat or back of the office chair, and were about 18 inches long and half the diameter of a nickel. However once sharpened they could and would be used to puncture a lung or a jugular. Each one would be sawed down into three to six inch shanks or two nine inch shanks. There was a small window of time, only two to three minutes when the prison staff in the observation vehicle that circled the prison would move out of sight, which is why I was brought on as a lookout. Apparently there was a whole arsenal of weapons hidden on the yard and this was just adding to the supply.

I made immediate friends with most of the top shot callers of all of the races and gangs as I had in Englewood. It was immediately evident that I had much more clout here in Florence than in Englewood or any other prison yards simply because I was white. I got a cush job doing a 15 minute trash detail every day at the 4:00 pm count that paid little but allowed ample time for my other business ventures. It required only 15 minutes of work per day running trash bins from the housing units to the main prison trash dumpster.

I soon made friends with Poncho the tar heroin connection. Poncho was pure Mexican. He obviously did not get high on his own supply. Born and raised in Denver he was trying to leave prison with lots of money to start a legitimate painting business once he left in four years. He was busted delivering 250 lbs of weed to a warehouse in Denver Colorado. Poncho was sentenced under a ten year mandatory minimum drug sentence and it was his first felony. He always said "This money is for my future and my family's future." After each batch came in he would gross over $8,000. His family would visit FCI Florence and bring heroin during visits in hard plastic cigar tubes greased with vaseline and he would slip them up his rectum at the visits in a secret spot outside of camera view.

Here in FCI Florence only a few people could deal with him, he and his front man liked my attitude and vigor for life. It helped too that Hog Head had vouched for me. It would have taken me much longer to establish myself in Florence if I hadn't known someone there to put in a good word for me.

I began building my business rapidly. Fortunately for me a second foot locker was available to inmates upon request. Mine was immediately full within one month of arriving.

I tried heroin again and again thought it was a waste and decided to stick to marijuana. However pot was much harder to find here in Florence than tar heroin and oddly enough easier to get caught with. The tar heroin that circulated throughout these walls was distributed in "papers" as in Englewood. This tar heroin was the consistency of soft licorice so that when it was opened it stuck to the sides of the paper like a wad of warm bubblegum.

To make a marijuana pipe in federal prison we would take a pencil and separate the metal portion of the eraser from the wood, then slowly twist the eraser back and forth until it came out of the metal in one piece; this would leave the round metal cylinder intact Next we would bite down on one end of the metal until it was nearly shut leaving the opposite end round and effectively creating our bowl. The sharpness of the pinched metal created the perfect tool to separate the glued seam of an empty toilet paper roll. It must be done gently with finesse or you risk ruining the whole process. Once inserted into one end of the emptied toilet paper roll, you load the marijuana in the tiny bowl, light it and take in all the smoke from the entire bowl and then exhale through another toilet paper roll stuffed with Bounce dryer sheets. The Bounce dryer sheets completely and entirely eliminate the smell of the marijuana, even though when you exhale there is a big puff of smoke going through the bounce laden toilet paper roll. The bowl is minuscule compared to the pipes out in the free world so finishing it all in one hit is never a problem. Pencils are sold in the commissary as are the Bounce dryer sheets and toilet paper rolls are everywhere so the equipment is always easy to get your hands on. When you are done you just rip it apart and flush it down the toilet then the evidence is gone, easy as pie.

There was also less cash and contraband floating around the prison here. In Englewood I'd had plenty of commissary and cash on hand (stamps), but in Florence a popular form of currency was penitentiary pussy. I was often offered a blow job as payment for tar heroin many times but I was not "gay for the stay" as the phrase goes. My personal preferences aside it was bad business. Too often had I heard about a shank coming out and blood being spilled because of someone messing with another man's punk. I wasn't spending my days slaving over the law books looking for a way out just to die in here because I succumbed to libido; my self-preservation gene was too strong for that. I quickly earned a reputation for being a product-only dealer. Besides since arriving at the county jail I mastered the art of masturbation. I could get myself off with amazing intensity and knee-buckling pleasure every time I wanted to orgasm. Nicky G in Englewood explained to me about the finer art of masterbation using two thick cotton socks, one inside the other and of course inside out as that side on the penis skin was MUCH softer than the inside of the sock. Nicky was in on a gun charge, 924 C, felon in possession of a firearm serving a mandatory minimum 15 year sentence. Upon getting aroused he explained to slip the sock "over your hard cock and vigorously go up and down holding just hard enough to move the skin covering the penis up and down at the same time as the sock was going up and down." Nicky continued to explain that "just before orgasm stop going up and down and press the edge of your palm closest to your wrist just underneath the tip of your cock as your cock pulses and shudders hot cum out of it," doing this he explained will intensify and lengthen the time of orgasm. It always made for an exceptionally intense prolonged orgasm. The result was as intense of taking a shot of heroin. If I waited two or three days between sessions the end of the sock would be filled with my juice every time, then immediately discarded in the trash.

FCI Florence was a good place to do the rest of my prison time. The law library had similarities to a university library complete with desks and typewriters. *The Supreme Court Law Reporter* was my favorite publication and ever since Sandstone, I read it voraciously. The law libraries were a big budget expenditure by The Federal Bureau Of Prisons for prisoners at the time of my incarceration. In the law library I would read up on any cases on point with mine.

Another convict who lived in my unit was a guy named Bogie Jovovich, he and I met often in the law library. A fellow inmate had mentioned that his daughter Milla was famous, although at the time I had never heard of her. He was in on a 20 year sentence for medical insurance fraud but maintained his innocence and like me spent a lot of time researching his case and similar cases for his appeal. In prison, he was not the high roller he had been on the outside and sincerely struggled with adjusting to this new reality. Like many of the men I would meet while in the system his anger at his situation would wear on him and he became more and more weathered as I knew him. Fortunately for him he served only five years of his sentence, convicted of a non-consensual crime stealing lots of money from taxpayers via medicaid/medicare fraud.

Despite how safe I felt while at FCI Florence there were a few incidents that could have potentially been fatal. The first happened one day walking back to my housing unit from the recreation yard during the end of the workday. That day I broke one of the three cardinal rules I was taught by Jim on Con Air and Pete Lafroschia in Sandstone: Do not discuss 1) your case, 2) politics, or 3) religion with anyone in prison. I was discussing my case with a convict named D. He was a muscular young minority inmate who I'd talked to a few times out on the yard or around the weight pile. I did not know him deeply and minus the tattoos he had a very honest demeanor about him. He was pretty young and served much of his sentence and was no fish. D responded to something I had said about my case.

"Fuck. They gave you 13 years for pleading guilty for 6,000hits of LSD." The tattoo on his neck near his jugular, a scrawled text read "Cut here" accompanied by a dotted line, bulged as he swore.

"Motherfucker, I took my case to trial," I said in a loud stern voice before he could continue.

He apologized and we continued to talk and walk. "I am sorry Blaze, no disrespect, I assumed the worst."

"D it's all good. Don't trip, it's cool," I retorted in a less threatening convict tone. This exchange was witnessed by a lot of other people as we crossed the yard just before chow time, soon the word had spread that there was a full-on conflict between two people of differing races. Conflict is a term not to use loosely in prison. It means fight which can in turn be a war of races if not handled properly. Even though whites would win the war because of sheer numbers in Florence, the whole prison would be locked down for weeks or even months if it turned to a war. All of this spread wildly without mine or his knowledge until at the end of chow that night, the leaders of his race approached me and apologized for him and said to me they did not mean any disrespect. Later that evening one of the shot callers for "our" team, Paul H, approached me to let me know that the incident was all squashed.

All of this business, the race discussions, the potential riot, occurred without the knowledge of D and I who'd simply been having a conversation that got a bit touchy. Apparently someone who had witnessed the exchange then related it to some of D's people who thought I disrespected him and another reported to some of my so called higher-ups who thought I was disrespected. In any event the entire negotiation was done outside our presence and in the end they (the other race) had to save face. I started to understand the seriousness of race inequality in prison, and specifically this prison. D and I still remained acquaintances and never mentioned anything about our respective cases again, but I think that both of us learned our lesson that day. When you're doing time on a real prison yard you have to be conscious of yourself and your actions. You're not as I thought of myself up until that point, just a grunion doing time, you are a representative of your race, whether you want to be or not.

The only convict code that superseded "You are your race," was that no matter what, it is always convicts against the man, meaning guards and staff first and foremost. Once during breakfast chow in Florence, a Native American inmate was found to be drunk and swung at a staff member upon the accusation. In response a slew of guards came at him violently beating him down to the ground and then continuing to pelt him with blows all the way through the cafeteria. It was brutal to watch. A quick decision was made by all races to each sacrifice a man in an attempt to keep them from crippling this poor Native American. One black inmate left his chow line and a white inmate came at the guards from the opposite side from the white side of the chow hall. The two men ran at the guards and began holding some of them back in an attempt to distract them from further beating the nearly unconscious Native American inmate they'd been railing on. The scene brought to my mind the atmosphere of the parking lot scene at a Grateful Dead concert at Alpine Valley in the early 1980's. The sense that it was all for one, one for all, people of all kinds, of all walks of life, united by one reason. Flowers of camaraderie in a desert of misery and long prison sentences. It was odd to be overcome by such a familiar peace in the presence of such a violent outburst. All three convicts went to the Hole.

Still, I struggled with this because I'd never thought of my identity in those terms. I'd always gotten along with people of all the races and sold to people of all races in and out of prison. I never understood discriminatory practices, especially within the framework of business. Why would you potentially turn down a market because of something as trivial as race? On top of being morally opposed to it, it was simply bad business.

This mindset got me into trouble though. Another incident prior to the chow hall incident that could have been serious occurred because racial rules even applied to selling: no one told me there was an unspoken rule to never sell alcohol to a Native American. One day I sold a half-cup of some recently brewed hooch to a guy (who happened to be an American Indian) in my unit. The next day he ended up in the Hole still drunk for nearly beating his cellmate to death and the entire unit was searched. Both my workout partners Paul Perez and Hog Head reprimanded me hard, telling me I'd gotten off lucky since the hooch wasn't found. "Dude what the fuck are you doing selling booze to an Indian?" Mother fucker they can't handle their shit!" Paul Perez belted out at me.

"Sorry man. How was I to know?"

"If they found our hooch you would have had to pay us the money we would have sold it for," potentially costing me a few hundred dollars, not a trivial amount in prison. "You lucked out, I love you bro, don't fuck up like that again."

"Understood, I am sorry bro."

The search put everyone at risk. I doubt the hooch would have been traced back to me, as I usually only acted as a middle man because I had the most connections. The entire unit would have been sanctioned for the hooch, since it was stored inside an air vent in the communal space. We had figured out how to climb up and unscrew the ventilation system, and I had easy access to the large trash bags needed to brew it thanks to my job on trash duty.

I could never truly escape the racial politics of prison despite how much I tried to ignore it and just bide my time. I had no say in whether to partake in the political game or not as my skin color spoke for me. As they so often do politics came into play during one of our poker games.

We had a great seven card stud game going in our unit. At least six or seven guys played regularly. We used chips as money and Hector ran the bank. We would play on nights and weekends and settle-up time was always commissary day. I never went to the commissary and although the stakes were small, a $10-$50 cash buy in, it was a nice thing to know I could con the cons in cards. I typically won unless Crazy Dave was playing.

Dave was the only guy I couldn't beat at seven-card stud. No one really knew why he was in prison or for how long. He would always say "It was a technical violation of the highest order." Dave was not a very threatening person and when he spoke it was captivating and intelligent, and never reeked of bullshit like a lot of so-called "jail house lawyers." Dave would preach the law and then give you specific law case citations for you to go read in the law library and see for yourself. He had great book knowledge with little practical applica-tion and was particularly keen on constitutional law. Crazy Dave had helped many a convict form a basis for appeal and I read many cases he recommended to me. During the day he read law journals like he was studying for the bar exam and at night he huffed paint with the same voracity. He often huffed paint or turpentine whichever he could get his hands on until he passed out. It wasn't uncommon to find him passed out with his bloodshot eyes often half-open which gave him a crazy and dazed look a lot of the time and was also the origin of his nickname. He was an incredibly intelligent guy forced into this dual existence by cir-cumstance. It seemed he was looking for anything he could get his hands on that would take him out of his reality, whether that was someone else's courtroom drama or a chemical high.

Dave and I were talking one night after a poker game when he said some very disparaging remarks about one of the shot callers for the whites. Some of the other white lieutenants of our race were standing on the the second tier. With a heavy heart I looked up and knew they'd overheard the remark. I got the look but the prison guard was in his office with the door open at the end of the tier close enough to interfere if anything went down then.

I knew what was going to have to happen. For the most part I managed to stay out of serious scrapes. I got along with everyone, never fronted the heroin I sold and was never ratted on for selling drugs, which I know because if I were suspected I would have been thrown in the Hole for investigation.

This was something I had no choice but to deal with head on.

Since Crazy Dave said it in front of me and to me and more importantly in front of other races, and since it was such a negative statement as interpreted by convict policy, I knew I would be ordered to "hit" him. The choice was to stab and kill Crazy Dave for saying such extremely disparaging remarks about a high commander in the white race or I would be hit for not taking care of business. Even though we outnumbered all races on the yard proper order had to be kept or so I was told and forced to believe. Any sign of weakness in the ranks could cost lives. I knew the unspoken rule: weakness was always eliminated. I was simply in the wrong place at the wrong time.

I was sent for. One of the shanks I'd helped Paul smuggle on to the yard appeared in my cell within 15 minutes.

The shank was sharp. I was 195 lbs, lean and stronger than I'd ever been in my life. When I arrived in prison I could not bench 100 pounds five times. Recently there was a weight-lifting contest with judges from the free world who ranked us in squat, deadlift, and bench press. I squatted 425 pounds, deadlifted 515 pounds, and benched 305 pounds. One day on the yard I won a bet when I deadlifted 405 pounds ten times, cold, with no warm up- that's four plates per side. I was strong and ready to snap this guy's neck. I couldn't risk my reputation by checking into the Hole under protective custody, and although I did not want to hurt Dave, for my own survival I had to do it. I had no choice. I won a small appeal on the LSD paperweight law but still had a ten year sentence. This was my home. I either had to take care of business according to convict law, or check into the Hole for protective custody and finish my time out in some other prison. If I decided not to go through with it and cop out, it was likely that in the next prison someone would find out why I had been transferred which would potentially be a much bigger problem for me.

It was about 15 minutes before night time lock down. My plan was to lure him to the laundry room as far away from the CO's office as I could get. I had my workout gloves on to protect my knuckles. Once in the room I was going to knock him out with a one-two punch then cut his jugular, ditch the piece, wash up, and go back to my room. This grease ball shit was a reality of being in a prison full of real hardcore seasoned convicts. I was not ok with this act morally or spiritually, but I had no choice. I was not part of any prison gang or group, but because I was white and there was such an overwhelming presence of white inmates I had no choice and was told so.

I tried not to think about his mother, his father, or his brother, all of whom he'd told me stories about. I tried not to think back to the times he'd sat with me in the law library helping me find new cases to build into my appeal or the games of poker we'd shared. I tried my hardest to clear my mind of anything but the physicality of the task on hand.

As soon as we entered the room the spotter gave me the nod— coast is clear. Dave had no clue what hit him as I turned quickly and gave him a left jab to the face followed immediately with right from hell. He flew backwards into the washing machines flying four feet from me. Dave was knocked out cold. I truly did not know my own strength. I pulled out the shank preparing myself. My spotter Jackie Blue (Jackie Blue was on point) opened the door.

"No. Five O coming up."

Before he could say anything else, the CO opened the door.

"Lockdown. We are counting a little earlier tonight," he said as he looked at both of us. He knew me by name. Neither of us dared look at Dave. I was sure any minute the lieutenant's eyes were going to travel to the floor where Dave lay unconscious in a crumpled heap. Then he looked behind me and simply turned around and left the room.

I hadn't given Dave enough credit as he was standing, or rather bracing himself against the washing machine I'd thrown him into looking the other way. The CO had seen us but it did not register to him that Dave was just brutalized. Within seconds of the door closing behind the CO, Dave's face began to show signs of swelling. The risk of doing anything more to Dave right now was too great. A sense of relief washed over me; I knew now it was over for now and probably forever. We picked him up and brought him to his cell.

By morning a guard had spotted Dave's swollen face when he was going for morning chow. When he wouldn't give me up they locked him down in the Hole. After breakfast I was back in the unit and Paul H came right into my cell with two brand new shanks in hand. Paul H was sleek with a face exactly like Pete Sampras. He had short curly brown hair, was always soft spoken and steady as a rock. He was also a career prisoner. He'd served almost all of his ten year sentence with the feds and after his federal sentence was up he'd be on his way to the state of California for a twenty-five to life murder beef.

He looked me straight in the eye. "We both are going to handle this like men. You and me in the TV room now." Paul had a cold look in his eyes, he was probably never going to see the light of day and probably figured if he killed someone he would not be sent back to the California prison system.

Paul Perez and Hog Head appeared They were standing guard outside the door of the TV room. The three of them all presided in other units. Though some COs were cool about it, most would lock you up in the Hole for going into a cell block other than your own. Their presence indicated the serious perhaps fatal, nature of this visit. This was the outskirts of humanity, everything started to seem a little fuzzy and surreal.

The word that people in other units got was that Crazy Dave said very disrespectful things about Paul H in front of me and other races and that I had done nothing in response.

Paul had only gotten part of the story and did not know of my forced attempt to kill Dave the night before. My spotter Jackie Blue who had been in Florence a long time was called into my room to testify. Eventually everything was straightened out; Paul apologized for the miscommunication and left me the shank as a trophy.

"Good work, Joel," he spoke as he patted me on the back.
Killing Dave would have meant a life sentence for me for sure. I was no longer such a stranger in a strange land— at least on the outside. Crazy Dave never told even though he apparently suffered a broken nose, two loose front teeth, and various contusions. I'd iced my fists for a few hours the night of the attack because usually when there is a beating and the guards don't know who is at fault, everyone in the entire prison has their hands checked for swelling and cuts. I lucked out, there was no inspection this time.

Shortly after that I had another close call. Poncho had just come back from another visit with a big cigar tube stuffed with tar heroin up his ass. Everyone on the yard who wanted heroin was getting high. I would buy a gram of tar heroine for $500 and have it pre-sold for $1,000 in $50 packages. At this time in federal prison you could only spend $180 on commissary every month but whenever a load of heroin came in, I would soon have over $1,000 of commissary in my extra locker. I was sitting pretty this round.

It was business as usual when I stopped in at Poncho's unit to score some heroin for one of my regular customers, Trotter. Not that we were particularly close, but I'd been selling to Trotter regularly and gotten to know him well enough to know he was trustworthy. He was an African-American and another career inmate. He'd shot at a FBI agent during a bank robbery so needless to say he was not going home for a long time. He acted as a quasi leader and elder statesman for the blacks on the compound. and no one really knew of his part-time heroin use.

As I was walking back to the unit during night time movement I saw a group of inmates standing together and didn't think much of it. Then I realized it was a group of Mexicans who were slowly closing in on another Mexican who'd recently arrived in FCI Florence. All of the sudden they began brutally attacking him. Less than three feet from me, I saw a shank come out. Someone must have dialed the deuces. When ever there is an incident, a staff mem-ber dials 222 on the inter-prison phone alerting all guards of the location and a warning bell goes off in the vicinity. All of a sudden thirty or forty prison guards were running past me to get to the action. I continued my leisurely gait back to my unit trying my best to go unnoticed. Typical procedure is that any time there is conflict on the yard any inmate remotely close to the scene gets stopped, questioned and more importantly strip searched. It had happened to me frequently before, enough that I was anticipating it and began to get really nervous about the heroin taped to the underside of my nut sack with scotch tape purchased at the commissary. I had to be conscious not to get too nervous. First, if I looked suspicious I would most certainly get stopped. Second, if I began literally sweating due to nerves, the heroin would fall right off my family jewels onto the ground and I'd miss out on my payment. That night though the prison staff just brushed right by me.

When I got back to the unit Trotter tried to give me one of the fifty papers of heroin as extra payment for going for him. I refused having recently tried heroin for a third time and coming to the decision that it wasn't worth the risk or damage. I explained that I'd just stick to good old marijuana instead. After he fixed himself a shot, I told him the whole story. It wasn't the first or last time that I found myself caught up in a seriously dangerous situation and getting out without a scratch. In this regard I was incredibly lucky. Sure I'd banked on that luck in poker, in dealing on the outside, but this was a whole new ball game. After all this was not a Grateful Dead parking lot; rather a heroine-stocked prison where you were only a knife-fight away from near death at any moment and being in the wrong place at the wrong time meant ending up potentially stuck in the system for life. Trotter and I both laughed at the absurdity of my luck in such a place.

Shortly before Paul H left to go back to the state of California for his murder charge, we decided to meet out on the yard for conversation. We both opted to go to the yard and not eat dinner. Our units were first and second for chow and the rec yard opened as soon as the chow hall did after 5:00 pm count. It was just us out there.

"Damn dude, where did you get such a cool duffel bag?"

"My row dog Sparky in Englewood made it for me as a gift."

"Fucking cool. I would buy it from you if I wasn't going to Cali for my state bit."

"Paul you would have to pry this from my dead hands."

"Joel I like you. You are real you do not try to front. You are you and act accordingly. That is very respectable and something very rare in prison. Stay that way now and in life."

"Thank you Paul."

Paul was more than likely going to do all day, meaning life without parole, and would probably never see the streets again. I respected him. We enjoyed the quietness of the yard together, talking and spotting each other on the bench press. Soon inmates and convicts started to filter out of the chow hall and come out. I would never see or hear of Paul H again. He said he had hopes of an appeal as all of us do. I always wondered what happened to Paul.

I had an opportunity to get transferred closer to home to a brand new prison that was just opening up in Pekin, Illinois. My first instinct was to stay in Florence. As time went on I thought that maybe that prison was even nicer than Florence. I started to seriously consider it. An old convict I'd befriended by the name of Herb had a talk with me. Herb was a bankrobber who voraciously played drums after lifting weights as part of his workout. Serving a 17 year sentence he had already been in for 10 years, he knew the fed prison system well.

"Joel, you're doing good time here. You got a great view of the mountains. Whites run the yard. Why leave?" He went on further to explain that Pekin would have all new guards who would not know what they were doing, and the numbers on the yard would be drastically different. He said because of its proximity to Chicago there would be a lot of minority gang members on the yard.

Race dictates some on the yard, but the higher security you go, the more it's about what gang you're with. Herb was trying to teach me this. It did not register though. Where your hometown is can help or hurt your affiliation as well. The dynamics of the location of this new prison, the fact that it was new and my obliviousness to this was the recipe for a perfect shit storm.

I never sat still when I travelled around with the Grateful Dead— seven months in St. Petersburg, Florida, nine months in Berkeley/Oakland California, nine months in Boulder/Nederland Colorado, and even my time living in those places were interspersed with trips back to Milwaukee and exotic vacations like Europe or Hawaii to see the Grateful Dead or Jerry Garcia Band. I loved to travel and part of me just wanted to keep moving. This time I got to transfer because of good behavior not because I got into trouble. I was going to be closer to my family so I would also get more visits. I had no clue what I was in for in Pekin, Illinois.

Joel Blaeser

Joel Blaeser
03491-089
U. S. PENITENTIARY
P. O. BOX 1000
MARION, IL 62959

Brad Blaeser
2304 N Oakland Ave #8
Milwauke WI 53211

Dear Brad   3/24/97

Thankyou for the address to the clerk of courts. That is most unfortunate about the books I sent. These savages are the ones to blame if it does not ever end up arriving. Yes it is very easy to criticize everyone as I do, I guess I can see alot more clearly than people think. And it turns people off because if what I say is true they dont want to deal with it. And yes if what I say is true I could be a little more tactful and helpful. However in theory that sounds good but in practice I am still in prison and we are all adults. If you need help ask, do you need help, do you want help, are you capable enough to diagnose yourself as needing help, we've been through this a million times. When I get out I will be working on my world wide operations and probably wont have nearly as much time as I do now. The bottom line is if its not broke dont fix it. Are you having fun and are you content. If so dont sweat it. However if you are not fully content and satisfied a 4-12 month retreat at a Buddhist or Zen Monastery might be a nice change that will help you in your next 30 to 40 years of existence on this

Beatiful planet. Your work would be happy to grant a temporary leave of abscence and may even pay for it. After all it would undoubtedly improve your ability and results with the Rug Rats. Most of all it would help you get to know you, your inner most self.

Well Marcia sent me a letter today. I am calling her on friday to touch base with her, I sent her a asskickin brief to incorporate with hers — She suggested a while back that if I have anything written up or a brief prepared — Then send it and she will incorporate it.

Whats new with you? Glen Biggus just sent me another book. This one is called The Civilization of Renaissance in Italy By Burckhardt. Basicaly it covers Literature and Arts to home life, fashion and superstition illuminating all aspects of the Renaissance. I am going to start it today Harry Wu was in that package — I was wanting you to read it so we coud discuss it some more, or was that Mom I wrote to about it. The drawing book was enlightening in more ways than one. Well Bro see you soon

Joel

11

All In on a Draw

I DROVE THROUGH THE Milwaukee neighborhoods of Riverwest and Harambee like a hungry lion approaching a watering hole, my eyes roving the streets for my next meal. This new addiction was far more thrilling than any of the alcohol, marijuana, cocaine, gambling, or drug-dealing I'd done in the past. It offered more adrenaline more risk more money and best of all it was perfectly legal.

As I roamed these neighborhoods I wrote down the addresses of buildings that fit my profile for making money in real estate. Then I would begin to research properties prioritizing them based on my findings. Much of the information I needed was available on the internet, either through the city or county website. I would collect information such as who owned it when it was purchased and for how much. I also checked the current tax assessment of the property the median value in the neighborhood and finally I'd collect the phone number of the owner which I would get from another website after I retrieved the owner's name. If the property was titled in a limited liability company I had a special website that would take the name of the LLC and reveal all members of that LLC. Next a call was made to see if they were interested in selling.

The majority of the buildings and land I was interested in were investment property (apartment buildings, mixed use buildings, industrial buildings and duplexes). More often than not the owners were all people in the same business as I was, interested in buying and selling properties.

"Hello my name is Joel Blaeser, I saw on the city website that you own that 18 family at 3056 North Palmer Street. That is a nice piece of property. Would you be interested in selling?"

Like clockwork they would say something like, "Are you a broker or a real estate agent?"

"No I am not."

Upon answering a few more questions they either said, "No," "Call me back in a little while," or "Yes I might be interested in selling."

I would propose a walkthrough and barring no unusual circumstances or discovery I'd typically fill out the offer-to-purchase (OTP) right after the walkthrough. I'd learned about the OTP process from a real estate broker who did time for bank fraud in FCI Sandstone. It is a blueprint of the entire real estate transaction: price, sale/closing date, if financed, how and things like what the loan payment is, terms of cancellation, repairs to be performed, what inspections are performed and when, how to settle disputes, etc.

Once signed and earnest money is received an OTP is extremely and unequivocally legally binding. It's more than simply money. The ramifications of failing to follow all the dates, deadlines, and responsibilities or check for errors in the building or land could be potential for a messy and long lawsuit for the buyer/seller. Additionally, a seller or buyer has no recourse to get out of the contract if the buyer and or seller fulfills all contingencies on their side of the contract. I discovered this first-hand when a seller tried to back out of a deal after we'd both signed a non-contingent cash offer. I always wrote my offers with no contingencies as I did my own inspections, closing in 28 days or less with no financing contingency. Once I was introduced to my bank of choice I basically had carte blanche for the types of properties I was going after and the only stipulation on the offer was access to property prior to closing for appraisal. By having a keen sense of the market from constant and continuing research and analysis I knew exactly what the building would appraise for with considered repairs or "subject to completion." For this particular deal during the window of time between which the offer was signed and the actual closing date, I reached out to a group of investors who'd been buying up properties in the area to see if they were interested in the building once I'd restored and rehabbed the building. The same investors upon determining when the closing date was turned around and contacted the owner and offered him $5,000 more than my offer. Fortunately for me we'd already signed the offer. The seller threatened litigation but in the end one call to his lawyer confirmed he had no legal leg to stand on. A very good lesson learned and insight into the types of characters I would come to encounter in the real estate industry, equal to and sometimes more sinister and conniving than people I met in prison or dealing drugs inside prison.

An offer to purchase can be intimidating to homeowners, which is why it became common practice to hire brokers or lawyers to fill them out for buyers and sellers. I purchased my very first property with all cash and knew every dollar counts, so I did not want to pay someone else to simply cross some t's and dot some i's. Once I'd decided to seriously pursue purchasing, rehabbing, and selling properties, I met with a local lawyer and had him further walk me through the process of filling out an OTP and more importantly, all potential legal loopholes. I then purchased triplicate carbon forms and filled out all of my own offers. By 1999 two years out of prison I carried nine blank offers on me at all time, three of each for the three different kinds of properties: residential, commercial, and vacant land.

It was pretty rare for a potential buyer to sign much less initiate a non contingency agreement, because it was what protected a buyer from any expensive surprises and held the seller accountable for any last minute corrections. But by the time I started carrying around OTP's I had developed a meticulous eye for detail, color, design, architecture, and had a natural ability for structural engineering. I became my own property inspector and though I admittedly made a few mistakes early on, I learned on the job. I had built a professional network of specialized contractors throughout the course of my endeavors so if I had a question or foresaw any issue with a property, (whether it was a phase one or phase two when dealing with dirty land or sophisticated legal maneuvers with a specific contingency in a offer to purchase or land option) it only took one or two phone calls at most to get the estimate or answer I was seeking. I found ways to negotiate down prices on nearly all my materials, having a few trustworthy lawyers and accountants on speed dial was a cost I never skimped on. With all that knowledge at my fingertips I was fearless. If the property appealed to me for my purposes I'd write out a non-contingent offer on the spot with a check for 10,000-$40,000 of non-refundable earnest money. The situation was beneficial to the property owners that I approached, I acquired around about 8-10% of the properties I set my sights on. Lots of rejections.

Most of the property owners I contacted weren't necessarily looking to sell, and rarely were they only homeowners. These were people who had made small and large real estate investments in the rental properties that were now nearing the end of their depreciation schedule. Of all 38 properties I owned between 1999-2009 none were ever in foreclosure or under any duress except my very first purchase from the U.S. Marshal Service. Typically the properties I chose were nearing the end of their depreciation schedule anyway. Many of the landlords I was dealing with were experienced enough with the process that they appreciated cutting through the red tape and hassle of a long drawn out sale to just being done with it quickly and cleanly with no or very little questions asked.

It was at my own risk that I wrote non-contingent agreements but I was eager to acquire the property and jump start the renovation/restoration process. Writing super clean offers only helped to get a better price and speed the process along. I loved the challenge of finding a building, examining it and finding the flaws; then researching and outlining how exactly to fix it. Then came hunting up the most economical way to do it. I was addicted to the bargain, think "extreme couponers" except I was dealing with flooring, drywall, and shingles rather than laundry soap and milk. Licensed plumbers and electricians were the order of the day, I was very tough and very fair, contractors came to learn that I always paid when the job was done, they did not have to worry about getting paid. There were and still are people who threaten litigation to get contractors to lower what they are owed or pay 90 days after a job is finished, that was never me. Often times to some contractors I would pay the remaining balance in cash, to entice a better deal on a future contract.

It soon became obvious that "restoring" a house to its former glory in a high rent/single family neighborhood took more time and money than doing a high quality "rehab" on a multi unit rental. I was expanding my search area to include neighborhoods with mostly white inhabitants. Although 80-90% of all properties I owned were in the Riverwest/Harambee neighborhoods (50-90% of these areas were minority residents) of Milwaukee WI. Ninety five percent of every tenant in my apartment buildings were minority. Constantly accused of overspending on my Rehabs/restorations, however the buildings were always full of renters or sold immediately upon being put up for sale.

DECEMBER 29TH 2003

Recently sober from alcohol and cocaine addiction, my efficiency of business re-lationships with people and a god of my understanding began to increase. This quality of life led me to flourish far greater than before. Though I was high functioning during my drug using years I was spiritually dying and not operating optimally in life with friends, family, or myself. I was a binging alcoholic who would drink heavily for a day or two followed by 5 or10 and even 20 days of no alcohol or cocaine. Once finding an anonymous 12 step program of people with a similar malady, life again took another turn for the better. The program helped and continues to foster a continuing clear connection to a higher power that I choose to call god.

I launched an operation similar to my landscaping company and did some of the work myself only using a skeleton crew of trusted laborers and specialists many of whom I had worked with on landscaping projects in the past. I attended each task with diligence, whether it was managing those laborers, the initial inspection, demolition, structural design, even the interior decorating, and orchestrating the marketing and selling process of every property I ever owned and sold.

Most of the houses and buildings I bought were over or near a hundred years old. Though I may have walked through many hundreds of houses, the ones that truly thrilled me were the ones with hidden treasure. I don't mean gold stashed behind the fireplace but rather remnants of century-old architecture and craftsmanship that with a little help from me could be restored to their former glory; some of the homes I viewed boasted treasures like the intricate wrought iron work of Cyril Colnik, unique stained glass windows, ornately carved crown molding made of plaster or genuine 1870's and early 1880's light fixtures and gasoliers, still burning gas. Details like these may have been overlooked by many of the tenants who inhabited the structure. Over the course of my real estate career I developed an eye as well-honed as any antiquities expert.

I had a new life complete with a new addiction, new job and new love which happened to be on in the same: purchasing, restoring, and selling property. I took pride in my work knowing that I was giving back to my community in the process by improving the neighborhood one property at a time. I made a point to build a reputation as a trustworthy, honest, and principled buyer, seller and landlord which you would think might be a lofty goal coming from an ex-convict but in comparison to the other sharks in the business during that time, I was a saint. The process of "flipping" a property was disgusting to me. Flipping as I understand it was buying and selling without ever making a change to or at the very least making superficial changes to a building whilst ignoring many of the more drastic safety and longevity issues. This kind of practice superficially inflated the value of homes partially contributing to the real estate bubble, driving up the property value and therefore taxes of a neighborhood without actually creating value or beautifying neighborhoods like I did… Moreover practices like it were spurred by greed, ignorance, and a general apathy toward local homeowners. Only twice in all 38 real estate transactions did I ever sell a property without making massive improvements.

Luckily, I'd built a good relationship with my banker, Peter. I'd been introduced to

Wauwatosa Savings Bank by my new friend and mentor John H. He saw my passion for wanting to save history and correctly "restore" older types of buildings and as a real estate investor himself offered some tips of the trade, including where and how to bank.

The loan format I chose to operate under was called Subject to Completion loans. Though complex and sophisticated it was preferable because it allowed me to borrow money based on the appraised value before future work was completed. The appraisal of the building for the loan was done "subject to completion" of restoration, and the bank required meticulous detail in order for me to be approved, initially. But I didn't mind the level of sophistication, in fact I thrived on this new challenge, eager to master it. For every building I bought I drafted a portfolio to present to the bank. I evaluated the building's value in comparison to the cost of the potential restoration projects in order to get an estimated budget together. I made sure to always add in an extra $2500-$5000 to every property for the inevitable "surprise problem" that would always pop up. "Be prepared for that construction surprise," John often said me, "it is the nature of the beast." Sometimes you don't see that the wiring isn't up to code until you tear a wall down. If there's one thing I've learned its that houses and buildings have secrets, and when you discover them it's often expensive; especially in the houses I was working on. I created detailed written descriptions outlining each project's cost, including labor, supplies, transportation, everything in the house that I planned to touch was accompanied with a written outline and intricate drawings of the improvement, from the foundation to the door knobs.

One of the benefits of working with Wauwatosa Savings Bank is that they only lent money from their deposits rather than loaning money loaned to them from the Federal Reserve. By not getting the money from the feds it allowed them more flexibility in the loans they gave and how exactly they were able to give them because they were not audited in the same way. It was not as hard. My credit was not the greatest and my very first loan from them was on a property that was worth $125,000 with no current leverage on it. They were not subject to a lot of the regulations that banks who get their money from the Federal Reserve or banks that make it a daily practice to "sell" their loans on the open market were. I was often approached by other bankers and loan brokers trying to get my business with loans that had a very low initial interest rate but only had a 1, 2, or 3 year guarantee. ARM loans, (adjustable rate mortgage loans). ARM'S turned out to be part of a deadly connection that caused the pop in the housing bubble. These loans certainly had lower interest rates than what I was getting at Wauwatosa Savings Bank but I could not get past how shady the people approaching me with these "arm" loans were. After the term of the loan, usually 1-3 years a new interest rate was imposed, as they had not guaranteed past the initial term rate, usually doubling, tripling or more. I believed that building relationships was better than saving a few dollars. Besides Wauwatosa Savings bank offered a 30 year guaranteed interest rate. Even though most often I was selling the properties within 60 to 120 days after closing, the "adjustable mortgages" concept seemed like a sham and if someone is selling crap then they themselves can't be far behind. In the end those types of loans and general disreputable behavior on the home loan market fed the derivatives bubble that would bring the entire financial world to it's knees. I eventually used one other local bank (Town Bank of Delafield, Wisconsin) for a few loans to hedge my bets just in case, two sources of money was good just to keep Wauwatosa from getting too comfortable with me. A little healthy competition always kept my rates and closing fees in check.

Shortly after I bought my very first house through the sealed bid U.S. Marshal auction, Is when I met John H in the Riverwest neighborhood of Milwaukee, WI, who was also a property owner. He walked me through one of his four family buildings showing me some of the improvements he'd made. It was refreshing to speak with someone who understood my vision, someone else who could look at a building and see its potential. He explained that all of the improvements he'd completed added value to the building itself and therefore he could charge slightly more in rent because the building was now better, cleaner, safer and more aesthetically pleasing. Specific improvements such as adding insulation or upgrading wiring not only made the building safer, it would eventually save the tenants money on their utilities, potentially even the cost increase in rent over the year, so it was a win - win for everyone. "Joel I see you really are eager to restore your house over there on 827 East Wright Street."

"I bought this four family for twenty thousand per unit unit. All the original wood-work is here. After we redo all four bathrooms and kitchens, consistent with its current architectural integrity, replace windows and sand hardwood floors we can get $650 per month in rent."

"How much for all that?" I quipped.

"Total considering building acquisition cost is about $130,000."

"Taxes, insurance, water bill, debt service is about $1600 total per month."

I instantly retorted, "So $600 profit per month for the whole building."

"Yes something like that but if you have 20 or 30 buildings it starts to add up."

"Yes I see I see," I said as we continued walking through the building. John loved to walk me through his buildings and I loved to hear him talk as he did. It was informative and downright inspiring. Sometimes he would share his contractors with me which was always a big help.

This kind of investment also drove the value of the whole neighborhood up, which was beneficial to him as he owned around 75 other properties in the vicinity (about 300 units). He kept the rent affordable raising it only slightly, but enough so that within a few years the extra profit paid for the rehab costs in full.

OCTOBER 2004

I remember thinking "I could never own a multi-family, that's far too much work." But rather than simply, buying, restoring and selling, maybe this idea of renting held some appeal. So a year later I started looking for properties that held renting potential. I focused on the Riverwest, Harambee, and Brewer's Hill neighborhoods of Milwaukee, partially because these were in or around my neighborhood and partially because I had an advantage with those properties. Milwaukee is one of the most segregated cities in the country and these were primarily African-American or mixed race middle and lower class neighborhoods. Entire sections of Milwaukee can be defined by race, and white landlords had a tendency to stay out of neighborhoods with predominantly black tenants. I actually preferred it because the neighborhoods offered comparable rent, but building acquisition costs were much lower at the time of purchase. After all what was to be scared of? I lived with all races in federal prison, sold them drugs, conspired and concealed with them, sometimes uniting with them against the "man." Often I was purchasing properties that would have doubled or tripled in cost six blocks away in a mixed race or mostly white neighborhood. Although I would raise the rent slightly after improvements, I was always very conscientious of making sure that it was still affordable and that my buildings were secure, and safe. The reality is that regardless of race, everyone wants a clean safe place to live. I always personally salted my sidewalks imme-diately after a snowstorm and at any time of the night I might show up at my 18 unit or one of my many eight unit all black tenant apartment buildings to mop the hardwood hallway floors. When tenants saw the pride taken in maintaining my buildings it made it harder not to pay rent. I was never sued by a tenant and my buildings were always up to code, never having work orders from the city and if one was written which was very rare or never, the problem was corrected within 24-48 hours. I loved my buildings like children, they were all soldiers of fortune spitting out cash like a busy ATM. If there was a long term tenant I inherited when I bought the building and their rent was lower than the rest I would not raise it, a good long term tenant is worth their weight in gold.

    While driving to my 8-family building on east Keefe avenue one day I noticed an attractive, albeit slightly dilapidated historic 18 family stone and brick building, and tracked down the owner in my usual manner. After I clarified that I was not a broker and that my intention was to restore the building, he introduced himself as L Jackson, a local real estate investor who worked for the City of Milwaukee. He mentioned he was retiring and he had 8 other properties for sale along with the 18 family. A seasoned owner knows that exposing the property to buyers or openly selling may cause strife among the tenants, so he was grateful for my plan and quick turnaround process. We both saved time and money by not using a broker. Though I had to empty some units while working on them, I still had an average monthly income of $26,350 in rent from all nine of the buildings i purchased from Jackson and only $17,500 in debt service for the loans on all the properties. In 2005 I was up to 72 apartment units in all counting a few others I owned, including a 120 acre grade A dairy farm in central Wisconsin where I rented the land to a local farmer. Truly, my profit came mostly from the resale of the buildings, the rent didn't hurt during in the interim.

    Jackson was a thrifty landlord, and very honorable. He had 61 apartment units in all, which takes quite a bit of work to manage well. Before we'd closed the deal he imparted some tricks of the trade for dealing with inner-city multi-family units. To start, he had a single master key which unlocked any door in any building he owned; basement door, furnace rooms, mop closet, apartment. There were 6 multi family buildings in this deal: one 18 family, one 9 family, three 8 family's and a 4 family plus three duplexes. Originally all had central boilers for heat (except the duplexes) and central hot water heaters which meant the landlord had to pay for the heat and hot water. Throughout the course of Jackson's 15 year ownership of all the buildings, he added separate hot water heaters for each unit and removed all the single boilers (except for one building) and replaced them so each unit had its own individual super efficient micro boiler in the basement using all the original radiators in each unit but adding brand new copper piping replacing the original steel and lead pipes. I had to hold my composure when I saw this because I knew this meant great savings for many reasons; with a central boiler if all the units are not rented it meant vacant units would be heated at a loss, and with really cold winters your heating bill would cut profits from the bottom line. It also meant that when I sold them I could command a premium because of the amazing value created by these customizations. In my initial assessment of the buildings I never even conceived of someone ever doing this and have not seen it since.

A fair amount of Jackson's tenants were on rent assistance and at the time people on rent assistance could also could get additional financial assistance for heat. This was a win-win for Jackson as he didn't even have to raise rent, a heating bill in those days was $400-$600 per month per eight family. Over the course of two or three winters he paid off all his costs for the retrofitting of furnaces and piping. The 18 family was the only one that was not separated, but that building had a extremely efficient steam boiler and in the worst winter months during 2005-2006 my heating bill was only $600-$900 dollars. The 18 unit building had very large 1 bedroom units with living and dining rooms.

As far as property managers go Jackson was a genius. He managed to make the most amount of profit without taking advantage of his tenants and still managing to take care of the properties. After 15 years of his ownership he more than made double his initial investment in rental income and payed off all the loans; he got value out of the asset and selling was a function of the market, price was dictated by current market prices. I knew that buying properties near the end of their depreciation schedule meant typically they would be in need of some repair but not derelict. Still, the competition for those nine buildings was fierce. There were guys just like me cold calling owners all the time, I would meet them around the neighborhood and see them working on their buildings. John H was even more savvy, every six months sending a letter that looked like it was handwritten to every owner in the neighborhood asking them if they wanted to sell. There were quite a few other interested investors with shady practices. They operated on a flipping business model; they'd buy the properties, over inflate the appraisals, and keep the extra money they would get at closing without doing the prescribed improvements to them. The lending culture became very lax, a bank lending money that was not theirs to begin with was more focused on getting the commission and servicing fees for the loan than building a long term relationship with the borrower. When I bought property my objective was to always buy, fix or restore, and rent to improve bottom line, then sell at a profit. I always finished my properties before estimated time of completion saving and thus making more money.

Real estate is an unusual investment; it is unique in that it produces income, appreciates over time to you but depreciates over time to the IRS, and is a tax shelter. Technically a variable risk investment that can be considered illiquid, I saw and experienced it very differently over the course of 11 years from 1999-2009. Because most of these buildings were at the end of their depreciation schedule and needed work, the owners were willing to let them go cheap. Another added benefit of buying buildings directly from a owner that were never official for sale is that when I finally listed it for sale a short time later after renovation, it appears as if it had not been "officially" for sale since the previous owners purchase many years before. The marketplace can and does react negatively to buildings for sale twice in a short period of time, appraisers and bankers don't like it and whether the risk is real or not red flags are raised. This is called seasoning, and because of it I was rarely in want of buyers for properties I had up for sale. All this coupled with already continuing rising real estate values made for a extremely synergistic effect positively affecting the bottom line.

There are many tax loopholes to encourage and generate pure profit. In 11 years I made approximately $200,000 in profit from the rent I was pulling in and although it is listed as income I did not have to pay social security tax on it. Capital gains from real estate sales are also exempt from social security, FICA and the like. My properties were an asset, but also a business, so all of my construction projects and rehab effort expenses were all a tax write off. The only profit I had to pay tax on was the profit from my initial sale after all expenses.

Like kind exchanges or a 1031 was another nice tool at the disposal of real estate investors used to instill stability in the marketplace and created in the 1930's. Technically called a 1031 that allows for any profit made from the sale of a property to be reinvested into the purchase of another property tax free. It was tricky and the rules were very strict, you only had 180 days to turn the money around into another property from the date of closing to the day of the purchase of the new property. There was another rule stipulating a maximum of 45 days to name up to three prospective properties to buy, but you had to specify the 1031 as the means to finance in the initial offer to purchase. The 1031 was beneficial to real estate investors such as myself because you pay 15% tax on capital gains from the sale from any property you own over a year but 35% on the sale of any property you have owned for less than a year. This way rather than paying any taxes on the income you gained from the sale, the income is reinvested into a new property without any tax implications as long as it has been at least 1 year and 1 day of time passed from the time when you bought to when you sold.

This was only sometimes useful for me as the turn around from purchase to sale was usually three months and in very rare cases up to six months. "Time is money and money is time," I often said to my contractors as they worked on my projects. Most of my money was redistributed into new properties over the years, partially feeding into the housing marketing crash that I was caught up in and my eventual demise as I should have been saving for the rainy day. The mindset of many Americans and myself was that the housing market was ever increasing in value as if the value of property would continue to rise ignoring it's proven cyclical nature.

My mother's new husband and my second father Larry Gray, a Harvard educated lawyer, traded on the stock market for a living. Although he picked some stocks long, (buying low and selling high) his true genius was in the shorting of stocks. Shorting is the practice of betting a stock will fall in price and profiting from the drop in price. We became good friends early on, when my mother wasn't home he would accept my collect calls from federal prison and we would discuss the stock market for hours. Later he warned me about the housing market. He recognized the bubble and made moves against the rising property values. Larry advised that I purchase properties with cash, saving the money from rent to purchase the next building.

I thought I was being careful. I always made sure that the loan payment was less than the monthly rent from the unit, or if vacant something I could afford from saved money in the bank, even though where I truly profited was in the resale of the building. I was selling my buildings and receiving $50,000 to $330,000 in profit per sale. I always had $150,000 in my checking account; I thought I was invincible.

In reality I was over-leveraged. Even though I was collecting about $26,000 in rent and only paying around $17,000 in mortgages per month, I had loans on all my properties. My cash on hand would never be enough to sustain the mortgages more than six months if disaster did strike, and soon once I had a little taste of wealth I'd invest most of my one million eggs into a single lake estate at exactly the worst time.

Joel Blaeser
03491-089
U. S. PENITENTIARY
P. O. BOX 1000
MARION, IL 62959

Rosemary Blaeser
1730 N Clark #4102
Chicago, IL 60614

Dear Rose   3/24/97

Hello There, I just submitted a partial brief to Marcia to include with her brief. I will keep you posted Sometimes I get a little too cautious — like in my last letter I did not want to fully go into what business I am going to start when I get out. Well I am going to go into the aquaculture business of growing fish in pen raised farms. This will have many purposes. One will be to ease the fishing pressure on natural stocks. And of course all of my fish will be raised organically and eco friendly to the environment. Two it will help the local economy where ver I decide to set up. Three it will supply you and I with a very stable financial situation. No matter what happens to the stock market or world economies people must always eat. After I set up shop on two or three different continents I may go into hydroponic organic vegetable. As far as the fish I will start with the basics — freshwater game/pan fish, bass, catfish, trout, then bottom feeders mussels, clams, oysters, these being a middle or lower class food then into shrimp and crustaceans. The industry is there and growing at a unbelievable rate. I can get up to a $100,000 loan from the small business administration when I get out of prison under the guise of being a disadvantaged minority (I.E. Convicted felon) It's a federal guranteed loan, To get it I have to submit a plan before its granted. If you come across any books, persons etc associated with Salt or fresh water aquaculture ties - check into it for me. I need information on this, specifically Techniques for the actual raising of fish. I wrote a bunch of people today about it. Eventually I will have all operations running on alternative fuels - Solar polar, electric generating windmills and natural gas from wells I drilled myself, or had drilled. I have my sights set, If not this summer then in July of 2001 upon final release. As Johny Cockrun said in the OJ trial I am Cautiously optimistic about getting out this summer. Dont forget to send me a recent picture of you, one where you look like you did in the playboy picture, or when you did when you came to visit me. I thought about you and larry visiting me, you might as well wait to see what happens with Marcia. See you soon

Love
Joel

12

He's Gone

FCI PEKIN WAS AN absolute zoo. Every Chicago street gang known to man had enough members in Pekin to be appropriately represented. Given that I was originally from the area, (born in the west Chicago suburb of Oak Park, Illinois and past resident) I had some local street credit but whites were definitely a minority on this prison yard. The unit sizes and overall structure of Pekin was very similar to FCI Florence except the total compound size was much smaller. Rather than a beautiful view of the mountains it sat on and was surrounded by flat land. I knew as soon as I set foot in the chow hall that I never should have left Florence. Factions of gangs and organisations were sitting all over, blacks and whites were mixed throughout with no clear lines of distinctions unlike all the other prisons I was housed at.

Not because everyone was getting along either.

Each table or mini subsection was being demarcated as this or that gang's area. This was something much more sinister than the other prisons I had lived in. It was very very loud, much louder than any chow hall I had ever been in, even ones that were bigger like in El Reno during holdover. There were 30 prison guards by the chow hall exit doors instead of eight or nine, indicating the lack of hierarchy within the convicts and factions of the prison. When there is tension in a prison, the chow hall is a dangerous, dangerous environment. The high ratio of convicts to prison guards coming together in such a confined space is conducive for rioting, beatings and fights. In Florence during chow it was relatively cordial and peaceful. In Pekin everyone of all races was vying for a position.

Members were flying their colors in creative ways. One member at a table might have a red bandanna and all the others had a red mark on their shirts made with a red marker. Some had blue bandanas and other groups had white. Lots of Mexicans were flying black. Both chow lines had different races going through them and there was no sense of order. It felt unstable, looked chaotic and sounded worse. Hundreds of loud voices rumbled in the metal box of the chow hall, reminding me of Penn Station in Midtown Manhattan during rush hour. As much as I was horrified at the division in the other prison chow halls chow lines I ate at, there was always a sense of balance and general acceptance to who was who, and with that came a certain sense of stability. Here in Pekin at this moment in the chow hall it looked, sounded, and felt like a lit powder keg ready to explode. Pekin was so new that no group had really established control over the yard yet. After all it just opened up months before. Herb was more than right. FCI Florence was the most comfortable situation I could have ever hoped for while doing time with the feds.

Of course, some luck would not hurt in Pekin. I happened to have a ten day holdover at El Reno on my way to Pekin and my cellmate there was a white convict named Rocky. He was a lifer, sentenced to over 100 years for some real brutal crimes. He was covered in tattoos with the demeanor of a southern gentleman. Rocky's hair looked just like Elvis's except fire engine red with a perfectly trimmed goatee and very light almost albino skin. Looking at him you would have thought biker except when he spoke his words they were elegant and gentlemanly with no swear words or half sentences.

"Hi my name is Joel, and I am on my way to Pekin."

"Pleased to make your acquaintance sir. You may call me Rocky, as I cherish the company of a man of my race in these confined quarters."

Rocky was very down with the white race but equally respected "all people of the Earth" as he put it.

He gestured at the beds and asked, "Joel would you prefer bottom bunk?"

"I am good on top Rock. May I call you Rock?"

"Yes you may," Rocky replied. "My last celly had a bad back and I was happy to oblige him with bottom bunk."

Rocky had been waiting for the next bus east. To pass the time, I asked him "Do you get high? I have two balloons of kind bud kiestered."

"I have been known to tickle that fancy on occasion Joel" he smiled.

Rocky was known but not affiliated with any gang or faction other than white people. Rocky had served time in most of the major federal prisons except Marion, and had a reputation throughout the system as a tough individual and a stand-up guy. He was 34 years old and had been in federal prison for 12 years already. While I was still at Florence I'd gotten my hands on some rare high grade marijuana from a close brother friend of mine but my transfer orders came in too quickly for me to be able to sell it. Out of necessity I keistered two big balloons and after getting along with Rocky, was happy to share my stash.

"Joel I have a sheet for the toilet and there is a hook over there for your convenience." He pointed to the wall opposite the bunks where he fashioned a hook made from a paper clip wedged into the frame of the glass in the upper center part of the solid metal steel cell door. I took the sheet and put the loop he cut out onto the clip and the other end of the sheet onto the corner of the upper bunk. This created a wall between the toilet and bunks and although still only inches from the bunk it still gave a sense of privacy. I had not went poo all day and had been shackled and handcuffed for the prior 12 hours. I lined the toilet bowl with half a roll of toilet paper so as to not lose the balloons when pushing them out. We smoked twice a day for the next ten days during holdover in El Reno Oklahoma. In gratitude Rocky said he would send word along to Pekin vouching for me. This could prove to be invaluable to my time there. Miraculously his transfer was switched to Pekin and two weeks after I got there Rocky showed up and vouched for me in person. In prison if you vouch for someone and they screw up or get into trouble for any reason by default you're involved.

At Pekin I found myself knee-deep in China-white heroin. I had never heard or seen of heroin this pure or potent. A guy could snort just enough to cover the tip of a match head and be very very high for hours. I tried it, got very high and was impressed enough to deal it but not enough to keep using it myself. Before too long I started building clientele including an order for three $50 papers from a white hillbilly named Kit.

Kit was serving time for felony possession of a firearm. He was yet another example of a convict who had been railroaded by mandatory minimums. If a convicted felon gets caught with a gun or just bullets, the federal government has a 15 year mandatory minimum sentence. Kit looked like a carny, unkempt, pot-bellied, dopey, tall, caring and dumb as a pile of bricks.

Kit was in the process of moving to a new house when a sheriff was called by Kit's wife for a domestic dispute. Consequently the sheriff ended up supervising while Kit loaded his boxes into the moving van. What Kit didn't know was that while he was loading his things his ex-wife was signing a statement saying that he had drugs in the vehicle and granting permission to the sheriff to search the vehicle which was in her name. The sheriff waited until he started driving down the road and then pulled him over for the search. Though he found no drugs he did find an old box of .22 shells most of which could not have been fired because they were so old. Since they were in his "constructive possession," under 924C (felon in possession of a firearm, federal statute), Kit was arrested and federal authorities were notified. With his prior small time felony conviction he was facing a 15 year federal mandatory minimum sentence.

Kit and I bonded at chow a few times over getting screwed by mandatory minimums. We were close enough that I was comfortable talking about my case and vice-versa. He showed me his case paperwork. I saw that he had appealed his case to the the Supreme Court and they refused to hear it. His only chance of getting out early was to turn into a prison rat. Of course that didn't occur to me the day he ordered the heroin from me. We set the deal up for commissary day. I gave him the list of commissary asking for half in stamps as requested by Little Bo, completely oblivious as to what I was walking in to.

The bell rang for 7:00 pm move. I had the three separate fifty papers of heroin in my pocket. I approached his unit walking quickly wanting to make it back to my unit before the end of the move. He looked surprised when I met him in front of his unit and blurted out that he had not gone to commissary yet. He was nervous and did not seem like the Kit I met two weeks before. I sensed something was not right.

"Where's the stuff?" he asked. His voice sounded shaky like when Marty testified against me in federal court at my jury trial.

I went with my instinct and I lied. "In my unit and where the hell is my commissary?" I said sternly.

Kit's expression changed. The center crease above his eyes tightened up. "Uh, let's do tomorrow. Same time same place?"

"OK," I said.

I hurriedly walked back to my unit. I put the three packages in the pocket of a dirty pair of shorts sticking out of my laundry basket and immediately headed to the TV room to find Little Bo my heroin connection. Little Bo was from Los Angeles, full-blooded Mexican who was 150 lbs soaking wet. I was introduced to him from a acquaintance of Rocky's from another prison. There was a growing demand on this prison yard for heroin from the whites who were not from Chicago or known by someone. I saw the opportunity and wanted to profit off of it. There were plenty of new unclaimed customers so I did not have to worry about getting into a conflict for stealing someone's customers.

I casually walked up to him. My face bearing nothing but a slight smile and offered a casual greeting.

Then my voice much lower said "I think that last deal was trying to set me up."

His eyes widened. "Where is it'?

"In my room."

"What are you doing here then? Go back to your cell right now and flush that shit down the toilet!"

"Fuck! You're right!"

I had only been back in my unit for all of a minute but it was long enough apparently. The second I stepped foot out of the TV room four prison guards and a SIS lieutenant were there. They took me to my cell where my celly was reading. They strip-searched us naked. All four of them had rubber gloves. My celly and I acted the part-very dumbfounded. Rick was my celly doing 25 years on a methamphetamine manufacturing charge. He was a non drug user, college educated and with no prison tattoos looked very run of the mill. 25 years my elder his long shoulder length hair was turning salt and pepper gray. We were the same height but he had another 30 pounds on me, all in his belly. A man of few words words with lots of respect, a true convict. He got caught making drugs for a well-known motorcycle group and never snitched. When they were done searching us they told us to go sit in the TV room and not to leave. One guard stood outside our cell keeping an eye on us as we sat in the TV room. The other three guards and an SIS lieutenant proceeded to turn our cell upside down.

As we sat in the TV room my celly and I came up with our story. Since the shorts were in a common area of our cell we knew unless I admitted to owning the heroin that a jury would probably never convict us because we could contend someone put the heroine in our cell. He absolutely insisted that we both play dumb and for me not to admit to anything, we both knew once they found it they were going to put both of us in separate rooms and say the other one said this or that. Nothing was in a locker and our cell door had been open all day. In an FCI the solid steel or wooden doors open electronically every morning at 6:30 am and stay open until lockdown at 9:00 or 11:00, depending upon if it was a weekend or not.

The clock kept ticking away, ten minutes, twenty minutes, forty minutes, an hour passed. Finally, after ninety minutes they came out. They came into the TV room and said we could go back in. To our astonishment they did not say "Turn around and cuff up," or "Let's go, you're under investigation." Every piece of commissary we owned was cut open—lotions, toothpastes, shampoos, hair tonic. All our food was opened and dumped out. They had special tools and took off the air vents to look behind them. Every piece of clothing was turned inside out and tossed all over the cell. It looked like a tornado had literally gone right through our cell. My green duffle bag was turned inside out but no seems were cut open. My mouth was dry. My knees began to shake.

I saw the gray sweat shorts where I had hidden the heroin. The pockets had been pulled all the way out. To my amazement, the heroin, three tiny paper packets of shiny white paper stayed stuck to the inside of the corner of the cloth pocket. My shaking intensified. My knees and hands were shaking almost uncontrollably. I could barely squeeze my hands. Still I managed to grab the three packets and throw them in my toilet, then pushing the button on the back of the standard brand stainless steel prison toilet in my cell. I continued to push the button, over and over until the stainless steel bowl started to get frosty because of all the condensation from the continual flushing. I had to have pushed that button about 30 or 40 times. I felt a strong presence in the room as if being watched by someone or something god like.

I had been sloppy. In Florence or Englewood there was a very established order of doing business. I was fresh on this compound and no one here knew Kit, yet I'd basically blindly trusted this guy. In addition I later discovered that prosecutors do successfully convict people in prison for possession of narcotics if found in your cell, even if it is not locked in your locker.

Within ten minutes of being back in my cell the same four prison guards came back into my unit and locked up Little Bo who I originally scored the heroin from. 25 minutes after that in the same TV room I got into a scuffle with an associate of my connection, some-one I never met before nor knew the name of. In self defense of my life, within 15 seconds I had him on the ground and was choking him to death. His eyes were popping out of his head.

"Guard is coming! Guard is coming!" two of my Chicago homeboys kept yelling.

I did not know they were yelling at me until a minute after they pulled me off of him. Tensions were high and the convicts on the yard would sure be wondering what was going on tomorrow at breakfast.

My combatant and I met in a cell later that night after 9:00 count. We squashed the matter in the guise of finding out who the rat was. Kit was surely the one. He ordered the heroin did not have the commissary and was acting very nervous. I did not sleep at all that night and in the morning when the doors opened the SIS lieutenant came in.

"Blaeser, cuff up."

"What? Why?"

"You're going to the Hole under investigation Blaeser."

"Investigation for what lieutenant?"

"We're investigating that too."

He wasn't going to say. Obviously it was the heroin. Someone was going to be made an example of.

When a new federal prison yard opens up a token stabbing and or killing helps to show what faction is boss and or has strong power. There were multiple factions in play at Pekin. Whites, Mexicans and Chicago was also represented, I was born in Chicago and claimed Chicago as a hometown upon arrival. The connection was Mexican and Kit a bastard child with no claims except his race.

Still the Hole wasn't enough for me to curb my behavior. I stopped caring and was losing my sense of self-preservation and self-worth. I was becoming institutionalized. I began saving sugar packets for one week straight while in the Hole in Pekin to start a batch of hooch in my cell. In the hole in a FCI you get recreation every day for one hour except weekends, during which time they would search your cell. You could refuse for as many days as you wanted but every seven days your cell would get searched regardless. On the sixth day they decided to search and I feigned having to use the bathroom and then started drinking the hooch. I couldn't get it all down so I tried to flush it. Someone on the cell block alerted the guards and they turned off the plumbing into my cell. I was given a shot for attempting to make alcohol.

Two days later very early in the morning on August 9,1995, I had an onset of terrible sadness. I had only felt like this once before in my life and it was three or four days before my father died in my arms. I remember sharing these feelings with my dad at dinner two nights before he died and explained to my father I thought he was going to die of a heart attack. It was a unique and specific feeling I could not shake. This same feeling overcame me while in the Hole in Pekin. Tears erupted as I sat alone on the cold dark cement and steel room. I was not sure why, Who died? I wondered. Was it my mother or brother? Hours later in the morning I heard on the radio that Jerry Garcia died. I was devastated. I felt lost and empty. Grief sat like a rock in the pit of my stomach.

As I sat stunned and numb in the Hole, a remarkable thing happened. The men in the Hole with me began shouting their condolences. My fellow convicts knew I was a Dead Head. It was also no secret the guards had forcibly removed my radio from my cell as punishment earlier and the staff were loudly berating me at the time. The entire day all the radio stations in all of Pekin Illinois and most of the country only played Jerry Garcia, Grateful Dead music or interviews with Jerry Garcia. My fellow inmates started yelling through the vents in the Hole telling me what was being said about him and updating me on the story. One of them even made some prison speakers out of cups and put it up to the air vent by the vent near me so that the sound of his radio was amplified into mine. I vaguely knew this person and he owed me nothing but blessed me with this unexpected display of prison camaraderie. Surrounded by a sea of wicked convicts, America's rejects, men who were labeled evil and removed from society and here they were giving me grace with little bits of love. I recognized that this kind of community is the same feeling I was overwhelmed with at every single Dead show I attended. It was a most appropriate remembrance of Jerry that these convicts embodied the spirit of his fans, even if only for a few moments.

I had taken great refuge during prison at the prospect of seeing the Grateful Dead and Jerry Garcia when released. It was all that I looked forward to in regard to getting out. At every prison I had been to, I wrote the local radio stations my requests to play Grateful Dead on Fridays, or during their "Dead Hour," (as most cities have once a week) and if they did not have one they created one. Often they would play my specific requests. I'd never lost touch with the sense of peace and community I associated with the Dead, Tony Brown the editor of *Relix*, the Grateful Dead magazine, always made sure I had the latest copy to read. Hearing that Jerry had passed away was, in a sense like losing my family, but more than that, it was losing my passion for when I got out.

Over time, my selfish grief, sadness, and hurt turned to joy and gratitude for the hundred shows I was lucky enough to have seen. I was blessed with the opportunity to see the Grateful Dead, and Jerry Garcia in places like Canada, Hawaii, England, Germany, France between the years of 1984 and 1992. I travelled all across the United States to see them. It was an amazing journey. In the days, weeks and months I reminisced to myself about all the shows I saw and how lucky I was to enjoy such free expressions of music, love, and community. I saw my first show about 11 years and one month from the day of Jerry's death.

Even more so I sat contemplating my life over the last 30 months. Just one week earlier, I was nearly busted for trafficking heroin. Getting caught with a single packet of heroin, just simple possession, would have meant AT LEAST seven to ten more years added to my sentence. Getting busted with three is trafficking, and that could be ten to fifteen additional years added on to my sentence. I was a first time, non-violent offender who had travelled the world with the Grateful Dead, had been in some serious scrapes in prison, had no extra charges on my sentence despite having sold heroin in three federal prisons, hadn't been raped, and was still alive - these were all things to be grateful for in prison.

He's Gone

My decision to leave Florence and come to Pekin was further exacerbated by a series of poor judgments and decisions that in the end helped me to see how bad I was getting. Before I went in, I'd quit selling drugs and begun to square up, and get my life in order. Now that I was in prison, I was selling drugs, and had no plan for when I was going to get released. I barely even went to the law library while in Pekin; I'd stopped caring about what I was going to become. I still worked out every day, and stuck to a strict diet, so physically was in some of the best shape I'd ever been, but my spirit was becoming dead, and institutionalized. No Pell grants, no manifesto. Every day seemed the same; Saturday was Monday, and Sunday was the same as Wednesday. I was losing touch with all reality; I was losing hope.

Although I had run-ins and serious issues in the other prisons, nothing seemed to compare to the run of bad luck in Pekin. Jerry Garcia's death was a wake-up call for me; I could not be a Dead Head my whole life, I would have to come up with a new plan for my life upon my release. I vowed never to sell drugs in prison or otherwise. I may smoke some marijuana in the next prison I went to, but that was it. I wanted to be sober and wasn't really sure how to. It seemed it was time for me to buckle down mentally and prepare for my release in about 80 months. I was lucky enough to have my sentence reduced over a law change, I had dodged enough bullets for two lifetimes. There had to be a reason for all that was happening. And if not a reason, then a message to take a look at my actions before I ended up doing something that would land me a life sentence or be killed.

"Talladega," my case manager told me.

"Really? How is it?" I shouted softly through the food slot in the solid steel door of my cell in the Hole.

"Not bad Blaeser," he continued. "I think you will do fine there. You are not being charged with anything as a result of this investigation." I just met Counselor Ross two months before and barely even knew him. He looked just like Mr Rogers, and I believed every word that came out of his mouth.

"A mid level FCI, Ross. I will be fine."

"Thank you," I told him as he waived and moved down to the next convict's cell.

My mother came to visit me in Pekin before I left. You get strip-searched before you leave the Hole, and then again in the visiting room cell after your visit is over but before you're returned to your cell in the Hole. After my visit, I was strip-searched and then I dressed.

"I will be right back. Hold tight," the prison guard said to me.

The next thing I know, the leader from a very large Hispanic prison organization came into the room.

Security protocols in prison as far as movement of prisoners are extremely strict in general population, but especially with prisoners from the Hole. It is rare for a visit to be denied, even if an inmate is in the Hole, but it is assumed that they are a extra threat of danger and therefore as a rule are not allowed to mix with general population inmates and convicts. He was obviously very powerful because prison staff allowed him in there with me alone.

I was very calm and not alarmed. This guy was trying to get a read on me. We talked about my connection that I got the heroin from the night of my cell search. It turns out he was pointing the finger at everyone else, when in fact he looked guilty himself. This shot caller and I had a brief conversation, and he got the information he was seeking.

During my visit, my mother wore a man's Swiss Army watch with a leather band. After the visit, I wore it back out. The shot caller commented on my watch. We had become acquaintances on the yard at one point. A couple weeks prior I did a favor for someone. I was holding a large package (seven grams) of China-white heroin for one of his associates. He thought I was solid but just had to talk to me one more time before I left.

The day I left Pekin, I had to do the whole property thing, going into a room with a staff member and packing up my belongings to follow me to the next prison. The watch was yet another prized possession. I also had my trusted green duffel bag from James, and I was offered even more money and drugs for it here than in Florence. Gym clothes, paperwork, workout gloves, water bottle, shoes, radio, and stamps.

I had not been in Pekin that long, and frankly, somehow I was glad to go. I was never charged with anything, or ever told what I was being investigated for. Now I was off to Talladega via El Reno Oklahoma, and the dreaded flight on the United States Marshal Service's Con Air…

Joel Blaeser
03491-089
P.O. Box 1000
Marion, Il 62959

Rosemary Blaeser
1730 N Clark #4/02
Chicago Il 60614

I spent some of the money last week and am going to spend the rest this week. Let's see 3 books of stamps, 2 Vitamin E, 2 Vitamin C, toothpaste, soap, conditioner, A whole bunch of powdered Milk, Garlic, tortillas + white Rice. This week more of the same. That way I will be stocked up on necessities for 2 or 3 months. I can't remember saying you looked much older as you mentioned in your letter. we can send pictures to each other all the time. If you or Jen have the program on your computer or the place that copies pictures does, maybe you can have them delete the pillow on the bed and the cosmetics on the shelf This takes away from the main contents of the picture.

Thank you for the $100 donation to the defense fund. How much is in there?

I received the books yesterday — Thank you!

In the quiet times and the small corners of the day, I think of you.

I want you to be happy for christmas

Mother

I received your letter today the one written on the Blue envelope. The camera is a wonderful invention, here is a picture of me taken 7 days ago, we get one a year. Please read the letter I have enclosed I have sent one to everybody and hope you all get together to discuss this matter. If it is not too much trouble a couple of copies would be nice, some other people asked for a picture also.

Joel.

03491-089
U.S. PENITENTIARY
P.O. BOX 1000
MARION, IL 62959

Brad Blaeser
2304 N. Oakland Ave #8
Milwaukee, WI 53211

1-16-96

Dear Brad

Here is that Atomp World I promised, I just got a letter from you from Dec. I love you and hope you are realy seeing whats going on. Your gig of helping mankind thats a tuff one. I like that idea, and being individuals as we are I am finding it hard to swallow for me. I help who I can when I can and how I can but realize that there is alot more to this world that meets the eye. How many Books have you read about the uprisings that happened around the world during 1798, 1848, early 1900's and late 60's early 70's. I am reading a book about it now called The imagination of the new left: a Global analysis of 1968. It goes into those other dates also and to my surprise the whole world had uprisings around those dates amongst working + middle class. If and when I am able to pursue what I want to do, things will different but yet the same fuck you to the american flag. Any way I have not heard from anyone but you and mom my mail has been very limited. I have not heard from Jenny in over a month. I asked for Pats address in my last letter I could not remember it and my phone book has been long gone for 3 months now. Anyway peace be with you, I love you   I got the book, thanks   love Joel

13
Poker and the Pop in the Housing Bubble

I'D GONE FROM PRISON to a posh house on a peninsula within eight years of my release. From a five by eight foot cell to a 6,000 square foot lake house. By 2005, I was making enough money from the rentals, and had sold enough properties in the last month to comfortably pad my bank account, which never dropped below $150,000.00. My last four checks netted me almost a million in cash, all made honestly and fairly. In all the drug dealing that was done between 1984 and 1991 (entire time) there was never ever more profit than 3-4 thousand dollars per month and that was my best month ever. At this point, I'd built up a crew of trustworthy contractors who were all on call if anything needed repair, and with my extra free time, I took a few vacations. I bought a one-way ticket to Australia to fulfill a long-time dream of mine. I became a certified scuba diver and learned to surf on some of the best beaches throughout eastern Australia, New Zealand and Indonesia.

This kind of money and freedom left me feeling invincible, despite all the warnings Larry had given me. He'd explained the concept of "the bubble" to me many times, starting back in 1999. The idea that a speculative price increase would eventually be recognized as unjustified was inevitable, he said. I was one of many Americans who'd begun investing in real estate. They all wanted to make as much money as I did, and all that investment led to an uptick in prices, presenting the perception that wealth was increasing, when in reality it was simply being redistributed. The already wealthy were getting richer, while the middle class got poorer but continued to support their lifestyle and increased spending by increasing debt. I got caught up in this idea of building up wealth and a future from the ground up in real estate.

Shouldn't you be able to make a lot of money by putting in hard work like I was? Well, let's examine that for a moment.

Things have changed since the 1950's. First, the market dynamic changed. It went from a goods market to an asset market. People use to put stock in things like vacuums and cars, and now people were converting their homes into assets. Their homes went from being a long-term investment to a commodity. The shift from a goods market to a asset market meant that if the demand went up, price would not go down. In an asset market, if the demand goes up, then prices go up. In a goods market usually demand falls as prices rise, conversely in an asset market, as demand rises, so do prices, creating a volatility. Sociologically the way to examine it is that in a goods market if everyone wants to buy this particular toaster then you're selling more of that toaster and the more you're supplying the less you have to charge because you are selling more. Technology plays a role as items are improved they can create renewed demand. Now if we look at an asset market, the idea is that the more people want it the more valuable it must be and therefore it should cost more. One could argue the entire concept is based emotionally in greed, envy, and jealousy.

Incomes had been falling throughout the 1980's and 90's, and people continued to borrow against their homes masking the lack of income growth. Carl Case and Robert Schiller, economic professors at Yale, created a home price index scaling from 1900/1980 to present day, called the House Price Index. They found that corrected for inflation over the last 125 years home prices had stayed relatively the same until the year 2000, at which point prices began a 100% increase. So as incomes were falling from 1980 to the mid-2000's, real estate prices were skyrocketing. In response consumers tended to borrow against their house, thus masking a lack of income growth all the while supporting their spending habits by acquiring more debt.

The result was a market supported by debt; not just mortgages but increases in credit card debt as well. Incomes were falling but spending continued on the same path causing increased debt, the result was that all but an elite few were becoming richer. The pop in the housing bubble is related to the rising income disparity. The last time there had been such a gap in wealth distribution as there was in 2006 was in 1929, shortly before the stock market crash that launched the country into the Great Depression. In 2007, 1% had 25% of all U.S. income. These same percentages are true of 1929, just before the Great Depression. In 1929, the inequality of the worker versus the rich was rising.

It's also important to note that during the golden age of America, the 1950's, wealth distribution was the most evenly spread in recorded history for the United States. Most any decent economist will agree that wage inequality slows movement of capital in any market. There was a gargantuan increase of installment credit in the 1920's to pay for all the new consumer goods in the markets - irons, vacuums, stoves, and automobiles, as well as real estate. Whereas in the 1950's the economy was primarily a goods market, rather than an asset market. Honda automobiles or vacuum cleaners don't skyrocket in price year after year and then drop dramatically. Asset markets can and do behave like that. In the 1950's the slow and steady appreciation of the value of a home allowed for upward social mobility. Not that there weren't real estate moguls then as well, but typically rather than transferring from owner to owner it was more common for a homeowner to live in the house for 10 to 20 years before retiring to the same property with a pension. Thus the house was used as a "good" not treated like an asset as such.

In response to the Great Depression, the federal government created the Federal Housing Administration. The FHA created and standardized low interest loans for the modern worker, creating a stimulus to the economy and making homeownership more accessible. The process of standardizing loans allowed the FHA to then sell those loans on the open market as a commodity. This conceptual process commodified mortgages which could then be resold to 2nd and 3rd party investors anywhere in America and thus was born the method and idea still used today of banks bundling and selling housing loans to investors. Now the selling of mortgages to individual investors or banks has been going on for over 100 years but the securitization process of mortgages or CDO began in 1987. Securitization of mortgages means bundling loans, any kind of loan, houses, credit cards etc., and then selling those loans. Essentially, debt was being sold off to investors; what they received in return is dependent on on how the loan is being paid back. the higher the risk the higher possible percentage of return. this process benefited banks because once a loan was bundled and bought by an investor, it freed up more funds with which the bank could give out more loans, not to mention that the bank made a profit on the process; collecting fees from a borrower at the time of loan origination and then getting fees upon sale of loan and servicing loan for keeping track of payments and other similar services. It became common practice for banks to participate in the securitization of loans, even small, local banks.

This practice had been going on for years, so why did it fail so drastically in 2006? Well, it partially had to do with widespread irresponsible lending and I think overall greed of the stock brokers and big time investors.

A majority of loans that were securitized in the 2000's were refinance loans, and second and third mortgages. They were not adding people to home ownership. A huge amount of the loans represented perceived equity in their home, allowing people to pull "equity" out of there homes. Additionally, banks started to lessen requirements for credit worthy or non-credit worthy people to get a loan. If you were breathing and an adult you had a good chance to get a home mortgage loan between 2002 and 2006. The majority of these loans were bundled and sold to Wall Street. In 2006, the $900 billion in mortgage equity withdrawal was the highest recorded amount to have ever been used for market consumption. In the previous five years it had been as low as $100 billion in a single year. 77% of the $900 billion worth of loans were subprime mortgages. Once all the equity was leveraged out of a property an owner had less incentive if any to stick around once they could not afford to pay the loan, or if the value dipped below the total outstanding debt for that property, owners had less incentive to continue to pay their mortgage even if they could afford it. This resulted in many bankrupt homeowners and a rapid "negative domino trend" of foreclosures. As fore-closures increased, confidence in the housing market decreased, thus affecting the confidence in bundled debt markets.

People who borrowed money from banks during this time now must take some responsibility for the mess. As my mother and grandmother have often said, "if you cannot afford to pay cash for it you do not deserve it." Larry had also tried to instill upon me the safety, or at the very least odds reduction of paying for real estate with cash and or bringing in a cash investor who takes equal risk for equal profit thus limiting my own risk and ensuring a future. If a property is paid for entirely with cash, even if the value drops significantly or you are faced with economic disaster there is no threat of not being able to pay the mortgage. You at least still own property as long as the taxes are paid. From 1999 until March of 2009, my sole source of income was from the buying, developing, renovating, renting, subdividing, and the selling of property. 95% of the 38 properties I owned in those ten years were bought, redeveloped, and then sold in six months or less, 30% of them in four months or less, even though real estate laws favor you for holding them in the long term. Despite all my precautions, banking with small local banks who only lent money from their depositors money, rarely keeping a property for longer than a year, and using my construction knowledge to make sure I never bought a money pit, I was not immune when the real estate bubble popped. I always reinvested into another property, and with the lake estate everything I had worked for since I left prison went into that property.

Partially, it was that the spiritual peace I'd discovered in Marion became more difficult to return to the longer I spent in the outside world. When I was released I slowly began drinking again and using cocaine. I was a binge user, meaning I could go a while without drinking or using, but once I began, it was an all-night affair. These nights could become emotionally and financially expensive for me, often averaging three hundred dollars to a few thousand per night at the bar. However, within two years and five months of my release, I had a real estate transaction every 45 to 180 days that would net at least $30,000-$350,000 in profit , so the money was of no consequence for me.

My life and habits were forming a spiritual black hole in my life. This was the impetus that led me away from the bottle and drugs to seek sobriety. I recognized that I was losing my spiritual consciousness. Even worse I was losing my time. Everytime that I blacked out, everytime that I couldn't remember where I was the night before, who I was with or what I'd said to them was a wasted day of my life. If I had learned nothing else from prison, the single most inescapable lesson which even the densest of inmates couldn't help but acknowledge is the value of time and how precious each day of your life as a free person is. "Freedom truly is a state of mind."

The loss of time which superseded even my loss of spirituality, the loss of money, or the wrecked and hurt friendships that would take years to repair, struck me the hardest and I realized that time is surely the most valuable asset of all.

Slowly but surely after I got out of prison I clouded my spirit and judgment, first with a drive to gain material things and money and now with drugs and alcohol. Juxtaposed against my fervor for life and appreciation of my freedom was the spiritual poison of greed and I filled the hole inside of me with drugs to try to feel whole again. By the time I finally got sober, I had been out of prison for six and a half years and had long since forgotten about the great spiritual strides I made while incarcerated in Marion.

Even with 18 months of not using drugs or alcohol I still had a long way to go to get back to a free state of mind. Then, in 2005 I made close to $1 million in a single year. My plan was to net $3 million and live off of the interest generated from it. I wanted to go to California or Hawaii, somewhere warm and full of sun. But the thought made me nervous; I was worried that I if I moved away this early in my sobriety I might slip back into using alcohol and drugs. Going out west without a firm spiritual foundation and almost a million dollars in cash was a daunting prospect. My spiritual advisor and sponsor agreed that it might not be the best option for my sobriety, so instead I chose to do the proverbial "one more deal" by buying a lake estate for $1.5 million instead. *I can make it back in real estate if I go bankrupt,* I thought. I was taking into account that I was a great salesperson and knew that by adding a bedroom and bathroom to my new estate I should be able to make at least $400,000, maybe even $500,000 on this deal.

At the time I purchased the lake estate my parents and even my banker Peter warned me about the market and to be careful, though Peter still loaned me the money to buy the house. I was living in a beautiful brick Dutch Colonial duplex located at 6429 North Santa Monica Boulevard in Fox Point, WI. I'd poured $100,000 into the property making it a single family home. After about two years of working on them, I decided that I was comfortable enough in my sobriety that I was ready to move west. I listed the Jack's Bay Road lake house for $2.9 million with a new friend, Sal Dimiceli. Within the first week of the listing a gentleman who owned 30 McDonald's restaurants told Sal he would give me $2 million in cash and close the deal in a week. I owed $1,180,000, and had about $220,000 worth of renovations and decorations of my own cash sunk into the property. I would have walked away with over $800,000, (about $270,000 in real profit) Sal said he would forego his commission to help me fulfill my mission. Promptly refusing, Sal continued to market the property.

In all of my prior 35 real estate deals, I would have never said no. Up to this point I had 100% success rates, yielding nice sums of money without having to put up any of my own money or very little of my own money into a deal. Deals I did put money into profited 300% to 500% in three to six months. One profited 4,900% in one week. I exposed all my hard earned personal wealth within the structure of my real estate business deals, Something I was not ignorant at the time of either. I thought I was invincible.

Three months later I got an offer for $1.75 million. Again I said no. The ship had scraped the iceberg, and I still thought we were at full speed. I was completely oblivious as to what was coming. The whole world was caught up in the derivatives bubble, and to exacerbate matters worse banks were lending to anyone breathing. My parents and more specifically Laurence Gray (my very brilliant 2nd father) were making tons betting the other way in the market place and he told me many times about what was coming. He was shorting bank stocks in south Florida. Ghetto taught me in Marion that the most important thing for me to learn was what I was not aware of. I came out of prison, worked my ass off to get where I was, made a huge blunder buying the house in the first place, then was lucky enough to find a multi-owning McDonald's philanthropist-type to give me a great offer, and in my blithering haste, I said no. There were times I lived in squalor while I renovated and restored a house, showering with a hose in the basement because the bathrooms were demolished to the stud walls, only to sell the house the first week it was listed for sale in the newspaper.

Perhaps I had lost some sense of reality. I was living in a 6,000 square foot secluded lakefront estate. I was still down to earth. Unafraid to pick up a hammer at a house I was renovating, despite that I had plenty of crew to work on it for me. I never drove a fancy car. I had a Ford Excursion for work purposes only, but mostly drove 3 year old cars like my Saab 9/5. But when it came to the real estate housing bubble I was in serious denial.

Around December 2008, I'd been forced to remove my rose-colored glasses and face reality. I recognized I was in a rapidly sinking ship and before I was fully submerged I wanted to make the most of the situation. At this point I owned three properties, 6429 North Santa Monica, 1525 North Marshall Street, a very historically significant house on Milwaukee's east side that I did an exterior renovation on and the lake house, and I was trying to sell all of them before the market crashed completely.

Desperate, I searched for an alternative means of income to continue to make my mortgage payments. There was a $15,000 buy-in no-limit Texas Hold 'Em tournament sponsored by WPT being held at the Bellagio called the Five Diamond World Poker Classic. Though I had played in three other 10k buy-in tournaments in the last two years, now I was struggling to make my $10,000 a month mortgage payment. The days of always having one hundred fifty to a quarter of a million dollars in my checking and savings account were gone. I had been playing poker as a hobby; now I'd be playing poker to save my skin, or more accurately, my house.

First place was around $3 million. I had just paid my mortgages before I left for the tournament, but my estate as grand and pristine as it was lost at least $1,000 in value a day. I was looking at walking away from it. That concept was hard for me to wrap my head around.

Previously I'd done well at some of the much smaller no limit hold'em tournaments in Las Vegas, winning first, fourth, sixth and ninth, (about $3500 for the first place finish at the Venetian Hotel and Casino in a $125 buy in tournament with 122 players in it) but had yet to pull off a big win in a major big buy in tournament. No limit Texas hold 'em is a huge action game and most agree the Cadillac of poker games. The game in tournament form is played with nine or ten people per table with as many tables as players have entered. Single elimination with no wild cards, royal flush being the best hand. Suits do not trump suits in this form of poker and once you're out you're out. Everyone starts with the exact same amount of chips. Each player gets two cards dealt face down (pre flop) only seen by him or her, a round of betting is allowed between each administration of cards and there is never a limit as to the amount you are able to bet at any point in the game, thus "no limit." Next, three cards are dealt face up, (called the flop or window) then another face up (called 2nd street or the turn) and finally one last card is flipped up (called the river). These are all community cards to be used by everyone at the table to make the best hand possible out of any combination of the two cards in their hand and or the five on the "board," making a total of 4 betting opportunities. The majority of hands in a professional no limit texas hold em tournament never go all the way to show down, thats the point at which both players turn their cards over. Meaning there is a lot of bullshitting and trapping and just plain good prison style bluff tactics to get your opponent to fold believing you have a stronger hand, or to feign weakness to get him to call your all in bet so you get all his money and knock him/her out of the tournament. Tables keep getting condensed as players get knocked out until there is only one player left, it is not winner take all, usually first place is around 33% of all buy in money with the rest going to the top 10% of the field, so finishing 10th in this tournament would still net a few hundred thousand. To reach 1st place means you've played 5 straight days of poker at 12 hours per day.

The main event started in a few days. I was back to my pristine way of living, like in Marion, eating exceptionally good, stretching, doing yoga every morning, working out, and feeding my mind and body good things. I attended a 12 step program three to five times a week and was coming up on five years of absolute and continuous sobriety. I prayed and meditated to a god of my understanding every morning and helped other alcoholics and drug addicts stay and get sober.

Getting off the plane at Las Vegas International Airport is almost like walking out onto a casino floor filled with slot machines. Bing bing bing of slot machines echoed out as I walked off the plane. Yes even the airport was full of slot machines, cigar shops and oxygen massage bars. Well this is Las Vegas I thought. As I made my way down Las Vegas Boulevard, the size and grandness of it all really started to settle in. As I headed north towards the Bellagio in a taxi you would see a hotel ahead of you that appeared to be a block away when in fact it was six blocks ahead. Because of the sheer size of the hotels, everything seemed closer than it really was. This was Las Vegas.

The casinos are the big winners in Las Vegas.

I remember the smell of the Bellagio. Most of the hotels on the strip in Las Vegas have a signature smell that is derived from a scent, usually inspired by the rain forest because it's so exotic and unlikely to be replicated elsewhere. A young entrepreneur came up with them and exclusively sells each hotel its very own signature scent. As you walk in, the smell is refreshing like a wild mountain flower or the smell of a gentle bouquet of hawaiian flowers. The ceiling of the front lobby of the Bellagio is a grand display of Chihuly glass floral sculptures in pink, blue, red, orange, and yellow hues. The Bellagio is the only five-diamond hotel on the strip and the service is amazing.

For the most part World Poker Tour (WPT) tournaments at the Bellagio commenced in the Fontana Lounge away from the main gambling floor. The Fontana Lounge is a posh hall thick with wool carpeting and huge windows that overlook Lake Bellagio and the fountain displays that go off every 15 minutes after nightfall. During tournament time, there are about 50 to 60 tables of ten players at each. Sadly it has since been turned into a nightclub and today poker tournaments at the Bellagio are held in the poker room.

I was about 15 minutes late. The opening "shuffle up and deal" announcement by Jack the tournament director was done, and the tournament was underway. I passed security and entered the thick concentrated silence of the lounge. Cards were shuffled and chips clicked as players caressed them while sizing up an opponent. "I'm all in," rose like a refrain from the packed tables, punctuated by the occasional "Oh no."

Most of the time you only hear what's going on at your table. There is a concentrated energy, each opponent eyeing the others and his chip stacks and taking mental notes as to how much they bet and in what position, and against whom. There is no Nash Equilibrium here. Most hands do not go to showdown. As in prison, if someone has a problem with you there is a good chance that the showdown will be avoided so as to not cause a war. When the poker hands go to a show down, you get more information on that particular player. It becomes a game of observation and intimidation by use of chips, very much like in prison, weeding out the weak and pouncing on them with bets or raising them with chips rather than knives and fists. In poker, you can play your hand, your chip stack, and you have your opponent. In prison, your hand is your race or "set" of people you hang with in relation to the percentage of that race in the particular prison you're at, and the relationship you have with that race. Your chip stack is access to weapons or other commodities you have— money, or drugs. Your opponent is the same as in poker. Is he tight? Is he weak? Is he connected with a gang? Does he have more people or chips than you to back him? I was a long way from prison, but the skills I'd honed there in regard to interpersonal conflict, my concentration and observations, were in tune full force.

The silence was only interrupted occasionally by a sweet, tall blonde who would quietly approach each tournament table and ask in a low hushed tone, "Drinks anyone?"

Within two hours I got into a very large hand with none other than Phil Ivey. He has an aggressive style of poker play as do I and of course one the the most well known successful cash game and tournament poker players ever, some say even as good as the late great Stu Ungar. I had not lost a hand yet. I had increased my starting stack of chips by about 55%. I was playing bad cards on the button. I put Phil on an ace jack, maybe a jack ten suited, but certainly something in that range. It was just Phil and I left preflop. He raised 2.5 times the big blind, 800 chips; in response, everyone folded but me. The flop came: jack, eight, six. I had a king and a six. The bets were small. I raised his bet on the flop and he smooth called it. He bet $1,500. I came over the top raising his bet to $5,000. The turn was a king. He bet about five thousand. I just called. Right now, there was about $14,000 in the pot and on the river was a six. I had sixes full of kings, a full house. I still thought he had an ace jack and was trying to bully me off my hand. I bet $15,000 Phil then raised me all in, another $4,000 more and I called. By the turn I had two pair and figured he was dead in the water with jacks. As he said all in, I said call and threw my cards over. He threw his over— pocket eights making eights full of sixes, crushing my smaller full house.

I misread him all the way, and really had no business in the hand to begin with. Preflop and in hindsight, it was a easy fold. Everyone folded after his initial pre-flop bet, leaving only me on the button and Phil sitting two to my left. I pushed my chair back and did the walk of shame out of the Fontana Lounge. I went up to my room, took some deep breaths then came back down to shake Phil's hand. When I came up to the table, I saw his chair was empty. Another player told me of Phil's demise. It seems as though someone else administered the same sort of beating to him as he did on me. I didn't feel so bad.

I would not think about my house until my plane landed back in Milwaukee. That $15,000 would only buy me a month and a half of mortgage. Yes, this was a long shot. Selling my house— at any price— was an even longer shot. My motto is, and always has been not to go through life wondering what if. There are no places in history for "what ifs." I gave the tournament my best shot. I was one closer to winning a big tournament. I tried to be the tiger for one day. That day, though, Phil Ivey was the lion, and I was simply the slaughtered sheep.

When I finally returned home, the devastation of it hit me. I could not stand the thought of losing my house.

I was in my living room looking out to the Mukwonago River. The landscape outside was as dreary as I felt; all the leaves were gone, snow covered the ground and frost snaked its way along the deck. Though inside I had the heat up 75, I was chilled. The walls seemed to echo with the memories of laughter and friendship, ghosts of the many lavish parties I'd thrown between these walls. I had so many parties here, even recently my 37th birthday party, a night full of amazing food and time spent with 40 close friends. Then there was the space itself, not just the memories. Waking up to the western view of the Tom's Bay, where cranes in spring taught hatchlings to fly. The identity of this house, and surrounding wildlife and land was imbued on me. For four straight years, this was my home, longer than any single prison, apartment, or house since I'd left the care of my parents.

I pressed my nose against the window to stare outside as I talked with my brother on the phone. "What an order!" I exclaimed. I felt I could not go through with it. Drinking was not even an option. I felt disgraced. I lost everything or I was going to lose everything. It had been 30 days since the Bellagio. My house was not going to sell. I had fine furniture and I knew Craigslist and eBay Ebay would produce some cash to live on.

I hung up with my brother. I wanted to die. The thought of drinking repulsed me. It was on par with having sex with a punk in prison. I started to think about how I could stop my heart from beating. Nothing was going to make me die with booze or drugs in me. My goal in life was to die sober and serene. I had been a binging alcoholic my whole life and on many of those occasions, I would partake in snorting and smoking cocaine. Dying contaminated with booze or drugs seemed like such a waste. I suppose it's a testament to my mental state that the thought of breaking my sobriety was abhorrent, but not suicide.

I'd never felt such strong and heavy despair as I did at the thought of losing the house; no break-up, financial loss, or even getting sentenced to prison had pushed on me internally the way the loss of the house had. Thanks to a beautiful spiritual program that helped alcoholics stay sober anonymously, I had found my sobriety, but obviously I was still lacking spiritually. I'd replaced my identity with the identity of a millionaire living in this house. When faced with the thought of losing it, I lost all sense of worth. Admittedly, now, the attachment to this material thing, the idea that it represented me, made me what I thought whole was.

I finally decided that the best way to kill myself was to jump off the Hoan Bridge in Milwaukee. It is positioned over the mouth of Lake Michigan and the Milwaukee River. The 285 foot fall would certainly end my life. I let go of everything I ever thought, felt, or held near and dear. I was as close to death on that bridge as anyone physically could be. Then I got out there, looking at the beautiful view of Lake Michigan, and was overcome with a sense of something greater than myself and that goddamned house, a huge god shot and a most fortuitous moment.

I realized that at least I could say I tried; I went for the gold with buying my house, with every property I bought and sold, with ever poker tournament I played in. This time I lost. It doesn't have to be the last time I play. I went for it and it did not work out the way I thought, and that's ok. The Anonymous 12 step program I am a member of has taught me that I am not the one driving the bus and I have to accept that. How I did not drink or kill myself that night is beyond me, but instead I stood on that bridge and told myself deep down that in the end if this house bankrupts me financially so be it. That house represented eight years of hard, hard work post-prison, starting with a $5.50 per hour job for 40 hours a week. I loved living every minute there and enjoyed it with all my friends, family and many girlfriends.

By April, springtime had arrived. By law the foreclosure wouldn't be complete for nine more months, and if at that time I filed bankruptcy I could postpone the process for another six to eighteen months my lawyer assured me. I had lived, laughed, loved in that exquisite location of a lake estate on an absolute pristine piece of land. But it was enough, and it was time to go. So I packed up some shipping containers and left April 15, 2009. I made peace with the land and the house. I thanked God for allowing me such a gracious gift, and launched the beginning of the healing process.

Joel Blaeser
03491-089
[redacted]

CARBONDALE, IL 629
PM

Rosemary Blaeser
1730 N Clark #4102
Chicago Il, 60614

Dear Rosemary and Larry,   11-6-96

Hello There, well it looks like ~~the~~ Billy Clinton won himself another and final election. He has his hands full though, ~~because~~ The Republicans are probably going to try to impeach him. and they do have control of both The house and Senate. Who did you guys vote for. It's legal in California and Arizona for doctors to prescribe weed, and in California doctors can also prescribe Heroin and other illicit drugs. Maybe This will be The start of a new nationwide trend. Most trends, social, economic, technical ~~and~~ etc, start on The west coast (CA) and work There way east. I would hope That you, larry your Sisters and Jen would have enough forsite and sense to vote for such a measure, if and when it does go to reffferendum in ~~Illinois~~. Ross was lucky to get what he got 8 or 9%, people perceived his so called tactical move to leave the race (in 1992) early as abandonment. He still pulled 14% then. He has regained some of the peoples confidence though. & Observing politics is all ~~that~~ The energy I wish to expend on such wretched people and Systems. These views were long held before I was ever entertaining The notion of prison. They have actualy mellowed due to less involvement of The free world. Most people think it's a great system, those same people base that on ~~their~~ There conditioned responses from the t-v and mainstream media publications. This media is part of The bigger corporate america That has most of The politicians in There back pocket and consequently

They (the politicians) work for them and not the proliteriate. Alot of people are content making 40, 50, 60 or 70 thousand a year. Money or externals dont bring happiness though. As alot of people are conditioned to believe by main stream media. So here's a system that does not work for the people 100%. Not even 50%. Here's a system that is completly backword to the truest sense of the meaning. 100 years ago you could drink water out of any of the great lakes, As of 1992 the Dept of DNR issued a warning saying that the fish ~~was contaminated~~ in lake michigan (all fish) is so contaminated that one serving will increase your chance getting cancer. Now here I am slamed down for 10 years for selling another adult something that he was (and me) using for his own benefit or harm (however you want to look at it) everyone who bought it new what it was and was using it for themselves. Now aside from the fact that he showed dishonor (and was rewarded for it) and I showed and live honor and was slamed. Aside from that. We knowingly used those drugs for ourselves, We did not ~~o~~ or act like Jim Jones or pour drugs into the water supply. Who polluted the water so bad that the water has to be treated in a 100 million dollar facility and one serving of fish will increase your chances of getting cancer. Those people who did that are not behind bars. That water affects millions and millions of people, there is no agency like the DEA or FBF who's main objective is to catch drug <u>users</u> and small time dealers, for crimes against nature. The list goes on. Politicians use the drug issue as a platform to get re elected. How about all the drugs prescribe for ailments that are a direct result from

Slavery was legal until 1864, did that make it right? all the contaminents in water and fish. By you and all those other citizens running around out there like tourists turning your back on the real issues, you are turning your backs on yourselves and on me, Here I am struggling to get a lawyer for a appeal I have never had, (My case has never ever been appealed) and you the people I rely on for many things want to come visit. leave well enough alone is that the rational or no I have a better one I can't afford it. Can you afford the 18% they charge you on your credit card. I put myself here and chances are when I get out of prison I will leave the country, but so what fuck a visit. You ~~████~~ all want to look the other way on the country and my case. I hear from all of you we don't have the money and then when can we visit. So when it suits your need you will spend the money? You and Jay have contributed alot and thus the most, but its still not enough. (Fuck Thankyou, Do you realy think I am not thankful) If I am your son then you are the mother, Dads gone so that leaves you with the leadership position. You should be the one getting on the family members about my situations. Your actions leave something to be desired. You have probably been more of a hinderince than help. As far as asking and putting pressure on family to contribute. On the phone to me you said nobody is contributing and you probably won't get all the money. That tells me alot about you. Yes it looks as though I've put myself on the hill and am casting alot of observations and I have haven't I. You daubt his credentials, well how much more money do you want to spend. What I am merely saying is this, And listen good. You casted a vote for someone

~~and~~ in this present election ~~and here~~ whats the sense by helping me (as you have) get a lawyer you have <u>started</u> to cast your vote for me (in a sense) and a vote against the's new revised roman empire. ~~Don't stop~~ Don't stop there though you deserve more and better!

Does larry still make you take the bus home, If I ever meet him I am going to check him on that. Where's your backbone. Can't you put your foot down. Are you with him more out of necessity than love. A little of both. These are rheotorical questions of course. You are the only living parent left, As you like to use labels, so where's the leadership.

I don't plan to come back to prison, and I have devised a rough detailed plan for whenever I get out. All of you except the obvious have written to me regularly and sent me plenty of money here and there. And I know things would have been real ruff going without that money, Now is now we live in the here and now, and rite now time is running out on this appeal. This is what counts the most. I need this lawyer and I am asking you to do anything and everything physically, financialy or whatever possible to help me. talk to the kids, say, mike, jen, Brad, and anyone else sisters, <u>larry?</u> If you are ~~sleeping~~ with him I don't see why you can't approach him about this. It's not like I have a terminal disease and am 3rd time offender. Is there something wrong with you or what! You <u>all</u> want to act like I have a life sentence.

How are you and larry getting along, Are you guys moving into another apartment. Did you guys plan anymore skiing trips.

5

You know since you informed me that Michael was breaking his word (not keeping me) about 8 weeks ago, I have written him at least 10 maybe 15 letters. He has not responded to one. It looks as though he has a communication problem with me, his family and most importantly himself. Which I took the liberty to point out to him in my last and final letter to him. He's behaving like such a rotten bitch Motherfucker that he would save alot of heart ache on his family and becky if he died or did a instant 180 degree turn around. At this point its hard to see him do the 180 degree turn. I surmise that he has refrained in killing himself (At the very least in part) because he see's and has seen the degree of my maturity, mental tuffness etc in doing this prison time. I also took the liberty of pointing this out to him. I am going to stop talking about michael to you, you have enough worries don't you.

Did that guy in arizona ever give you a new pair of sunglasses or your money back? Do you guys roller blade in the winter time. You being physically fit, eating healthy and thinking positive doesn't cost any money and will prolong your life longer than any medicine or health insurance. Yesterday at 12:00 Am I came off of a 66 hr fast, I missed my goal of 72hrs (3 days) by 6 hrs. I drank water and ate a little bit of salt. For the last 4 weeks I fasted every Sunday now I am going to fast every Sunday for 24 hrs then every 4th Sunday fast for 3 days. It's really

6

not that hard. It realy drains out the impurities and toxins that build up from the dirty air, water, food etc. Your mind becomes clearer ~~and~~ and quicker in this process, which is a real nice bonus. Food is one of the very few things people have control over in here. Besides all the benefits above, being able to resist food for 3 days builds even a stronger Iron Will, resoluteness and direction.

Well mom + larry peace be with you, enjoy yourself.

Love Joel

were you or are you able to fulfill my book requests. I need books real bad

14

Black Box

Though I left the compound a burnt and crumbled ruin, my first impression of Talladega was that it was as neatly arranged and manicured as a suburban neighborhood. The brick buildings seemed to almost shimmer in the hot sun air as we pulled up.

I had no idea what to expect out of FCI Talladega, but after my time in Pekin, I was looking forward to a chance to get my act together. I'd had too many close calls in Pekin. At one point, I was holding a half ounce of pure china white heroin for a friend whose friend's cell mate went to the hole for investigation. It was just getting passed around, and I held it for nine long days. I could have easily been stuck in prison until 2020 if I got caught holding it. I had to change. I had to prepare a future.

I talked with my new case manager Mr. Allen upon arrival in Talladega, and he assured me if I could go 24 months without a shot or any other trouble whatsoever I I would be eligible for the federal prison camp in Montgomery, Alabama. This was one of the few remaining places a federal inmate could attend a real college while incarcerated. "Blaeser you are young and seem savable. No tattoos… You might have a shot out there once you go home."

"Allen, I can do 24 months clean."

"If you make it to Montgomery boy, you can go to Alabama State full-time if you please."

Me? A college boy? BOY!" I just met this guy and did not know what to think, but what did I have to lose?

"This is your fifth prison in 33 months Blaeser. You better keep your nose clean. You got seven years and a wake-up. It's up to you..." The meeting with the case manager left me with renewed vigor and a brighter outlook for the future. There was a carrot at the end of a stick and it looked good. College, women, degree, prison camp, no fences. The thoughts of a prison camp and college were intoxicating. It was a very strong incentive to not get into any bullshit over radios, weed or whatever. Bide my time and keep my nose clean was the mantra. To my surprise and benefit, I soon found out Paul Perez my old workout partner with Hog Head from FCI Florence was transferred to FCI Talladega for dirty urine six months prior. He told all the right people on the yard that I was a solid convict and to look out for me. He introduced me to Dean, another super huge muscle dude who needed a workout partner. I read, meditated, occasionally smoked some marijuana, worked out a lot, and kept my mouth shut. Talladega was a just a regular ol' medium prison and was very low on the scale of notorious happenings. Except for some cuban detainees going crazy in the hole in the 1980's It had a reputation as a pretty docile prison.

One day I headed down to the recreation yard for a workout. Naturally, I grabbed my beloved green duffel bag, the one Sparky had made for me back in Englewood Colorado. I always appreciated how it was made out of a wool blanket with double straps and a thick chrome zipper; looking like it was from out of a store. I had just entered the yard when one of the prison staff called out to me to stop. I looked over, expecting to see a CO and to my surprise found myself staring up into the sneering face of a lieutenant. A correctional lieutenant is one of the higher-ranking officers who is head of security and emergency response on a federal prison compound.

"Where did you get that?" he barked, gesturing to my workout bag. "Those are not allowed here. STOP!" he continued in a stern, condescending voice. His eyes flicked over to my ponytail and his voice lowered, "You dirty hippie-long-haired rat." That was the worst thing you could be called in prison and next was getting physically assaulted and not fighting back, all this in front of at least 100 other convicts moving about during lunchtime. As he was throwing me to the ground, he put his hands on the green duffle bag.

My back slammed on the cement path leading to the rec yard from the chow hall. His left hand sat on my chest while his other hand was ripping Sparky's sacred gift away . I was in shock, horrified and angered so deeply I was seeing red. I wanted him to hurt. I yelled out in screaming agony as he ripped the duffle bag completely out of my hands, "YOU FUCKING BITCH NIGGER... GIVE IT BACK!"

"What? Oh my God, what did you just say? Motherfucker! BLAESER! You are in for it." His voice got louder and his grip on my chest tighter and stronger. "Turn over and CUFF UP! You're going to the hole for investigation." In the melee of emotion I forgot I was in a federal prison. Even if I won the tug of war with the bag, I still had nowhere to go.

My green duffel bag was taken and I was escorted to the Hole for verbal assault and investigation of contraband. As soon as I was in the Hole, I demanded an appointment with my counselor to start filing a grievance. Federal inmates are afforded a grievance process according to the Code of Federal Regulation 28 (28 CFR as its referred to). The process starts with a discussion with your assigned counselor. It could be lost or damaged property while in transport from one prison to another or something as serious as abuse or staff misconduct. Any inmate who wishes to take court action because of a prison issue must exhaust the administrative processes, which in this case is called the BP process. Relief could be granted in part or in whole at any point of the process. Once, some of my property was lost in transit from FCI Sandstone to FCI Englewood. I received a property slip when I left Sandstone, and when compared with property slip I was issued upon arrival at Englewood, it was obvious that the Bureau of Prisons, who was responsible for shipment of all prisoner property, was at fault for the lost property. I was given a $45 credit at the commissary. Even though I was seeking $90 of redress, I settled for the $45 credit.

Most inmates make a point of knowing this process, and it is standard in every federal prison but USP Marion. After the Tommy Silverstein and Clayton Fontaine incident, Marion was put on permanent lockdown, and the Marion administration was afforded certain rights and privileges that superseded other federal prisons or regional offices.

Though inmates are aware of the process, few ever make it through to the end of the process when it's regarding staff misconduct. The staff have a way of dissuading inmates from pursuing legal means. In reality I was in enough trouble and by all accounts should have just let it go. By the time I was released from the Hole about 35 days later, my complaints were gaining traction at the regional level. All I wanted was my duffel bag back. It was listed on my incoming property slip when I had entered Talladega, so according to the BOP's own policies, I had a right to it. Having it was not a security breach, and it was no threat to the orderly running of the prison.

My case manager at Talladega called me into his office after I was released from the Hole.

"Look Blaeser, don't file the BP-11. You're barking up the wrong tree with that lieutenant," Mr. Allen said.

"I'm going to pursue it. It's my property and I have a right to it. I didn't provoke him, and wasn't causing any trouble." I shook my head, and looked at my case manager. "I'm in the right here, and you know it."

Now it was his turn to shake his head. "That may be, but it's dangerous territory."

The very next day the aforementioned lieutenant called me into his office. He was a large black man, about 6'5", and he sat comfortably, even casually behind his large desk. There, on the desk between us, was my green duffel bag. He did not invite me to take a seat.

"Blaeser if you do not back off I will have you sent to Marion for the remainder of your sentence." His face was a blank stone as he said it, but his eyes glittered with a sinister gloss similar to a blood crazed convicts eyes after a designated murder.

I really thought about it and all the stories I had heard up until that time about Marion. The threat was real. I'd played enough to poker to recognize a bluff, and this man was no bluffer. Talladega was my 5th prison and I was in my 35th month of incarceration. I recalled everything I'd heard about Marion; I was a believer and decided that I should back off.

He picked up the bag from his desk and threw in my face. I smelled the green wool one last time. The bastard lieutenant looked me in the eye.

"It's not worth it. Let it go."

I looked at the bag one last time, and set it on his desk. He was right. I said, "Lieutenant, I am deeply sorry for my terrible name calling. I lost my temper. I do not know you. I was wrong and I am so sorry."

Then I shook his hand, and forgot about the whole thing.

Joel Blaeser
K.C.D.C.
303 Court Street
Covington Ky 41011

Rosemary Blaeser
1150 N lake shore drive
Chicago Ill 60611

Jan 4, 1993

Dear Mom + Jen

Whats up. Still hanging in there. I cant wait to read that book that u got me Jen. I should be sentenced in the next 2 months then I will get shipped. Thankyou for the extra cash mom. I decided I am going to wait to get good shoes, because the ones I have are not wore out yet. I need to conserve as much as possible. I need socks and underwear. The rest of the 30$ you sent me I will save for food or toteries. As soon as I get to the Fed Joint I am going to run everyday so I will need to get some good running shoes then. Dont forget mom when and if you do come down when I get sentenced to bring my tax forms. Also can you make sure I put a valid address on them. Also one of them I have to send money with and one I get money back on well I am going to roll See u later

love u Guys Forever

Joel

Letters from Marion

MOM   FeB 21, 1993

I Also Asked HI, Hows IT going. I Thought About the
That He might lawyer The one in texas, and IT occurred to me
not be as when god IS on your side IT doesn't matter
good as the who your lawyer IS. So lets JUST go with
one I paid but the court APPointed one he will Be Fine. IF
Best Anyway Something doesn't work out I can Always
Fire him and get Another one ITS my right.
BUT I am sure He will Be Fine. don't
worry JUST Pray, I know I will Be out
In 3 years. I have Been using Prison
to increase my human Spirit not Break
IT. I cant wait To get shipped to the
Fed Joint, Good food, fresh air, and of
Course I can Start my Education. well
Mom when I get out The First Big money
I make I am not going To Ask myself what I
want BUT I am going To give you what
you need + deserve So you can retire and do
what you want. I cant wait For That
day, I love you say hi to Jen For Me

P.S.   love Joel
on the letter That IS
Addressed to Room of Class
JUST Put your Address
No NAme - ok.

15

Acceptance

NOVEMBER 1990

THERE WAS ALWAYS A woman. It's the beginning of an old dimestore Pi novel, and as an attorney friend of mine stated, an inherent part of every indictment.

"There's always an ex-girlfriend," he'd said in response to me telling him about my indictment.

This particular woman's name was Sierra. I was introduced to her by Rainbow's son Josh at a Grateful Dead concert in Denver, Colorado. I was in love the moment I saw her. She was studying chemistry and business at the University of Colorado Boulder and living in a little cottage at the rear of her uncle's property. She'd been to a few Dead shows and enjoyed the scene, but hadn't caught up to my extensive resume of shows yet. I convinced her to travel to Las Vegas for a show with me. It was one of the last of the season. When we returned to Denver, she invited me to move in with her. I looked at it as fortuitous.

In retrospect, I was not yet mature enough to support someone else emotionally, financially, or spiritually in a relationship, but I suppose with ex-relationships it's always in retrospect that we note these kinds of things. It was a rather odd existence; the two of us lived in a small cottage on her mother's property and split the $250 per month rent. During the day she'd go to school, and I would hang out with friends. For the most part my friends liked her, some of my Grateful Dead family members were unsure of her. The truth was that the two of us fought a lot. When she drank sierra would threaten to leave me for other men and there were times after we fought that she wouldn't come home. But I was young and new at this live-in relationship thing. The fighting and drama had an all too familiar ring to them offering a skewed sort of comfort. Within four months of moving in, I proposed. A few weeks later, I returned the ring.

Sierra knew that I sold LSD, though I didn't share much with her about it. Shortly after I'd moved in, I started some pot plants with very good seed from Neville the seed king in Amsterdam. One day Sierra and I got into a fight and she threatened to call the police. The plants were half grown. I played it safe and removed the whole grow room in less than one hour and threw it away. I knew I couldn't trust her with any information. She might be spiteful enough to use it against me.

Eventually the fights became more frequent and more volatile. In the end her infidelity and my immaturity got the best of us. It was a bitter breakup and out of spite I betrayed her confidence to some of her friends. In short, I drove her to hate me.

After the breakup I traveled with the Dead again. Not that I'd stopped while I was with Sierra. We went to shows in Chicago and the Milwaukee Jerry Garcia shows, which is when I'd introduced her to my family. But now that I had no strings I could once again follow them from show to show.

I saw my blood family less and less. Between Dead tours I would stop in to see my mother on Mary Ellen Place, a sleepy little block off Honey Creek Parkway in Wauwatosa, Wisconsin. All the houses are 1920's two story brick or stone homes with long driveways and big garages. The front door was always open. I remember one summer after Dead tour around noon, I sneaked in to say hi to my mom. My beard was four inches long and my hair nearly to the middle of my back. My mom had never seen me with any more than a 5 o'clock shadow. She was washing dishes when I snuck up around her to hug her and say hi. She screamed to high heaven and dropped the dish she was holding, shattering it on the large porcelain sink as the water was still running.

"Joel! I barely recognized you!" she exclaimed as it finally set in that I was her son, and she embraced my hug.

"Just popped in to say hi," I responded as I kissed her cheek.

"We need to talk." She gestured toward the butcher block kitchen table, and took a seat herself.

"Sure mom, what's up?"

"It's about the letters."

Every time I flew on a plane she would receive one of them.

My heart dropped. I knew this wasn't going to be an easy conversation.

"Mom, listen I-"

"No Joel, you listen." I stopped abruptly. I wasn't expecting her to raise her voice.

Her voice was clear and her eyes bright. "I only have so much of this life left, and I don't intend to see any of my children in the ground before I'm there. If what you are doing is dangerous enough that you have to send me letters to ensure I can identify your remains then I think you need to reconsider."

"Well mom, it's only if the plane goes down. You can't tell me that Jennifer and Michael don't fly. They have just as much of a chance of dying in plane crash as I do."

She looked at me for a moment, letting my argument hang in the air between us.

"That may be true, but they don't send me a paper reminder of their mortality every time they do it. Do you understand that it takes days for the letter to reach me? That the time between your call and the letter arriving I can't help but pace the house, fretting over you? No longer about you dying in plane crash, but what you are doing out there. And with who."

She sighed, and I watched her shrink before my eyes under the weight of her words, as her sentences brought forth all the feelings of those days wrought with worry.

"It may be true that you aren't my only child to fly, but you're the only one who feels the need to do so using a fake name. And why Joel? Why do you keep putting yourself at risk like this? Is it for money? I would be happy to help you if that's the only reason. You have to understand that it's not just your death I worry about, there are fates worse than that. At this rate, on the path you are on, you are either going to end up dead or in jail, and along the way you'll have pushed aside everyone who cares about you. You keep me at a distance so that I can't be a part of your life, but that's all I want- For you to have a life, a good one, with a future."

Her head fell into her hands on the table. "Joel, I won't survive many more years of this kind of worry. If you don't stop selling drugs, I'll die."

I remained silenced. I'd never really given it much thought, and I'd never thought she would be this upset. I had always been the black sheep of the family and just sort of assumed no one cared that much. Of course I'd always been close with my mother, and now that she was alone, I suppose that my absence hit home that much harder.

I reached across the table to take her hand into mine. "Mom. I am so sorry. It's not as important as you are." I gave her hand a comforting squeeze as tears welled in her eyes.

"I can't come home right away. I have a few things to take care of. But I'll move home soon, and I'll quit soon."

I made my way home later that year, in November of 1990, intending to start a life without drugs. I had not sold any drugs for some time, for a few reasons. Shortly after the conversation with my mom, I'd gotten a call from a client of mine named Marty.

We met the previous year, in the summer of 1989 in the parking lot of a Dead show and talked for a couple of hours. Most of the time I used a fake name when I met people, like Tree Limb or Jupiter. After all, I rarely saw them again. We started doing mail orders right away, using the prescribed method to send money and LSD.

We had a sporadic business relationship from then on out, doing about six or seven deals over the next six or seven months— about 10,000 hits total. Until one of Marty's customers got arrested for 25 hits of LSD, and Marty called me to say he wasn't going to sell anything for a while, but to call him in three to four months when the storm blew over. Paired with the conversation with my mom, I took it as a sign from the universe that I had reached a good stopping point in my selling career.

Meanwhile, down in Kentucky, very shortly after that call, the local sheriff came to Marty's door just to ask him some questions. He was not under arrest or under investigation. I taught him to cover his tracks well. There was no physical evidence because he always burned the envelope after he took out the LSD. There was nothing leading back to him except the word of a caught person. Then, right on the front steps of his house he broke down in tears and told the sheriff ever detail of every deal he'd ever done. The local sheriff in Kentucky had never heard of such an elaborate way to sell drugs; a process that enabled me and others to sell LSD all over the world under various names, using Western Union as a traveling piggy bank. Marty agreed to go with the sheriff and make his statement on video.

Down at the station this country Kentucky sheriff could not believe the way Marty had been buying the drugs, but he did believe he was guilty. He video-taped Marty's entire story and in the morning was smart enough to call the DEA. The DEA informed him that he just admitted to 15 years of crimes and if he did not cooperate they were going to put him away.

He must have remembered my real name although I never remember giving it to him, and remembered the Western Union transactions but not the fake names he sent the money in. The DEA began to sift through records from different Western Unions throughout the country. It would be months before they finally found records for the money he remembered sending under all those false names. Back in Milwaukee, I was unaware of the target on my back. I was going about my business, working as a landscaper for my brother, and reuniting with friends I'd long since since lost touch with. shortly after I got back to Milwaukee, I walked into the Up and Under Bar on Brady Street and noticed two girls and one guy strategically placed around the bar. They were actively avoiding eye contact with each other and any of the other few patrons in the bar. Their behavior seemed very suspicious to me, and I immediately recalled some of the sting operations in the Dead parking lots.

I took a shot in the dark. I walked up to one of the girls, a friendly smile on my face, "How do you like working for the DEA?"

They played it off well. At that point I had not been selling anything illegal and was just starting to get by. I suspected they were there for me, but they could have been staged for anyone. What I didn't know was that they had been following me for a long time hoping to catch me with a large quantity of LSD and try to get me to hand over big name manufacturers. It was very rare for anyone in the scene to have seen or dealt with LSD in its pure form, most people get the LSD already on the paper in liquid form or on gel tabs. I however was trusted and respected enough to have seen and scored actual crystal LSD. The DEA was hoping to get enough evidence to convince a grand jury to indict me because they suspected I knew some of the select few people actually who manufactured LSD and if they could get some names from me it would be a huge feather in any prosecutor's cap. And they really liked feathers.

There was a big rock show coming to Milwaukee and along with them some of my connections. I'd since lost contact with Dan, but had access to Rainbow's product via Michael, aka the Nederland Colorado King. Since Sierra and I had broken up, Michael and I became very close. He explained that he never trusted Sierra, stipulating that "If she was ever put to the test she would break down like a cheap shotgun." Michael had already had two of his biggest dealers go to prison and not say a word about their source. He was a good judge of character.

I couldn't resist the temptation. I met up with Michael outside of the shows and did two quick deals, one for one hundred sheets (ten thousand hits) and one for fifty sheets (five thousand hits). This was the biggest amount of LSD I had ever sold in such a small amount of time profiting a total of fifteen hundred dollars, providing some savings over the coming winter.

It had been quite some time since Marty had told me he wanted to back off, so I gave him a quick call. We discussed ordering some front row Dead tickets for an upcoming Dead show, but something seemed off. I became incredibly nervous at how shifty Marty had seemed on the phone and decided not to send the LSD this time. Still, the conversation was enough for Laura Voheers Klein, an ambitious up-and-coming federal prosecutor based in Kentucky, to convene a secret federal grand jury.

An indictment and grand jury are different from trial in a few ways. A federal grand jury is often conducted in secret, meaning the accused is not present or provided any representation. To be indicted there must be demonstration of preponderance of evidence, rather than guilt "beyond a reasonable doubt," the well-known requirement for a guilty verdict at trial. In addition, rather than being a unanimous verdict reached by all grand jurors, only two thirds of the jurors have to vote in affirmation or non affirm. Also, it is interactive; rather than acting as observers, Grand jury members are allowed to ask questions. Months later, when I read the Grand Jury transcripts and encountered the questions the grand jury members asked the prosecution, it was evident they barely got two thirds to affirm, whereas in a trial, all must vote guilty or innocent, or it is declared a mistrial.

The prosecutor had no physical evidence of any LSD, only Marty's story and our conversation about Grateful Dead tickets. Then, my ex-girlfriend, Sierra from Denver offered testimony against me. She was never charged or questioned, but apparently at the prompting of her mother offered to come forward with a story. Although she produced no physical evidence, she corroborated bringing me to the Western Union one night. She was a cute, sweet girl, who was a straight-A college student and very scared to be in court-- the jury fell for her nearly as hard as I had. In the end, the grand jury had enough votes to indict me on nineteen counts: nine counts of money laundering and ten counts of distribution. With no less than a 90% win rate my chances of going to prison were huge.

They still followed me around for another month or two before they arrested me. That morning of April 24, 1992 was average. I was up early, had breakfast and was waiting for a friend before heading to work for my older brother at his landscaping company. I heard the knock on the door.

I lived in a three-plex on Humboldt Avenue on the east side of Milwaukee, right across the street from Scaffidi's Hideout Bar. Unknown to me as I opened the door, there were two DEA agents in the front of the building with pump shotguns. I heard after the arrest that there were also two agents in back with what appeared to be AR-15's.

"Surprise, surprise," one of them said when I answered the door.

As this was happening, my whole life started to pass right in front of me. The shock of what was happening made my ears ring. I opened the door, an automatic 45-caliber gun was put to my forehead while simultaneously being pushed backward all the way down to the ground, during which, this gun barrel was firmly pressed to my forehead. He rolled me over onto my stomach, the gun never moved, touching my ear and then the back of my head. As he cuffed me, he asked if I was Joel Blaeser. After I made an unintelligible sound of assent, he sat me in a kitchen chair and threw a nineteen count federal indictment into my lap.

While I was being cuffed my roommates were woken up. The entire apartment was gone through. Chairs were overturned, pictures taken from the wall and removed from their frames, sofa cushions were torn apart; they left nothing unturned, including the kitchen cabinets, which had a three small cups of water with tiny sprouting marijuana plants in them, but they looked right at them and left them. They must have been really focused on LSD.

The DEA agent who'd tossed the indictment at me was a burly five foot nine, and had a face that was mostly concealed by a bushy brown beard.

"Do you know Sierra such and such and such and such?" I was still in too much shock from having a gun put to my forehead to answer him right away, but he didn't pause for a response.

"You're in deep shit, Joel. If you help us set some people up, we will let you go today," he said. "All you have to do is agree to help us, we will work out the details later."

I thought of my dad, his lectures about honor; his definition of honor translated to taking responsibility for one's actions, and more specifically not telling on anyone. I recalled my mother poking fun at me for being 'such an honest John' and my younger brother Bradley, who was always telling on me, and usually receiving a beating from my dad because of it. I thought about Michael, Dan, Tim, and all my other Grateful Dead brothers. I thought about every prison movie I'd ever seen and the odd thought 'at least they have weights and I'll be able to bulk up finally' crossed my mind. Then another thought occurred to me, at least I did not have to worry about getting caught, meaning no more paranoia or looking over my shoulder. Somehow in the midst of this chaos while my apartment was being torn apart and this nightmarish lumberjack with a piece was staring me down, I had started to find a few silver linings. I was already beginning to calm myself down. I looked the large DEA agent in the face and calmly explained that I had nothing to say. He remained stoic, and simply looked at me.

"You are going to spend all of your twenties in prison and maybe more," he said. The reality that I was freshly twenty-three years old slapped me in the face. My demeanor wavered for a moment, but he continued. "That is the absolute best part of your life. Don't let it go down the tubes."

It was a compelling statement I felt sick to my stomach at the thought of living in a prison through my twenties. But setting someone up was a life sentence of dishonor and I could not capitulate.

I thought about taking my mom to her first Dead show in the summer of 1991 at Soldier's Field with my brothers, and smoking a huge joint of kind bud with her. We found seats in the tenth row. It was festival seating meaning anyone with "floor" marked on their ticket could sit in any row. I was on some very good LSD, and so was my brother though I didn't find that out until years later. I remember dancing and grooving to the Dead with my mother.

It was then and there that I was overcome with the conviction that somehow I was not going to serve more than five years, and that I would survive it all.

"Take me to my cell," I said. I have no idea where the strength behind those words came from, aside from the strict sense of honor instilled in me by my father. While I was refusing to give up any of my contacts I could envision him standing near in a white collared work shirt commanding me to take responsibility for my actions. I did not admit to anything and knew the evidence was weak; I had stopped selling all drugs about 18 months prior because of my paranoia about Marty and not wanting to go to prison. With a good attorney I would have a shot at beating the evidence. Though I felt fear and trepidation about what was around the corner, oddly enough I felt protected in my convictions.

SEPTEMBER 8TH AND 9TH 1992

My trial lasted just over two days. I never took the stand, but simply watched as my youth was sentenced away.

My trial judge was William O. Bertelsman, appointed to the bench by Jimmy Carter. He had not been the judge on any of the earlier proceedings. Years later before I went home, I came to realize that if I had a bench trial I probably would have never gone to prison, a very rare exception to a jury trial. There were many subtle nuances in my case with regards to the rules of criminal procedure that I believe the judge recognized and disagreed with.

The majority of evidence they had and used were the recordings of Marty Waters and I talking about transferring money for Grateful Dead tickets. The prosecution included dozens of tapes in evidence, most of which had come up with unintelligible recordings or blank. Before trial we tried to fight this, but to no avail. The amount of tapes made it appear as if there were many more incriminating conversations between Marty and I when in reality they only had a few scratchy conversations about payment for tickets.

When Marty came in to testify he looked terrified. He had dyed his hair Ronald McDonald orange and testified that he had been placed in the witness protection program. I wondered why, as it's not as if I had ever threatened him, not in all the years we had known each other. I'd never even been to his town in Kentucky. His voice shook as he read all of his answers to the prosecutor's questions off of a piece of paper. My lawyer asked him some of the same questions as the prosecutor and he answered differently which gave doubt to some of his testimony and great drama in the courtroom when Gatewood my lawyer pointed it out.

My ex-girlfriend who came on her own free will, had some holes in her testimony as well. She showed very little emotion on the stand, her face unreadable as she recited her answers to the prosecutor.

Gatewood Gailbraith had command of the whole courtroom during closing arguments. I felt like he really put on a good show. The two main witnesses, especially Marty, were really made to look like liars because of their incongruent answers. Gatewood's handiwork was reminiscent of a Perry Mason trial, each face turned to him as he revealed the holes in testimony and insufficient evidence against me. Then, at one point the judge told the bailiff to withhold the jury and proceed to scold the prosecutor for introducing "other act evidence."

After closing arguments the jury was out only three and a half hours.

Guilty on all eighteen counts. In this federal court they did not ask the defendant to rise when reading the verdict.

I cried, cried very hard and very wet. I was a young twenty-three year old facing a prison sentence of up to 293 months; I was potentially going to lose over 24 years of my life.

We tried to get an appeal bond—a bail of sorts, until the appeal could get settled. Sentencing was set for about thirty-five days out. As I lay in the little courthouse holding-cell, I remember a distinct conversation I had with my aunt, Georgie Blaeser, my father's sister. She is a nun for the Sisters of the Sacred Heart, Catholic Church. She offered to take me in and hide me. She said I would probably end up in Italy, or another foreign country. She was serious, and was firm with her offer, but I would never be able to come back to the United States. That was a scary thought and until I lay in that holding cell, I could never fully appreciate the offer. There was no turning back. Not coming back to the United States as a young twenty-three year old seemed like a certain type of sentence of its own, but definitely the lesser of the two—way lesser or so I thought at that moment.

In the holding cell in the courthouse that night I couldn't sleep. I poured all of my emotional distraught into sexual energy and masturbated. I ended up having an incredible orgasm. I told myself to get used to it.

Acceptance

The next morning, when I woke up in the county jail I was totally and utterly numb. The sight of food sickened me and made me instantly nauseous. I gave away my whole tray. I was twenty-three and was probably going to get twenty years. With good behavior that meant I would be forty when released. I had just lost nearly twenty years of my life. I had to adapt, overcome, prepare, decide, and act with every move I made.

When I was found guilty in the courtroom during trial, I asked for a court-appointed appellate attorney. Judge Bertelsman said Kurt Phillips was a great appellate attorney who he knew from law school. Who knew this appointment would come back in spades. I thanked him.

Once convicted, federal defendants get a direct appeal, which goes to the Circuit Court of Appeals. If denied, then the Supreme Court of the United States is the last stop for those issues you originally appealed. If on direct appeal you get shot down at the appellate level, and before an attempt at the Supreme Court, you can appeal your case "en banc," in which a panel of appellate judges rules on the issues being appealed. Anywhere along the line if you the prisoner win, the prosecutor will appeal again unless decided by the Supreme Court. Once all those avenues are exhausted, prisoners per the constitution get what is called a writ of habeas corpus, or 2255. When filing a 2255, the process starts with your trial judge. My trial judge was as fair as they come. Once you exhaust your appeals, you're pretty much stuck unless there is a law change. The appeal outlets are vehicles into court and not to be squandered. The fact is that I had a range of outs with regards to my situation. At the very least, it offered that opiate of the masses—hope.

We fought the way my sentence was calculated. There was no physical evidence at my trial, and no lab reports. I was not charged with conspiracy. I was convicted of selling six thousand hits of LSD and laundering six thousand dollars. Transfer of money through Western Union over state lines is considered a form of money laundering if the money was from drug proceeds.

We also challenged the severity of the LSD charge. LSD was calculated by weight of the carrier medium, and for my trial they used the paper from the person who got the LSD from Marty. There were two different people's hands the drug actually went through after I'd sent it on, not to mention that the last person to have it, Marty's client who'd gotten caught, was not at my trial to corroborate whether he had made any changes or additions, or whether the piece of paper was the same weight as the other product they assumed I sent along. The weight came out to thirty-nine grams. One gram of LSD is ten thousand hits, so thirty-nine grams was a ridiculous amount of LSD and far more than I had sent Marty or sold over the course of my life. The result was that I ended up receiving a level thirty-four on the chart of sentencing guidelines, which only goes up to forty-two.

The prosecutor, Laura Voheers Klein, on her own put a motion in for a two-point enhancement for leader organizer and a two-point enhancement for continual career enterprise, putting me at a level thirty-eight which results in a 235-293 month sentencing range. Judge Bertelsman on his own volition (at sentencing many months later) said he did not believe I was a leader organizer, or that the two-point enhancement for continual career enterprise was warranted. That put me down to level thirty-four—151-188 months. Judge Bertelsman said that if I ever came back in front of him with any appeal-able issue, he would see to it that I would get reduced to no more than five years. He explained that because there are mandatory minimums set by Congress, his hands were tied by the mandatory minimum sentencing laws. In 1984 President Reagan signed The Comprehensive Crime Control Act, which took a lot of power from sentencing judges. Before this, judges were given wide berth in drug cases, which often resulted in deviations in sentencing even among very similar drug sentences and even by the same judge. A sentence in a similar case with the same judge could have a difference in range of ten or twenty years. Congress continued with more and instilled the Anti Drug Abuse Act of 1986. This ushered in the "New Law." Parole boards would be phased out. There would be no indeterminate sentences either. The only way to get below the mandatory minimums once convicted was a 5k1.1 motion, or a "Special K" as we called them inside the walls. This means the defendant must provide substantial assistance to arresting authorities and become a rat.

Judge Bertelsman decided on his sentence. "151 months," he said sternly. I was ecstatic; It had been five long months since getting found guilty, I clapped my hands together and thanked him. I knew immediately it meant twelve years and seven months, or with good behavior one month shy of serving eleven years. It was still a significant part of my youth that I would never be able to reclaim, but it was a whole lot better than the twenty years that I was expecting. Judge Bertelsman reminded me to contact Kurt Phillips for my direct appeal.

Acceptance

Days later, my lawyer sent me an article from a local Kentucky newspaper. It stated "Judge Bertelsman sentenced a Milwaukee man on an LSD case to 151 months. He stated that in his opinion the drug laws were too stiff, and that if he had discretion he would have sentenced the accused to five years."

I was already well into the first of the three distinct phases everyone in prison goes through. (everyone that is who adjusts "well") implosion: You cannot believe what has hap-pened. You're sort of numb, and don't know what to do. The second is explosion and would soon follow.... You're furious. You want to escape, kill swear, whatever outlet you can find for the emotions that are running rampant through your body. the third would come in full force and extreme delight in Marion............. which was acceptance: You acknowledge your present state, the reality of what has happened and your part in it. For I have found acceptance to be the only way to ever achieve peace of mind again.

Joel Blaeser
03491-089
P.O. Box 1000
Sandstone MN 55072

Rosemary Blaeser
1150 N Lake Shore drive
Chicago Il, 60611

Dear mom & Jen   April 10, 1993

What's up. Here are some articles that have been in the paper recently. There were 3 other ones but I could not locate them, but I did read them, and they were along the same lines. I have not recieved my trial transcripts yet, but they should be here soon. I started computer's on Thursday and it goes slow but I am learning. The drug awareness program is finally going to get started next week. The weather here is finally started to warm up here. I would appreciate it, if you could write the sentenceing commission in Washinton and ask them to please make "the LSD law Retroactive. They vote on it the 19th of this month. I hope you enjoyed your stay at Florida. ~~~~~~ did you get a tan I hope so. In 2 months I get a BP-15 which is a prison classification. Presently I have a Low In custody but I should get a Low out within the next 2 months. This will enable me to be eligible for a camp. ~~~~~ Maxwell Air Force Base in Alabama is the be top camp for education. They even have a masters and graduate program along with Bachelors too. When I get Reclassified I am going to write the judge and ask him if he can write the BoP (Bureau of Prisons) and reccomend to them to send me to Maxwell. Oxford prison is excellent for education purpose's but it is a medium prison and that level is higher than my level classification. The campground, does not offer the school that the prison does, it has no school. Well tell everybody I say Hi love you

                                                Joel

P.S.
did you send my letters
to Chris and Ron also my friends
mom sent you info on Families Against Mandatory Minimums (FAMM)
you will also be getting some letters to sign and send to congress
can you also in your next letter write me the Addresses of those talk shows but disguise it in your letter

Joel Blaeser
K.L.D.C.
3 Court ST
Covington Ky 41011

Rosemary Blaeser
150 N Lake Shore dr
Chicago Ill 60611

Dec 24, 1992

Dear Mom Merry Christmas ☺

    Thankyou for the gift I appreciate it. You shouldn't be worried about buying the kids gifts. If I had money I would buy you everthing I could and anything you wanted. Life does go own as you mentioned in your letter. Hope you had fun at Barbs and Judy's A ski club sounds interesting, I think it will be easy for you to learn since you already know how to water ski. It would be a great advantage for you to quit smoking, I care for you deeply and would hope that you would. Who knows maybe you will even find a boyfriend or something. If you were going to get me a birthday present please don't. Just knowing that your healthy and happy is enough. The 3d/30 was unexpected and greatly appreciated. Please stay strong and heauthy

love U, Joel

P.S.
Please tell Jenifer I love her and hi

Joel Blaeser
KG, D.C.
303 Court Street
Covington Ky 41011

Brad Blaeser
S/O West Walworth
Whitewater WI, 53190

Oct 3, 1992

Dear Brad

What's up. I am Bored to death here, I am just Awaiting Sentencing. Gatewood Gave me the names of 4 Prison camps, I can request were I want to Go. The 4 are Marion camp-Ill, Oxford camp-WI, morgan town-west virginia, and Eggland Airforce Base-Fl. These are the newest And Best ones. They dont have any Fences The one In Florida even has tennis courts. I will also Be Going to school here Along with working. In some instance you get to leave during the day to go to school and return at night. I am realy curious as to when the next dead show is when (If you do) write me Back can you tell Me when & where the next tour or show is. I Bet it will Be Halloween or New years. Also can u check The microfilm and see if I was in the paper. I was Arrested the First time on April 24th 1992 and the second time Around the middle of may. But the article will Probaly Be on the 24 or 25th of April Because that is when I was officialy Indited. I saw The last 2 Packer Games There looking Pretty Good with Faure as Quarter Back I also saw The Bears choke Against NY. Well Signing OFF   love U
                    Joel

Joel Blaeser
K.C.D.C.
303 Court Street
Covington Ky 41011

Brad Blaeser
510 West Walworth
Whitewater WI 53190

Feb 24, 1993

Bradley
 Whats happening, So your going to the shows say hi to the band for me. I was thinking how sometimes (and it happens to all of us) you feel down about someone and you want to say all the bad things and wrong things about them and it's only cause u care. Well take that same energy and exemplify the good and try to help that person been after all it's because you love that person. No one is perfect. I think that I am going to stick with my appointed attourney. Why pay someone to do the same Job either it can or can't be done. your poems sound real good and one day you will have them in a book I am sure of this. If I were out rite now I would sell books at the shows. especially the ones I am reading. Well I am out of here Be good and Be thankful for what you have love you Joel

Oct 26, 1992

Dear Brad,
 What's up. Sorry I took so long to write back. I am waiting for sentencing. It is on the 17th of November. I can't wait to get to the federal prison and get this bit over with. I also have a chance at the appeal courts. I am not holding my breath. Though I have 3 good main reason for the appeal: Insufficient Evidence, Inadequate Representation, and Misuse of Federal Guidelines.

 It was really warm here today, we had outside recreation, I didn't go though. I read that book Wise Guys by Nick Pileggi it was real good (Based on all true accounts) It took me 10 hrs to finish it. I hope you can get out of your trouble, If you take it to trial and cant afford a lawyer they appoint you one. I thought

I trained you well enough. You did not have to open the door unless they had a search warrant. Then even if they did you could have made them wait until your lawyer came (if you had one) to read it and make sure it was proper.

I didn't remember you mention about the microfilm of newspapers, to check to see if I was in the newspaper. I would appreciate it I was arrested on April 24 1992. 9.AM. I was also curious - remember we went to the Jerry show in Shy Town what was that new song he played, I think someone else sings it too. I have been trying to think of it for a while. has the dead played any shows, are they going to do Halloween. I hope you + Lisa are getting along. I am going to go

love U
Joel

P.S. Thanks for the drawing, I have it hanging on my wall.

Whats up Bro, Thought I would drop u a line. I am pretty sure I have seen that kind of fish before. I will probably be able to get jewelry when I get to the Federal Pen, But not now. I think I have seen Phish in Boulder one time but I cant remember for sure. The pot necklace looks good. Any thing with a pot leaf should sell. I remember the song I was thinking about that Jerry played in Sky you it was Shinning Star. Your P.S. said take a look at your first ad, what did you mean on the envelope? Show it to me again. Next time you write me can u please print or type it is very hard for me to read your cursive.

I dont know if you heard or not But I got my sentenceing postponed till mid decemb we need more time to protest the Pre Sentence Investigation that is what the Judge bases the Sentence on. It looks like I might get 15 to 20 years. I just got done with another book Cold kill, a true Murder Story about 2 lovers who conspire to kill the girls parents. I just started another Book Megatrends 2000. A awsome Book on world & economics and upcomeing trends. I want to get that Book. What a long strange trip its Been. Mom told me that you were wanting them to read it. Well I am Signing off love u Bro

Joel Blaeser

P.S.
A buddy of mine
new the founder

16

Crime School and the Single Cell Organism

OCTOBER, 1995

THE FIRST NIGHT'S SLEEP in Marion was surprisingly easy. I awoke around 5 AM, with a very aroused euphoric energy vacillating between extreme fear and wild wonderment at what lay ahead of me in the days, months, and years to come... I felt a certain sense of convict privilege with a overwhelmingly sinister sense of fame now being one of Marion's alumni. USP Marion was the Super Bowl of all America's prisons in the 1990's, full of Olympic-grade criminals and convicts, How was I to survive among the top 383 most predacious and sophisticated criminals in the entire country? I basked in the glory. My ego loved it. After all, I had to play the part or else become fodder for Marions finest. I had seven more years before I went home, if i made it home. The mania felt like a cocaine high. I would see and hear unreal events unfold in front of my very eyes such as the violent fight between John Gotti and a east coast gang member on an adjoining recreation yard. Beatings, stabbings and viscous brutal attacks on convicts by prison staff at Marion were the order of the day. I paced the tiny cell trying to recall everything I had ever learned or heard about USP Marion. What was general population in Marion going to be like? Who was here now? Somehow this ended up being the genesis of a new spirituality for me. Intuitively I knew if I did not adopt some sort of healthy spiritual practice to fill my time inside this solitary space I would surely go crazy. Aryan Brotherhood Capitan Big Mac Michael McElhiney would teach me yoga through books and discussions. Bruce Pierce, Matrin "Ghetto" Trevino Vargas, James H. "Doc" Holliday, John Gotti, Tyheem, Death Row Gary, and many others would mentor and teach me through my journey through Marion. Lots of the convicts in Marion could be and were cold blooded killers. Even if they befriended me and taught me, it did not mean I was in the clear. In fact, the trickery and sophistication of these men was far beyond anything I had ever encountered in my life, inside or outside the walls, for they could surely outsmart and kill me. The ones who murder you in prison are usually the ones closest to you. After all it was my closest convict associates who told me I had to "hit" Gary in FCI Florence or I would be "dealt with" all for a perceived slight. I would not be so lucky in Marion. If someone had a problem I would be killed or offered up as fodder for another race or gang to do with me as they pleased. I needed to cultivate a stronger convict persona that would keep me safe from convicts and guards alike or else.

I was so so very grateful I did not have to worry about encroaching someone else's territory. In every prison I'd been in, I'd had a cell mate. No more stage fright going number two on the toilet during lock down, every single cell was built for one man only.

Having my very own cell brought a sense of security and privacy not afforded me anywhere else in my life. This at least was one good part about being in Marion.

I had always been a private person, but was forced to share a room with my brother for 17 years. Between my childhood and prison, I rarely had my own room, and was truly grateful to have the solace of my very own space.

My cell was just long enough for me to do a push-up, and just a hair over 5 feet wide. The beds in Marion weren't really beds at all, instead they were six foot blocks of con-crete molded to the floor and wall, only reaching two feet high. To combat the cold of the unforgiving concrete, we were given a three inch thick aqua colored plastic mattress. The bed had standard accouterments. Both the fitted and top sheets were standard prison issue, a grainy cotton and linen mix and were complemented by two gray, very thin wool blankets folded neatly on top of the bed. Finally the odd single luxury USP Marion provided us: a plump, pure down feather pillow, beige with thin navy blue stripes. About three feet above the pillow was an 18 inch cement shelf* mounted to the concrete wall. These shelves were stocked by occupants, most often with a prison TV, radio, and books, as well as the occasion-al personal item. In Marion everyone had the same drab black and white eight inch TV. At the other end of the bed, closest to the bars, was another cement shelf protruding from the wall, which functioned as a nightstand and created the perfect space to read or write while sitting at the end of the cement slab.

Opposite of the cell bars and cell door was a stainless steel outcropping from the wall, consisting of a toilet connected to a stainless steel cabinet, and on top of that a steel sink. The bright blood red cell bars were reflected in the wax of the dark gray floor. The walls were painted a creamy yellow.

The area directly outside the cell was referred to as the range or tier, a fifteen foot wide corridor. Opposite the cell bars was a wall with huge opaque windows with 25 foot high ceilings. As I remember it, each cell block sports 96 cells in Marion, 48 per side, with 24 upper and 24 lower per side, each assigned a letter of the alphabet A through G, It was only during our outside recreation days that we could see people in adjoining recreation yards but did not have physical contact with them or people on the opposite side of our prison unit. We only had access to people in the tier directly above our cells on the second tier. Inside recreation was divided into two groups, morning recreation for upper tier and afternoon recreation for lower tier and outside recreation was both upper and lower tiers every other day.

In summer it was extremely hot and humid. There were no fans and no air conditioning and in winter it was on the cooler side, never warm, but maybe 65 degrees inside the unit. Occasionally for extra punishment the guards in Marion would throw the windows open in the middle of winter dropping the temperature by at least 20 degrees. It at least meant that there was fresh air on the cell range.

Soon breakfast was announced. It must have been 6:30 AM, a sound that would become very familiar while in Marion was the distinct loud clicking noises when all the cell doors were simultaneously opening up along with some guard with a strong southern drawl yelling "Chow!" or "Come and get it!" According to protocol at Marion, we were never to leave our cells for chow. We were instead supposed to receive our meals on enclosed plastic trays handed to us by prison staff through a small slot in your cell door. This policy was pri-marily implemented for the safety of the guards. The only possible contact between prison staff and inmates during chow would be if someone shoved a hand through the single meal slot where the trays of food were pushed through. Otherwise, staff were barricaded behind two rows of thick bars, which were also surrounded by Lexan, a bulletproof plastic glass. There was a complex system of pulleys, levers and gears, sheathed in metal above each cell door, which allowed the prison guards to control individual cell doors, or the entire cell block, without ever having to step foot in the actual housing unit. Instead, they operated the doors from outside the cell range, even during chow.

Still, about half the meals we had in Marion were retrieved by the inmates instead of receiving food in our cell. I don't know whether these mealtimes were granted to our cell block as a reward, or if they occurred because of sheer laziness on the guards' behalf. Or perhaps it was simply an attempt at entertainment for the guards; after all, meal time was one of the most dangerous times for convicts in Marion.

Unlike every other prison I'd been to, there were no separate lines for chow; all inmates, white and minority alike, would line up to grab trays from the slot. There was only a two minute window to grab your food before the large metal cell doors would slide shut, and you were expected to be on the right side of those doors, whether you got food or not. Cell doors would open and you would proceed down the range to the front of the unit to receive food trays through the slots and then have to go back to your cell and after all trays were handed out the cell doors were all closed at the same time. I would later learn all cells in Marion had bars on the front of them except the boxcars in the hole. Convicts could gang up on a weaker man, enter his cell and once locked in proceed to kill or rape and no one would notice for another 40 minutes. There were plenty of convicts locked away in Marion for over a decade. In any case, a hardened criminal locked up for 23 hours in a shoe box made for some creative entertainment, most of which was violently brutal and heinous.

Despite the limited time frame to retrieve the trays and get back to your cell, chow was when the most violence occurred. The moment you walk to the window to grab your tray, your back is turned to the entire unit. Often, the weapon was something simple, like the wooden prison-issued radio put inside of the prison-issued heavy webbed laundry bag, then swung overhead in a twirling motion as hard as possible just as someone turns to grab their tray hitting them on top of the head. This happened once or twice a month while I was in Marion. If someone was killed or brutalized in any unit, all of Marion's cell blocks would go on lock down and convicts would be confined to their cells, with no chance at coming out for any reason whatsoever for at least 3 or 4 days and sometimes up to 2 weeks.

People did not just randomly get beat up, raped, or killed in Marion. Such a small window of opportunity meant it was almost always pre-meditated. If someone had a problem with you they would very rarely challenge you to a fight here or anywhere, but instead just take you out, often for something as trivial as perceived disrespect. The most valuable weapon in Marion was surprise, which in turn meant your odds of defending such attack diminish significantly. This environment fostered a sub-conscious hyper-awareness within me; I made a point of constantly being aware of everything around me at all times. My best chance for survival here was to be a politician as opposed to a warrior.

In Marion when the "deuces are dialed" about 70 prison guards flock to where the fight is. They enter the block yelling as loudly as possible for everyone to get down on the ground, batons swinging mercilessly. Usually the combatants continue to fight. You will immediately regret it if you don't hit the floor in time; not only will you get beat down on their way in, the guards also give an extra beating to anyone they catch standing. They are relentless in the punishment of the inmates caught fighting, it's payback for putting the staff in danger. A fight is the only time prison staff in Marion will be next to un-handcuffed, and unshackled general population convicts. Even if you are laying on the ground, they give you a couple of a shots to the ribs with the baton just to show you who's boss.

During the two minute meal-time tray retrieval we also had access to a hot water spigot. Unlike all the other prisons I'd been to, Marion did not have a microwave. This was because a microwave could potentially be very dangerous. A 32 ounce coffee mug available at the prison commissary for $1.50 could become a weapon in and of itself. If filled with the appropriate liquid, such as a combination of baby oil and hot water, it essentially became a heated bomb. Once thrown on someone's face, the oil would stick and burn the skin right off. Skin grafts would be a necessity if you lived through the beating that would follow the hot oil assault. That said, the 185 degree water from the spigot would certainly disfigure someone, and distract them long enough for a potentially fatal beating.

We were counted every four hours and the numbers are reported and passed along to the Bureau of Prison's headquarters along with data from every prison in the Federal prison system. That first morning after breakfast, a blond guard with a severely burnt face walked the cell block incessantly counting us.

I foolishly made a wisecrack about it as he passed my cell. "Red face when do we get recreation?" I said.

He must have been sensitive about it because he literally bristled, but his voice remained calm as he reminded me "You'd better tone it down if you don't want any trouble." Despite the fact that the demonstration at our arrival was still fresh in my mind, I remained disillusioned about the true freedom exercised by the guards here in Marion. I also felt part of something bigger having been sent to Marion because of the crack law riots, and that sense of belonging gave me a false sense of security. I still held onto a misplaced faith that the system would protect my most basic rights.

Meanwhile, I settled into a nice routine in Marion. We passed the time by listening to our prison-issued radios, or watching the six channels on the prison-issued television. I read most of the time, worked out, and did yoga. TV did not come on until after dinner except on weekends. I was having thoughts that Marion is just what I needed to get me ready for the free world. I sold heroin and marijuana in three other federal prisons, and although I wanted to get out, I had just enough distractions at those other prisons to keep me from putting 110% into getting out of prison or preparing for it. Jerry Garcia's death was the beginning of my wake up call and that was only 65 days ago. Marion was my sixth federal prison. I stopped selling drugs before I went to prison because I did not want to end up here. Certain thoughts again started to creep in my mind, the declaration to my family that I was going to stop selling LSD because I did not want to go to prison, followed by getting federally indicted on a 19 count federal indictment about nine months after that declaration, for something that happened almost two years prior.

I started a grateful journal within days of arrival, my first ever, writing in it every morning 10 things I was grateful for, 10 toes and 10 fingers regularly made the list, along with healthy private bowel movements.

While in Marion, my physical, internal, and external health were becoming even more exquisite. I woke up at 5:30am every day drinking 32 ounces of water the minute of awakening. Then 45 minutes of deep breathing, proceeding into an ancient style of yoga that was basically formed from the 900 or so positions a human baby does naturally in the mother's womb before birth.

Soon after my arrival in Marion, I befriended a very high-ranking shot caller from an extremely well known notorious american prison gang. One day Big "Mac" Mike McElhiney came by my cell during inside recreation. "Hey Blaeser! You ever practice yoga? I am Mac. Call me Mac."

Mac's reputation preceded him. Days earlier, during inside recreation, Death Row Gary mentioned Mac was a major shot caller and captain for the Aryan Brotherhood.

"I am Joel, and no, I've never really done yoga before. I stretch a lot though."

Mac continued, "We do yoga everyday, good for the mind and body. It will help you. You look like a good white dude and you have a outdate."

How did he know I had an outdate?

Having a outdate was good and a curse, as most of the people in Marion have a life sentence and sometimes they will kill you just so you don't go home, this is only out of jealousy because they are leaving in a pine box. It was almost unheard of for any inhabitants of Marion to have a outdate.

"Thank you Mac,"

I said as he rested a book in between two of my cell bars. Mac was heavily tattooed with huge hands on a very lean and muscular body. His voice was deep, confident and steady.

The Aryan Brotherhood along with the Black Guerilla Family and La Eme are all elite prison gangs and forces to be reckoned with in the higher security prisons especially USP Marion.

The book was called *The Complete Illustrated Book of Yoga"* by Swami Vishnu Devananda.

"Joel, I do yoga every morning and I suggest you do the same. I am going to workout now. See you later!"

"Thank you Mac."

I read the book that day and started practicing the next morning, slowly incorporating the book's positions into my morning routine. I never felt better in prison. Ironically, the horrors of incarceration were introducing me to myself in a way like never before. I was trying to make progress in all areas of my life, mind, body and spirit, and even though this was the scariest place on earth, I had the most secure feeling when inside my cell, even more than when I was physically free. I felt almost more free in the mornings practicing this yoga routine than I had ever felt in the free world.

My nightly dreams were clearly helping me forgive my father and all his outrageous beatings of me as a very young child. We would meet and talk it out or I would end up saving him after my furious bike ride home. I had no cravings for drugs or booze, and although I wanted to desperately get out and go home, there was an overwhelming sense that everything was going to work out, and that I would not serve longer than five years of my 12 year and seven month sentence. (Which was reduced to ten years because of a LSD law change.)

Staff at Marion were always arbitrarily moving convicts from unit to unit without any warning whatsoever. About two weeks later during inside recreation, Mac came to the front of my cell and pulled out a piece of sharp thick stainless steel and asked if I could "hold" it for him. I was stunned and amazed that he had this piece of steel in such a high-security prison. By this time, I was starting to become more of a seasoned convict, but this scenario represented an extreme dilemma. I had an appeal under review based on another recent law change and if I won I would be instantly released from prison. On the other hand, if I were to get caught with this piece of steel, we were talking at least three years added to my sentence, not to mention a severe beating by Marion's finest. But Mac was white, and I was white. Weapons were good to have because you never knew when a battle might arise. To stay alive in Marion I had to think critically and act critically. I respected Mac, but would have been stupid to not be intimidated by him at the same time. Taking this piece could save my life in a fight or get me an extra ten years because the courts might perceive it as murder. Telling Mac no could mean adversity from him and his set also causing me to get into harms way or lose any chance of protection. Conditions and politics changed immensely since Sandstone and I had to adapt as it was happening. As Mac pulled the piece of steel out it was as if all time stopped. Yes was not an option, but I had to be diplomatic.

I looked him straight in the eye.

"At this time I cannot hold that."

He replied with a perfect poker face,

"It's all good, don't sweat it."

He took the piece of steel and continued down the tier.

"Later Joel!"

"Word Big Mac!"

Right or wrong I felt more awake for life during that decision and in Marion in general. I was feeling awake and present for the very first time in my life, looking at each and every decision I made and how it could or would affect me. Mac had the piece of steel and I knew it. That was a big enough liability in it of itself. I had access to it if i needed it. I didn't need to hold it as well or so I thought.

There was never any mention of it again. During outside recreation, Mac and I would play tennis after I got done running. It was the oddest thing. The balls were old, courts slightly cracked, the tennis rackets were rickety, and the nets were barely hanging, but we played anyway. C unit was the only unit that had access to the larger prison rec yard, all the other units in Marion had their own yards, about 1/8 the size of the large yard. If I missed a shot I was in trouble,

"Mother fucker I will throw this racket at you if you miss another shot,"

Mac would bellow out. It was Mac's way of being a brother to me in a hard knock sort of style. And sometimes he would throw it at me anyway, but only when he missed a shot. We would then laugh incessantly.....On a real good day the guards would let us stay out for 90 minutes or even 2 hours. Within three or four weeks, Mac was mysteriously removed from C block to another unit. He was a good person to be allied with in prison. I was aware that I could easily be killed or offered up if Mac and I got into any sort of conflict for any reason, yet he befriended me and I survived Marion so far.

Once a month prison guards would drop off a box of recent popular magazines to each cell block. On this lucky day we were first out to inside recreation and I had my pick of the litter. I chose a few women's magazines and a men's health magazine. There were 25 or so to chose from and I chose three. Once finished I would pass them down the line to the other convicts. Many of the women's magazines had sample pages of the latest fragrances in them. Champs Elysees by Guerlain was my favorite. Once the tore out flap was glued on my cell air vent via toothpaste my whole cell would smell like a sensual woman for days. At night when I masturbated it made for even more of an intense orgasm as I could pretend there was a woman with me.

All of my property was destroyed in Talladega, except for my legal paperwork which I'd grabbed right before the guards rushed our unit during the riot. I would regularly read and reread my trial transcripts, focusing especially on the part where the judge had dismissed the jurors. It had to have been something significant for him to have had the jurors leave the courtroom, but the only instance recorded was that he had asked the prosecutors how they planned to prosecute the case without physical evidence.

In Marion, your access to the law library was through written request only, and they would bring the specific law books to your cell. This severely slowed my process as I was scouring law books on a variety of topics regarding criminal procedure before I found what I was looking for. I literally yelled "Eureka!" when I found what the judge was referring to during trial: other act evidence. The prosecutor's main strategy was using other act evidence, which at the time was not allowed unless specifically asked for during the discovery process (which happens before the trial) and getting permission granted from the judge and defendant's lawyer. I was charged with ten counts of interstate commerce, and nine counts of money laundering. The case was tried like a conspiracy case and had very little other evidence at trial. I was never caught with drugs ever in my life—no pipes, no paraphernalia—nothing ever. I screamed so loud in Marion the whole cell block heard me. I quickly remembered where I was.

"Blaeser what happening down there?"

Big Moe shouted back at me.

Dirk piped up,

"He must have drained his blue balls with a knee buckler Moe!"

"No no, I just read this letter and my family is doing well and they sent me some dollar bills, that's all."

I said in a calm steady voice.

Moe and Dirk came on the bus with me and were heavily tattooed, huge, muscular members of a Los Angeles street gang who were busted for trafficking crack cocaine.

"Ok, sounds like you might be going home or something."

"Yeah I wish!" I quickly yelled back."

Jealousy and envy can be brutal when everyone has 25 years or life. This was hard at first but now my life depended on it, no one in Marion could know the truth about my case at all, it was bad enough I only had 7 years to go.

When you're locked down for 23 hours a day, and want to pass a note, an item, or a secret message to someone, you go fishing. You unthread part of a bed sheet, make a long line, tie the item with a small weight, like a piece of soap, two or three pencils, or a rolled up empty tube of tooth paste. Then you reach your hand out the bars on the floor, fling it down the tier, and then pull the line up with the item to the cell you are trying to reach. You watch with your small plastic mirror (purchased at commissary) to make sure you get it where it's supposed to go. Usually other convicts will help to get it where it needs to go.

Some of the American black prisoners were masters at communication and have this sophisticated and rare form of dialect of ebonics depending upon what city they came from. This was in addition to speaking perfectly fluent english. I first really became acquainted with this form of communication in FCI Englewood. It is fascinating and confusing to hear, something I could never ever understand, sort of a cross between pig latin and real broken English with a twist. It was rare to hear and for the most part if you wanted to get a message across, prisoners were relegated to "flying a kite" as we say in the big house.

I got one such item, and the red-faced guard walked by and yelled at me. "Blaeser if you fly any more kites you won't get recreation for a week!"

I quickly retorted,

"What ever you say red man."

He scowled at me and then walked off. I was waiting for books to be sent. The law library finding was good for me, but the wheels of justice were slow at best. I still had my 2255 habeas corpus appeal, which could be appealed again for years to come, and could easily eat up five to seven years until finally settled. My strategy was to get out now. In hindsight, with all the big players I knew, I could have easily called the FBI and turned state's evidence and got out that way., it could not get any worse I thought, and being a rat meant a life sentence of dishonor., I felt a certain sense of nobility not telling on anyone and taking my sentence like a real man, like John Gotti, Doc Halliday, Big Mac McElhiney, Bruce Pierce, Death Row Gary, and most of the people I came across in Marion, in direct contrast to the percentages of people in all the other state and federal prisons. Well over half of the people in Marion at this time had taken to their case to jury trial, starkly contrasting the national stats of more than 90% who plead guilty in their criminal cases. This strengthened a weird sense of belonging and self-recognition within me.

Outdoor recreation occurred every other day. November came quick, and with it came lots of cold, rainy weather. When the weather was bad, almost no one went but Rigo, a half black, half Puerto Rican convict and I. On one particularly cold rainy November day, the guards left the two of us out for three and a half hours. I was overjoyed. Having been born in Chicago, and lived a long time in Wisconsin, I was very acclimated to cold weather, so this was a treat. I never let on how much I enjoyed the cold weather on outside recreation days. They surely thought they were punishing us. Rigo started to complain about his frozen feet as we were walking the track.

"Joel my feet are freezing! I want to stop walking around the track."

"Rigo, no no. We must keep moving or you will freeze., wiggle your toes vigorously as we walk, ok?"

"What are you talking about?"

"Did you put the commissary plastic bags in your shoes like I mentioned yesterday?"

"Yes I did."

"Ok so your feet are dry. "come on, just keep walking and wiggle the shit shit out of your goddam toes. it will increase circulation."

"Ok white boy, we'll see!"

Rigo was a puerto rican gang member from Queens, New York doing 38 years for 15 kilos of cocaine and major weapons charges. He was in Marion for an escape attempt during the Crack Law riots in FCI Tennessee. The cold rainy weather continued all through the month and soon I was the only one going outside for recreation. The very next session of outdoor recreation, I was told to get ready by Red Face. About thirty minutes had passed, and everyone else declined rec. I started to yell for my rec, and Red Face came by my cell and said I wasn't getting my rec that day. I welled up with anger I let my emotions get the best of me, and I retorted back in a loud surly tone,

"Motherfucker, I will do you like Tommy Silverstein if I don't get rec today."

He stood stunned in silence.

"Oh ok, hold on a minute,"

he said.

Within ten minutes every single prison guard in the entire prison of USP Marion was paraded by my cell. One by one they walked by in a huge line stretching from one end of the cell block to another, well over 75 of them. Red Face told the guards as they passed my cell. They all looked me in the eyes and said,

"You fucked up, motherfucker. We're going to get you. Watch your back, asshole."

"Who in the fuck do you think you are? "....

"You're leaving in a box asshole. "

"We going to send Big Black Larry into this cell block., he loves nice smooth skin on long- haired white boys like you."

Big Black Larry was legendary throughout the system and until now I thought it was part myth, but apparently Larry loved to perform fellatio on younger looking men and if you did not let him do the deed, he would beat you down or knock you out until you did, only to wake up with him sucking you off and one of his fingers shoved up your ass going in and out......

The remarks continued,

"Who do you think you are Blaeser?, Your asshole will be filled with cum before you leave here!", " Piece of shit! We will get you!".

Other convicts were stunned and reminded me of how someone could be killed by the the "Brand" (code for Aryan Brotherhood) just for mentioning Silversteins name on the tier.

Moe, my cell neighbor, said

"Blaeser you got balls but I would not want to be in your shoes, not for a million dollars."

"Blaeser what the fuck did you say or do!" other inmates yelled down the tier. I sat silent, numb and in shock.

I had no clue as to the seriousness of what I just said. I knew the whole history before I ever got to Marion. In my naïve, hippy-ish, ignorant way, I still thought I was untouchable. I had no clue how bad I just screwed up. It would be many weeks before I had a sense of the wound I opened up.

The day before New Year's Eve, a tall blond guard yelled through the front of the cell block loudly

"Blaeser, you got a visit!"

Our tier was out at inside recreation, but I was allowed to go into my cell and comb my hair. It was very long (twelve to fourteen inches) and all the same length. I had not started working out yet, so I was not sweaty. I had never had a visit here in Marion. It was cold out, but the sun was shining. The dull hue of the cell block walls had a slight glow to them because of the sun shining through all of the windows-a definite plus.

Holidays in prison were tough at best, an air of melancholy would engulf the prison when the holidays like Easter, Christmas, New Year's Eve, 4th of July, and Halloween would come around. It was almost tangible. Fighting would die down, people would talk less, laugh less, the chow time was quieter, prison staff was a little nicer, the food was little bit nicer, bigger meals with better cuts of meat. Christmas was especially difficult. Barely a word is uttered during chow or in the chow hall. Everyone attending is somber, and intense. During Christmas time there was always some sort of Christmas basket that each prisoner would get from the prison, usually a basket of some specialty food items like crackers, jellies, cookies, cheeses, nuts, etc. It was this weird juxtaposition of humanity and severity. I was always grateful to get it and dumbfounded at the same time.

    I always kept my hair in a ponytail and still did not cut it. Roy's warning 25 months before still resonated in my mind...."If someone gets a hold of a piece of your hair while you are not looking, you can easily be brought down to the ground, and or distracted while someone else cuts your jugular vein". Roy continued "Ninety-five percent of the body's blood passes through these veins, and that's why, on average, it takes 30 minutes or so to fully stop a shaving abrasion on the face, or a cut to the mouth from chewing tobacco". Expounding further during my first shot of heroin he assured me jugular veins are not protected by bone or cartilage, which makes them susceptible to damage. Due to the large volumes of blood that flow through these veins, damage to the jugulars can quickly cause significant blood loss, leading to hypovolaemic shock, and then death if not treated. With a large cut to the jugular, you have three to four minutes before the majority of the blood is out of your body. This is common knowledge among most prisoners, Once cut inside a prison it will take a minimum of three to four minutes just for staff to arrive and assess the scene, and another one to two minutes to get you to the prison infirmary (if it is not a larger incident). Being that there is very little protection for the jugular, it is quite easy to sever it with a little pre-dawn practice in your cell. A sharp knife or point fashioned from a pencil or piece of plastic and the element of surprise, and you're 80% there. The jugular vein is on both sides of the head, running up and down from the back of the jaw (bottom of the ear) down the outside of the neck to the shoulders. I was always taught the left side was the best to hit because it is the closest to the heart, and would empty the body's blood faster.

    So, I proceeded to undo my ponytail, combed my hair, and pulled it back into a ponytail again, brushed my teeth, and yelled to the guard to open up my cell. Everyone was out on the range working out, or talking to people on the second tier. It was not unlike any other day of inside recreation for us.

    I thought to myself about what the visit was going to be like. I remembered Ghetto telling me to give John (John Gotti) his regards out at visit if I ever saw him there. I proceeded towards the front of the cell block, down by where we get food next to the showers. There was a double set of bars. After I walked through the first set of bars, one guard yelled to the other one at the controls with a big brass handle, "Clear!"

The first set of bars slid closed, blocking me off from the rest of the unit. There was another set of bars blocking me from prison staff. There was a small slot on the bar door waist-high, and a small slot ankle-high. About two weeks earlier I was called for a visit and I flat out refused. I knew no one was coming to visit me and I suspected it was a ruse to get me out of the cell block so the guards could retaliate against me for my stupid emotional outburst. This time I knew my mother was coming to see me. My rationale was that as long as I was around other inmates, I could at least have witnesses to an incident if they tried to get to me. I believed that with a real visitor I would be ok.

"Cuff up and turn around. Get your back against the bars Blaeser!" As I did, I could feel the heavy cold steel of the leg irons go on (pretty much a larger version of handcuffs with a chain about twelve inches long). Then, instead of handcuffing me behind my back, they put a belly chain on me and handcuffed me in front. I suspected why. It turns out all prisoners are brought out to visits with belly chains so as to not upset people from the free world who come in to visit. I had never witnessed anyone being brought in or out of a cell block in Marion handcuffed in front. Even when we went to outside recreation we were handcuffed behind our backs and outfitted with leg irons before we left our cells and came in contact with prison staff. It was at least two guards per convict, and three if they suspected you of potential danger, which was basically everyone. We were always handcuffed behind our backs, and had leg irons, with one guard holding the cufflinks, raising them so you were forced to lean forward as you walked. The leg irons only allowed you to take small steps, and then two guards flanked you with long, thick, combat-grade, wooden nightsticks lined with heavy gage steel rods for bone-breaking ability.

"Are we going to have any trouble out of you?" Blondie asked when I was done being belly-chained and handcuffed. He had his nightstick out and was swinging it into his hand, and was staring straight into my eyes.

He was the one two weeks prior who tried to lure me out for my supposed visit. I knew my mother was coming today, but really started to wonder if that was such a good idea. I shook my head to Blondie.

"Nope, no trouble out of me."

"Good. Because if you give us any trouble we will kill you," he scowled out with a disturbing grimace. I played a lot of seven-card stud poker in prison, and although I did not plan to give any more trouble to staff in Marion, I knew he was not bluffing. Clutts, the prison guard who was murdered by Tommy Silverstein for being mean to him, must have been friends with Blondie, or perhaps Blondie was just down with his pack of wild dogs. He and one other guard took me out to the visiting room. Biesner was your typical hillbilly. He smelled like cheap musk aftershave and was about five feet ten inches tall with a receding pepper gray hairline. He had a decent beer belly and weighed maybe 220 pounds. He wore a blue clip-on tie, with a white short-sleeve shirt tucked into blue polyester slacks, and a thin black belt with a square chrome clasp. He also had on black leather loafers, and a thin silver name tag above his left shirt pocket. Blondie had the same uniform on.

I took comfort in the fact that my mother was here for the next three days, and that they couldn't possibly do anything now because of my visitor. As they spun me around, there was a big flight of stairs in front of me—about six steps. The cement was dark and grey in color, not like the shiny waxed look of the cell block floors. The lighting was dim. The box with all of the gears in it was open—I could smell the gear grease—and the big brass handle* that stuck out. I gazed with wonderment. This intricate contraption that was powered by hand. The big brass handle was connected to a gear, and in turn that was connected to another set of gears. At the top were levers in a steel frame with notches in it. It looked like some weird hand powered motor with lots of gears, wheels and pulleys in it.

Blondie put his nightstick on my shoulder with a pretty good thud and said "Keep your eyes forward! Inmates are not allowed to see inside the box."

"It is a security breach!" Biesner broke his silence.

They were now talking to me in a normal tone of voice and it eased my fears of them beating me up or killing me. As the door closed to the box, the third guard locked it up with a big padlock, and it just looked like a very large box sticking out from a wall with a lock on it.

We proceeded up the stairs, around a corner, and passed a little office where they would sit, and into a very brightly lit hallway painted in bright white, with light blue speckled linoleum tiled floors that were buffed to a super high gloss.

We went through a series of similar hallways and locked steel and glass doors, through another hallway, and out to the visiting room. The visiting area consisted of a long row of booths, individual from one another on the prisoner side-a big Plexiglas box framed in thick steel with a steel door to enter. Opposite the door was a huge steel framed Plexiglas window, and on the other side of that is where the visitors would sit. There were partitions in the visiting room on the visitor's side so each visitor from the free world side was quasi-separated from the person next to them. The partitions only stuck out about 36 inches from the Plexiglas. On the convict side, you were in a glass box. You could look left to right and see all the convicts who were there visiting, and you could see the people who were visiting the convicts next to you. The visiting room was a bright room with waxed linoleum floors, and looked like freedom. There were no real signs that one was in a prison, looking out.

It just happened that John Gotti was right next to me, "Excuse me Mr Gotti, my name is Joel." He turned to look, "Ghetto asked me to send you his regards."

"You must have saw him in the hole," he responded.

"Yes."

"Thank you. Tell him I say hello."

"I will. Sorry for disturbing your visit."

"Don't worry about it."

I sat down to say hello to my mom.

"Hi Mom." She was a little star-struck and could not take her eyes off Gotti. "Mom!" I said loudly. "Here I am! You are visiting me! Stop staring!" We talked for six hours straight. Her hair had gone all gray since I had entered prison 39 months earlier.

I sat down on a metal chair welded to the floor. There was a phone that you had to hold during the visit to talk through. We talked about a whole range of subjects. I was happy to see her. It was a great visit. I had a prison meal during the visit. It came in the same three inch thick insulated plastic tray as in the cell blocks with a multi-course prison meal of corn, beans, rice, bread and meat loaf with juice of course. No fancy spices on it but, salt, pepper and some imagination.

When visiting was over, there were convicts to the left of me, and convicts to the right of me still in the visiting booths, but for some reason they took me out last. When John Gotti left he said "They must have some special interest in you, taking you out last for some reason."

"Yes, just my lucky day I guess." Another peculiar thing was they handcuffed me behind the back this time. Biesner had a really disturbing look on his face. Burns was putting on the leg irons when a wave of fear came over me. It quickly came and went. I thought about my visit with my mother tomorrow on New Year's Day. The outside of the visiting room was eerily quiet. There was no one around, and silence except for the chains jingling. They opened up the door and they said to step back. I stepped backwards and one of them grabbed my handcuffs and the other one had his nightstick out. We began to walk back the same way we came many hours before, through the first set of doors to this big room, which led to a very long hallway back to the unit. Halfway through that room, I felt a big tug on my ponytail from my left side. I started to fall to the floor. I double stepped, but to no avail. I tripped and fell straight to my side. As I fell onto my left side straight to the floor, I could feel Biesner hitting me to the back of my jaw—he wanted to break my jaw and knock me out. I still couldn't comprehend what was going on. For a second I thought someone attacked me from behind. It was a fleeting thought. The only thing I could do was to try to curl up in a ball. Burns had my handcuffs firmly in his grip. I pulled my knees up to my stomach in the fetal position as I hit the ground, and kept trying to roll away from the punches.

Burns and Biesner were Southern hillbillies at their finest, as Biesner was repeatedly hitting me in the jaw and side of the face. Burns was beating my feet with his nightstick. All of a sudden I heard the body alarm go off. The body alarm was a GPS signal that brought all the other guards running. I must have accidentally kicked one of their walkie talkies and armed it. Before I knew it, 50 more prison guards would be barrelling down on me. I knew there would be a brief increase in people beating me, but it also meant it would soon stop. Hearing the alarm this time was music to my bloody ears. After they subdued me-which was a joke because I was already shackled and handcuffed—they stood me up and I could feel warm blood running down the side of my face. My right eye was swollen shut. My jaw was definitely not broken, but my ear, lips, and cheek on my right side were swollen. As they stood me up, I could feel the warmth and numbness of the swelling on the right side of my face. My feet felt like they had bee stings all over them. Intermittently they went numb.

"He tried to head butt us," Biesner said.

I retorted that they had attacked me. "I did not they attacked me."

Some petite brunette, very good looking prison guard wheeled in some sort of re-straining wheelchair contraption and wheeled me off to the hospital. I was wondering how they were going to cover this up. In the infirmary the doctor sat me on a bed. I did not have enough strength to keep my back straight, and was slouched over. The doctor felt my jaw, teeth, feet, and looked at my nose.

"You're pretty lucky Mr. Blaeser—no broken bones and no loose teeth. How did this happen?" he asked. "You have very nice straight white teeth, you're young, and have a whole life ahead of you."

As I sat there, my fear turned to rage. I knew it was over, but wondered about seeing my mother tomorrow. They got me back for what I had said. I knew this would be another badge of honor among the convicts of Marion. I felt disgust for Burns and Biesner, and thought about exacting my revenge in the form of brutal violence.

The staff lieutenant had an incident report for assaulting an officer, and a statement already prepared with this elaborate confession written out. This proved this was in fact a multi-part conspiracy to get me back. I thought about whether I would be able to see my mother the next day. There was no way they would let me see her. I was beat halfway beyond recognition. Biesner and Blondie suddenly appeared and started getting in my face saying if I didn't sign it, they would kill me. Blondie started swinging his nightstick with full force right next to my head. I could feel the wind from it. It kept getting closer and closer, finally just barely nicking the back of my skull.

"Blaeser I reiterate. You're a good looking fellow, and will be going home in a few years. Just sign it," the doctor pleaded in a more compassionate and convincing tone.

He was so calm and straight faced, as if everything was hunky-dory. I thought about how I was such a good convict at all of the places I did time—Sandstone, Englewood, Florence, Pekin, Talladega—because of the fact that I never told or cooperated and took the government to trial. I thought that signing the statement was weak. I thought if I didn't sign it, they would hang me up and make it look like suicide. I thought about what my mom would go through if they murdered me and made it look like a suicide. The hardest part of doing time was what my family—specifically my mother-was going through, thinking about what I was going through inside these walls.

I did not want to sign it. My head was numb and warm. I would not have felt much more pain. As the nightstick nicked the back of my head, I relented and signed it. They then brought me to the hole; they brought me way to the back, down a bunch of steps, to the dreaded boxcars. Once there, I was shackled and chained to a cement slab, one with no green mat and it had big iron hooks sticking out of the cement, probably something like the bow-els of a slave ship from the 1800's. They were called the boxcars because it was a room inside of a room inside the hole. The larger room was Plexiglas and steel, and the second in-side room was bars and Plexiglas. It was such that the prison staff could reach in and unlock the leg irons from the big steel eye hooks on the cement slab by my feet so I could go to the bathroom and eat. They kept the handcuffs on but put them in front of me. When they first brought me there, they strapped me to the cement slab, handcuffing and shackling me to the hooks overnight. My neighbor was Tyheem, a convict who was a native Brooklynite. He had just got into it with another convict over the morning newspaper and beat him up pretty bad, so they threw Tyheem in the boxcars while the other ended up in the prison infirmary. He had a strange sort of respect from the prison staff in the hole.

In the morning they said they were going to keep me shackled by my feet onto the hooks, but would unhook my handcuffs from the side hooks. Tyheem convinced a morning guard to give me one of his ex-tra pillows. "Yo boss man give him one of my pillows. They beat that man halfway beyond recognition."

The pot bellied-southern guard who I never saw before said, "Blaeser this is your lucky day. Don't say I gave this to you neither." Lord knows how Tyheem got it. I was so thankful.

"What's your name?"

"Tyheem"

"Thank you Tyheem."

"What happened to you? Who did you fight? What's your name?"

"The guards got me back for something I said."

"What did you say?" Tyheem yelled out.

"I will tell you tonight when no one else is listening."

With this standard, prison-issued, down feather pillow, with dark blue stripes, I was ecstatic. Now the cement slab would not feel so hard. When feeding time was over, I still had my handcuffs on, and they could reach through and lock my leg irons back to the steel eye hook.

Tyheem was a character and we talked into the wee hours of the night about a lot of subjects. It was very dimly lit by the boxcars. I was an instant celebrity with Tyheem for having taken such a whipping from the prison staff. Later that night, after I told him the whole story he was in disbelief that they did not kill me just for saying Tommy Silverstein's name to them, let alone threatening them with his name.

By the third morning, the prison staff removed my leg irons and handcuffs. I still had to sleep on that cement slab for 11 more days. I was given a ticket, or shot, for assaulting the staff, a pretty serious infraction, and I knew it would follow me around in that prison and others if I was lucky enough to leave MARION alive. I was also assigned a disciplinary hearing, at which I was given 90 days in the hole, 12 of which I'd already served. Ultimately, I would spend six and a half months in the hole, with no phone calls and no way to tell my mother I was ok. No radio, no TV, no commissary except absolute necessities like toothpaste and shampoo, and of course only getting recreation for one hour on Mondays, Wednesdays, and Fridays. Again, we did not get any recreation after a fight or beating in another unit. Being in the hole we would usually see some of the carnage after a fight or brutal attack because the convicts would get sent to the hole after the incident and the entire prison would again be on indefinite lockdown until staff arbitrarily lifted it.

Tyheem and I enjoyed each other's company for about 14 days total. We would rile each other up intellectually, broaching every subject under the sun. He loved to read the section of *USA Today* that talked about the favorite books of big corporate CEOs.

"Joel I have this book, *Christianity Through the Ages*, and this dude who turned that bankrupt airline all the way around? This is his favorite book."

"Sounds like a good book Ty, It sounds like its about how Christianity was marketed all through the ages."

"You a smart white boy, hey!" If it is good enough for that CEO it is good enough for me. I am half way through it. It's in my temporarily confiscated property, and I will get it back when I get out of the hole."

He was soon to be going home and vowed he was done dealing drugs. He continued, "I want a real life, with barbecues and ball games, waking up with morning breath next to my girlfriend with morning breath. I am a believer!" he exclaimed.

He had about 9 months left on his sentence. I was in Marion about 70 days and already had a first-class ticket in the boxcars.

He told me about the supposed crack riot in Lewisburg, Pennsylvania. He said that all the convicts on the yard made a pact not to riot, but that prison staff was trying to instigate a riot so all of the prison staff could get triple time pay, as a riot is the only time prison staff can get triple time pay. The fact that Lewisburg Penitentiary was such a high-security prison, not having a riot was miraculous in and of itself. After it was clear that they weren't going to riot, a full 24 hours after Talladega finished rioting, the prison staff locked down the prison, and started removing prisoners from their cells. Tyheem and many other convicts allege they beat them in front of the other prisoners and then charged that as a riot. This served two ends. One was to instigate other prisoners to be violent towards other staff, and to get Lewisburg on riot status in order to get triple time wages.

"Wow that is quite a story Tyheem."

"Yeah. They wrote shots for like 200 of us for instigating a riot and shipped eight of us to Marion. None of us were charged in a outside court because it was all a ruse to get triple time pay."

After I left the hole, and upon interviewing other people from Lewisburg out in the general population, I got the same story. Each prison sent between five and 20 of the so-called instigators to Marion. Marion itself was on the verge of closing down before the riots occurred. It had been discovered that there were mass amounts of asbestos and lead in Marion, and I was told a federal judge agreed with a lawsuit brought about by an inmate. However the mass riots that occurred in the prison system caused Marion to get a waiver from the courts and stay open. The other convicts I interviewed about Lewisburg all told a similar story, and most lived in different housing units.

There was a silver lining to all of this. The first was being graced with the presence of a man named Ghetto, aka Martin Trevino Vargas, one of the most intelligent men I have ever met. A career criminal by trade, I'd met Ghetto when I first arrived in Marion. I was put into a unit temporarily for only a few days, and it was there I made Ghetto's acquaintance. He struck me as an intelligent and cunning, but kind, individual. We instantly hit it off as a father son type of thing. Then without warning I was moved to another unit, and didn't see him again until now. He was a American-born Mexican who spoke fluent French, English, Spanish and Italian. He started getting into trouble a long long time ago and first cut his teeth on the streets of East LA. Ghetto had been in the hole for quite some time and the prison staff feared him being alongside other convicts and inmates. He was very smart and that meant he was considered extremely dangerous by prison staff. He was sent to Marion under suspicion of undue influence upon staff members at another high security federal prison, though his original crime was armed robbery.

Time has a different pace, and different value in prison. In Marion especially, where you are supposed to be limited to one hour a day of human contact, it seems especially slow. This can and certainly has driven men crazy. But freedom also has a double meaning. There's the tangible, being out of these walls and into the real world, and then there is freedom as a state of mind. Most convicts inside the walls have a hobby, a project, or a dream to keep them sane. Often it is something like working toward their appeal or developing an interest in law. For Ghetto, it was becoming a teacher of philosophy and the world, and I was an ideal student. I had a burning desire to learn, and there was an entire scope of the world I hadn't experienced at 26. While I was in Marion and in the hole he fed me books like a baby being spoon fed pureed blueberries. We read and discussed many books he suggested, including: *Secret Teachings of All Ages* by Manly P. Hall, *Imagination of the New Left* by George N. Katsiaficas, *Justine* and *Dialogue Between a Priest and a Dying Man* by the Marquise De Sade, *Tracking the Jackal* by David Yallop, *The Prince* by Niccolo Machiavelli, the Bhagavad Gita, *The Hundred Thousand Songs of Milarepa*, the Koran, the Torah, *Art of War*, and more subjects by Confucius, Thoreau, Keats, Kropotkin, Dostoevsky and more. He encouraged me to read these texts, and then afterward we exercised our critical thinking with long discussions about plot, theme, and philosophy.

"Joel, prisons are universities of crime maintained by the state," an obvious quote from Peter Kropotkin, one way of testing me on some recently read material or spoken material from him.

I had always had problems concentrating in school, even after a new diet had been prescribed for me many years earlier. Occasionally, I still had problems concentrating on certain tasks in prison. On a few occasions, I tried a small shot of instant coffee from Ghetto and it would seem to temporarily focus me on our topic of discussion. I used coffee very judiciously and would drink maybe a half of cup every couple of days. It seemed to help me to digest all the information I was learning from Ghetto. We would stay up into wee hours of the night discussing philosophy of the Marquise de Sade or the kill range of a Kalashnikov Dragunov sniper rifle. I wanted to learn everything all at once. One day I asked so many questions Ghetto retorted loudly,

"Joel, answering that would be like feeding a steak to a baby. Let's start with the basics first, but we will get there."

One night we were talking about guns. I learned about the myleesh, (russian pronunciation) for little boy the myleesh was a baby AK 47 the size of a machine pistol,

"It's a true killers gun Joel", Another interesting one was the FIE LAW 12 gauge semi automatic shotgun with a nine shot clip with tri burst, 3 shots fired for every one pull of the trigger, Ghetto assured me

"you could damn near cut a car in half with that one," or the Scorpion, a eastern bloc machine pistol

"Joel you could sew someones lips shut with that one." Ghetto was obviously well versed in planning and executing a robbery plot.

"Joel, the hardest part is to be ready to kill someone if they resist. We never plan on it, and try to avoid it like the plague. We are not killers, but we do kill and have to be prepared to do so without hesitation. For it is this hesitation, Joel, that permeates all other actions with the act and that can cost life."

"We had to blow the kneecaps off of one of those sorry sons of bitches once and he was still going for his gun. We got away without killing him. He got real lucky."

Ghetto assured me if I could not cross that mental threshold I would never make it as a big heist robber.

"even if I were robbing someone without guns," he maintained "you must be ready to kill, but only as a last resort."

He showed me an article about how the United States Postal Service was the largest transporter of money, more than equal to any and most all armored car services of the day and even today, The article was about how a post office outpost was hit and millions of dollars were stolen from unsuspecting and unarmed postal workers. No one was injured, and no one was ever prosecuted for the crime. I am sure Ghetto was the one who did it or directed people to do it. He taught me that when you get shot, even if you have a bulletproof vest on, that you go into shock and usually lose control of your bowels for a few days because of it. Ghetto told me how years before he escaped from FCI Talladega and robbed several banks while out on the run before they caught up to him in Miami, Florida.

I learned about how easy it would be to hijack a commercial plane at 35,000 feet. "Joel, if I can make a shank in my supermax prison cell, I could make a very sharp knife and killing instrument on a commercial flight within 90 minutes of takeoff. I assure you Joel, our air space is very vulnerable, and almost anyone could hijack an airplane The security is much higher in other countries because of guys like the Jackal."

I listened intently as I looked at a picture of an eastern European sniper sitting behind a Kalashnikov Dragunov sniper rifle, my birthday present from Ghetto.

New York is not safe either. Those buildings are very vulnerable to an air attack and so is Washington. Heck, you could easily take out any plane on the coast with a heat seeking portable rocket." We would drift around from military and criminal subjects to deep philosophy and what it really meant to be honorable.

The other benefit of being in the hole was the birds. The guards would leave the windows on the whole cell block open in the winter as a form of punishment, the cold air adding insult to injury. Most of us didn't mind though, because each morning the open windows brought us a gift from the free world. Here, in this hellish jail within a jail, full of men who'd forgotten what beauty looked like, what hope felt like, the world shared a glimpse of both with us. As if they knew this part of the prison was where their presence was most needed, each morning songbirds would flock to the windowsills of the hole and serenade us. It was such a gift to see and hear them celebrate life and their freedom.

One morning after recreation Ghetto and I were once again discussing philosophy, when two birds took roost on the sill. Both of us stopped to simply enjoy the presence of these two songbirds. I was taken away for a moment, enjoying the feeling of simple appreciation as they settled in a nearby window. I thought Ghetto was listening and watching them too, but it was confirmed when I heard his voice, hushed in reverence for this moment of peace, whisper "Free as a bird." In the silence of our cells, his words seemed to take form themselves and fly out the window to join the clear notes of the birds along the wind.

As I was peeking out the bars down the hallway I saw something that piqued my curiosity. A salt haired guard was creeping down the tier toward our cells. It was almost comical the way he had his beer belly hugged up against the wall, a look of concentration on his face. What on earth was he doing? He finally reached the edge of the sill, still out of sight of the birds who continued to chirp their duet. He reached around over the top of the window hugging his beer belly as tight as he could against the wall so as to not alarm the birds. A sudden sense of dread and horror filled me as I realized what his intention was, but before I could have let out a shout to intervene, he then grasped the top of the window and in one motion slammed down the window with immediate and brutal force. The chirping stopped instantly, but he did it again two more times for good measure. Now the only sound on the cellblock was the loud stinging sound of cold metal on metal slamming into each other. As he slammed the window I witnessed feathers puff out of the window and a jet of blood squirt to the floor. He laughed as he walked away and said, "Free no more! I am going to have sweaty sex with my wife tonight! HA HA HA!"

This moment stuck with me as the most sinister example of the cruelty of the guards during my entire time in prison, even more so than when they beat me mercilessly and coerced my signature onto forms admitting my guilt. I was overcome with sadness for the birds, but also for the guard. My sense of bewilderment for this person was soon overcome by a sense of gratitude and compassion, gratitude for me having a date that I could get out of this rather than being trapped by a life sentence, and compassion for that prison guard who obviously had committed himself to a life sentence here in Marion. I wondered about his home life; did he have a wife and kids? If so, was he capable of that cruelty toward people? Can any of the guards really escape the hatred for humanity that is drilled into them by this institution? Are they capable of compartmentalizing their cruelty? Do their children look up to them and model that behavior later in society? Pondering these questions instilled a sadness in me, and compassion for this man welled up inside of me. I said a prayer for him, and in that moment confirmed a question I didn't know I had about myself: I was still human. Years later, as part of my alcohol recovery program I would formally learn that saying a prayer for someone is the best antidote to remove or forego a resentment toward someone, and that resentments are a poison that destroys the serenity and sanity of the person holding them.

"Joel, he's a real winner!" Ghetto exclaimed in a tone showing clear disgust at the actions of the guard.

"I will say a prayer for him Ghetto."

"Joel was the green duffel bag worth it? What about that black lieutenant? Where do you think he is now?"

Ghetto loved to get me going, and this was Friday night. A little cup of coffee, and we'd be up all night.

"Your journey needed to lead to Marion. This was your destiny Joel."
"That green duffel bag and your smart mouth led you right to me Joel. First to get here to Marion and then to come to the hole right next to my cell. Joel, did you get the radio station tuned in yet? Where's Jerry Garcia Joel? Ha ha ha..."...

I had been in the hole almost four months so far. After the first three months in the hole the guards gave me my radio back. Ghetto was in the hole for the last 20 months under continued investigation and had his radio for a while. Ghetto knew it was Grateful Dead hour in Marion. I had written the local radio station a few weeks prior explaining some of my situation and asking them to play some live Grateful Dead. Ghetto knew the address by heart to all the local radio stations, or so he led me to believe. Most towns have a Grateful Dead hour or they're tuned in to a nationally syndicated one hosted by David Gans, called the Dead Hour. All the other prisons got some form of the Dead Hour just because where they were located. We were sure they were going to read my letter or mention me on the air, a huge security breach I would later learn.

They played a great live Grateful Dead concert and mentioned me by name and prison number with a strong dedication to me and "All the other fallen comrades living behind the walls of Marion."

I had asked for a specific date and time and although we were not sure we planned for it just the same. Twelve hours later on Saturday night the investigative lieutenant came to my cell scowling and yelling…

"Blaeser, you lose your radio for 90 days. That was a major fucking security breach. I could have your fucking ass. Cuff up and let us in to get it."

It was a small price to pay. I hadn't heard any Grateful Dead for many months and that was an epic show, one I did not see on my travels either.

"Thank you lieutenant. It's all good, I just needed to hear some Dead."

"Fucking hippies, never thought I would see one come through here."

My hair was still very long but I did not look like a hippie and had no tattoos at all. Someone connected to the prison must have heard the show or my name being announced. I wouldn't get my radio back for five more months. Every Friday they would play some Dead and I would always listen to it once I got my radio back.

"Well Joel, you've done it now," Ghetto bellowed out as the lieutenant walked off the tier. We laughed like drunks at the lieutenant. Ghetto had warned me when I sent the letter and it made perfectly good sense. After all this was the only level 6 federal prison.

Getting in trouble like this was always a badge of honor amongst convicts in Marion. Emotional support and general praise came from all cells on the tier when they took my radio. My face still showed signs of my beating from Marion prison guards Burns and Biesner.

It was impossible for men to be unaffected by forced isolation, and not every man's constitution could stand up to it. Being stuck in a tiny room for 23 hours a day, month after month, year after year, with no form of escape aside from sleep, and only yourself to keep you company forces your mind inward in ways that some couldn't cope with and at times I couldn't cope with.

I was not immune to the strains of self-analysis. There were days when I pinched myself, to ensure that this was in fact my reality. Sometimes when I woke up in the morning, it would take me a second to remember where I was, and how I got there. My mornings varied from waking confused, then taking in my surroundings with a momentarily crippling horror, to an immediate recognition and acceptance of my situation. Sometimes my time in Marion was speckled with surreal calmness; I became aware of peace for once in my life.

When my sentence for "getting into trouble in Marion" was over and I was allowed to leave the hole, I was glad, but I would dearly miss Ghetto and our caffeine-fueled late night discussions. Upon arriving at my assigned housing unit after leaving the hole, I met and quickly became friends with Bruce Pierce. Bruce was associated with "the order." In other words, he was a white supremacist, and a famous one at that. He was on television more than John Gotti was. If this was being a friend of the devil then so be it, I had to sur-vive. In this cell block all the whites had to stick together; there were only eight of us out of 48 inmates on the cell block. Knowing Bruce was a sort of currency that in the future could hurt me, or save my life. The environment I was in at that exact moment called for lots of currency if I wanted to stay alive. Aligning with Bruce Pierce was being in Rome, and doing like the Romans. It helped that he was in Bruce Lee shape but he was also a scholar and a gentleman to me. He taught me new martial arts fighting tactics. Ghetto had acquainted me with dim mak, the art of delivering secret strikes that cause your opponent to die or become ill, Bruce taught me secret moves he developed in

Marion, and passed covertly from convict to convict like an occult secret. Bruce would show me a couple of moves and I would practice in my cell at night. If he were to get into a conflict I was going to have to back him up. I was not asked to join any organization. The fact that we talked and he taught me things meant we rode together.

Bruce and I broached many subjects throughout our discussions. He truly believed in separate but equal with regards to race.

He was convicted of the murder of Jewish talk-show host Alan Berg. Bruce was also connected to large armored car heist in which none of the $3.5 million stolen was ever recovered. The robbery took place on a secluded stretch of highway in Ukiah, California. Bruce had a 252-year sentence and was very respected by all colors of convicts, and of course by the southern hillbilly guards.

Despite my affiliation with Bruce, I still got along with the majority of the others on the cellblock, including the leaders from the other races. As I had in all the other prisons I had served time in up to this point, I was amiable, friendly and more optimistic than most while still being humble. Miraculously, I started to make friends.

I was so happy to be out of the boxcars and the hole. I saw some familiar faces back in C block and a whole lot of new faces. My new neighbor was an acquaintance from months before named Death Row Gary. He had been on death row in Florida, (or so the story went) but the case had been overturned. He was initially busted for a bank robbery, and his girlfriend and her family members made incriminating statements to the police. Then, just before his trial, his girlfriend and two of her relatives were found dead, shot execution style on a beach in Florida, a very long way from his Indiana home. The murders were a death penalty case, but the majority of evidence at his trial was a jailhouse informant from Florida who was later discredited. He still had to do the federal time for the bank robbery. I've often wondered how he lured all of them down there, but that isn't something you ask about in prison. Or was Gary bullshitting me the way some convicts do? He had to do something really heinous to get here. No one talks about being guilty of something you barely got away with, despite the way it's portrayed in the media. He said as part of his deal, once the death penalty case was dismissed without prejudice (meaning they cannot retry it), he agreed to serve federal time on the alleged bank robbery. He even sported a small newspaper article chronicling the overturning of his death row conviction. I had no way of knowing if it was really him. There is every kind of con artist in prison for every reason.

I also made fast friends with Richie. He was a shorter man who, with his freckled face and friendly demeanor, resembled Paul Newman. He was a semi-truck driver who sold marijuana, and ended up getting caught with eight tons of his own product. He was from out east, but loved Green Bay, Wisconsin. We quickly became workout partners and typically would do the Marion prison workout that was passed down among the convicts in Marion over the prior decades. There were no weights in Marion, only a steel pull-up bar, so it was a combination of that, a sophisticated floor routine then running ten miles in about 80 minutes when we had outdoor recreation, (only on days they gave us extra time outside). Every day, Richie and I got stronger and had more endurance. This workout was what I had heard about in the other prisons, invented out of necessity, tried and proven by the hardest of hardcore convicts here in Marion.

There was a convict by the name of Alex. I started to get into long talks with him about the Koran, including fasting, diet, and prayer. He was disposed towards non-violence, but a true warrior nonetheless.

"Knowing when to be a politician and when to be a warrior is paramount to being a good leader Joel."

Alex was a great leader for his people. Soon after we met, I did my first three-day fast, just drinking water. It was amazing. By the third day, your senses are more acute than four days earlier when you started. I found out on my third full day during my morning yoga stretching I was much more limber than three days prior. Alex and I talked a lot about our diets. Alex would go on 14-day fasts with just water and a little juice. He was a staunch believer in the Nation of Islam, but not in a militant way.

Rodney Davis who came with me from Talladega was in C Unit as well. I never really knew him in Talladega. He was arrested when he was about 23 years old, and had 20 years. He was caught selling a kilo of powder cocaine to undercover DEA Agents. The crime of selling a kilo of cocaine with the federal government carries five years. The undercover agent convinced Rodney to show him how to "crack" it up. He put the kilo in a big pot of boiling water, added some baking soda, and voila! — Crack. He was facing 20 years with the same drug, and the same amount. The agents did this to try to put some pressure on Rodney to give up his connections, but to no avail. Rodney stood to be released from prison as soon as the crack law was going to be passed. He was understandably bitter towards the system. After all, now he would be getting out when he was 40.

None of the other prison guards ever messed with me after my beating. Sometimes Burns and Biesner would try to get me to lose my temper at them by taking my milk from my morning tray of food. But by now I had been there for over a year and had adjusted physically, mentally, and spiritually. I still followed the same morning routine as months before, yoga, deep breathing, and 32 ounces of water upon awakening. I read and tried to discuss with Bruce abstract concepts like the Nash equilibrium, Von Neuman's theory of games and economic behavior, or the theory of relativity in a state of nothingness. I made an entire wedding plan for my future bride, including a seven-song medley for the bride and I to dance to which featured three styles of dancing. I wrote a business plan for a radio and print media company.

I needed to keep my mind busy so that I didn't focus on the fact that my appeals were losing momentum. I had lost my direct appeal and the Supreme Court case appeal for my specific case that my case was held in abeyance too (Neal v UNITED STATES No. 94-9088). Somehow from somewhere, I had this deep knowing that I was only going to serve five years, a vision and feeling that was imbedded into my psyche the moment the jury found me guilty. Like an uncontrollable reaction to something, it was with me like the memory of my father, it just never left me and I could not shake it no matter how many appeals I lost or how bleak it looked. It then became through grooming and positive affirmation a strong unshakable feeling that overrode any doubt my mind would and did try to muster up along my prison journey. I had been in Marion a little over a year, and had been in prison for 49 months total. Being in your cell 23 hours a day made for a lot of examination of your mind, and a lot of meditating, imagining, and thinking. It was a beautiful thing in its own right. I had not lost my mind. I was growing spiritually, mentally, and physically. Some people that came to Marion with me from Talladega were totally losing their marbles, mumbling to themselves, and doing very off-the-wall stuff. Solitary confinement is not for the faint of heart, or weak of mind. Monks choose it. We didn't. Somehow I was able to be in complete acceptance of the situation, not forget where I was, and have gratitude for my life. I was forced to be there; however, probably similar to some of what Buddhist monks endure. I was finally becoming settled in my mind. I never achieved this state of serenity in life until I reached Marion. The prior 26 years, at best, were not even close. I was finally understanding beyond words or thoughts that less is more, and what it really meant to let go absolutely, forgiving all, living in the now, embracing each day with a refreshed enthusiasm, living each day to the fullest, and yes, still laughing everyday at least once. Leo on the first plane ride assured me if I laughed on average once a day I could leave prison sane. I had this certain kind of peace within myself. I didn't care about anything. I was neither happy nor sad. I was not fearful, cocky, or confident. I was an observer, and a observation being observed. I was not a saint and did have some bad days for after all, it was Marion. I really came to kn ow that my family and especially my mother were the ones doing really hard time in the suffering they would endure thinking of my situation.

"Beauty is truth, truth beauty," I remember writing in a letter. ("Ode on a Grecian Urn" by Keats of course Ghetto's all time favorite) Although I did not remember it at the time, Ghetto's teachings penetrated my psyche in more ways than I knew.

It was then that I saw the suffering my mother was going through over me being in prison. I would silently meditate for her well being. Freedom is a state of mind, and oh how sweet it was for the first time in my life…

I was moved yet again to another unit in Marion. I was going to miss James Doc Holiday, and some others on the last tier I was on. Doc and I had long discussions about the finer points of laws and federal rules of criminal procedure on a federal appellate level. He claimed he had won federal appeals before and was in prison for being part of one of the biggest crack cocaine empires ever.

Something did not seem right with this move. I just received a letter from my lawyer Kurt Phillips. There was a new law passed called the Safety Valve Law. There was a wide range of application to this law. It was very differently applied depending what circuit you were in. There was no doubt the Supreme Court would settle the inter-circuit conflict. The law was set up for people who were first time, nonviolent offenders. If the court deemed that they fit all the criteria under the law, it allowed sentencing judges to reduce the defendant's current sentence under the mandatory minimum; however, the defendant was required to give up all pertinent information in regards to his or her case. Some circuits found that if the defendant had no useful information or could not remember details of his or her case, this did not preclude the defendant from enjoying the benefits of this new law, as long as all other criteria were met: first time, non-violent criminal.

I was being remanded back by the appellate court for re-sentencing. Unknown to me at the time of the order by the appellate court, USP Marion filed a motion to my sentencing judge, trying to stop the transfer, saying I was too dangerous to be moved, and cited my so-called attack on staff (which was their cover for beating me). The judge rejected the motion. Because the court calendars were so full, my court date was set for an unknown date months away.

Kurt Phillips, the original lawyer Judge Bertelsman recommended at my sentencing for an appointed appellate attorney, was brought back in to represent me. Though we'd lost the direct appeal, and the case that mine was held in abeyance to in the Supreme Court, the Sixth Circuit of Appeals found that I was eligible under this new law to be re-sentenced;

however, it remanded me back to my trial and sentencing judge, Judge Bertelsman. Final determination was up to Judge Bertelsman. The prosecutor, Laura Voheers Klein would definitely weigh in on this as well. During all my conversations and letters with Kurt Phillips and his office, I always contended and stated that because of my trauma of being in prison, and because of the people I bought or sold LSD to, that I had no other useful information to give. The people I met had names like Tree Limb, Sunshine, etc, and I was always traveling and only met people once or twice at the most. Kurt urged me to stick to my story and not to worry on my last legal phone call to him before I left Marion to go back to court.

"I know the judge, Joel. Trust me" he said in a very confident tone.

"Ok, ok, Kurt."

It seemed very odd for him to say, and later I would learn what he meant by it.

Some of the circuits were refusing to apply any sentence reductions if defendants didn't substantially assist with new unknown information. I was not going to leave prison a rat. If I had to tell a white lie, so be it. I had been involved in very extreme situations. I watched as a building at FCI Talladega burned to the ground. I was brutally beaten by prison staff in USP Marion. In Florence I was forced to "hit" someone only to be saved by a eager guard wanting to go home a little early. My time in FCI Pekin almost got me a new charge of heroin trafficking and an additionalten years in prison. I currently lived in the worst, and most notorious federal prison, built for the most sophisticated and predacious, escape-risk convicts known to planet Earth. I would make it. I was not going to become a rat—not now. Part of me was forever hardened. Seeing another man getting stabbed to death, or seeing another race brutally beat down by one of its own touches you in a way that is indescribable. Your first instinct is to help them. The first time I saw something like that I had to fight it off with all I had to turn away and do nothing, otherwise you risk your own life right then and there, or later by your race's shot callers for getting involved in a conflict that you had no business being in, and thus jeopardizing your own race. Part of me also had this amazing and pure appreciation for the simple things in life. In prison, and today, ten toes and ten fingers always make the top three or four on my morning grateful list. Time is more valuable than anything, as anyone in a prison cell surely knows. After being in Marion, I understood why convicted felons could never own guns again. After being treated so harshly while living in a pit of evil, you have a greater propensity to kill. It made sense to me.

It was June of 1997. I had been in Marion for 21 months now, and I had served almost five years. It could be months before I was sent back to court. Because of the high-security nature of Marion, Kurt was ordered not to tell me specific dates.

After my phone call with Kurt, I ran into my old cell neighbor Gary out on the yard. He asked me if I got action back in court, and I cautiously confided in him about the Safety Valve Law and my chances. He said he asks a question of everyone who gets a shot at appeal or early release.

He looked me in the eye, and asked, "Will you ever come back here Joel?"

"I do not know, Gary. I do not want to come back," I said without hesitation. "I will try my hardest not to."

He patted me on the back and said, "Shit Joel you're only the third person that has ever said that to me in over twenty years."

"I am only the third person who has ever said that to you?"

"Listen here Joel. Everyone else says no, never, or I'm never coming back." He went on to tell me about people in that block, and all throughout his years in prison who have all been back one, two, and three times on probation violations or new charges.

"Don't worry, you'll do fine," he said.

"That is a humble way to look at things. After all, no one can predict the future.

"Wow thank you Gary."

There was this one peculiar incident right before I left Marion. One day I was moved to a cell furthest from the front of the unit. This new guy who was constantly mum-bling and talking to himself was moved right next to me the next day after I was just moved. It was about three weeks before I left for court, not that I knew that. I had no idea when I would go to court; the day they told you to pack it up is the day you leave.

About ten days after he arrived in our unit, we started talking. He said he had been in Marion for the last 11 years, and that he was tired of playing their games. I asked him to explain and he told me the prison staff had moved him into this unit so he could kill me before I left for my appeal. He said he wasn't going to play their game anymore and was not going to start anything. It was surreal. I was not scared, shocked, happy, or sad. I did not know whether he was just crazy, or they really had put him up to this in response to my re-marks about Tommy Silverstein, or both. Nothing surprised me at this point, and anything was possible. Within days after him telling me that, I was off to court.

I was on my way back to Covington, Kentucky. It was late July 1995, which meant I had served almost five years to the day when I left Marion. At the early hour of 5am they arranged for my transfer, most of the cell block was asleep. The marshals came just for me, so I alone was marched through the long front hall. I'd only seen it once, the very first time I'd came to Marion; a day so fraught with shock and mayhem that I'd forgotten most of the details. Looking at the first tendrils of morning light reflecting in the mirrored-checkered floor tiles flooded me with memories of our arrival almost 23 months prior. Then, the moment I'd dreamed of. The marshals led me right through the front doors. The gentle kiss of the fresh, cool morning breeze on my skin is a sensation that can never be surpassed.

Blondie just happened to be on duty the day I was leaving. As I stepped into the rear of the van, he leaned toward me and said softly. "If you ever come back here, we will kill you."

I found out later how hard they'd tried to keep me there. After my re-sentencing hearing had shown promise, Marion officials filed another motion to the district court to have me remanded back to Marion even if the judge wanted to release me immediately. The motion again referenced my attack of a guard while being taken back from a visit. They warned the court that I was a danger and not equipped to re-enter the real world. Marion officials requested that if I won my appeal, that I be sent back to Marion so they could "ready me" for freedom.

This kind of motion was unheard of. The judge and the prosecutor at my hearing asked me what happened regarding my time in Marion and with the guards, and informed me of the petition. Neither of them had ever heard of or seen such a motion get filed. The fact that Marion officials had the audacity to file a motion to the court in anticipation of me getting released could only mean something much more sinister. Fortunately for me, the judge and the prosecutor were not fooled by Marion's motion. Like a lot of things in Marion, the motion was daring and bold and in the end not successful.

I gave no outward response to Blondie's words that day, but inside I chuckled. His words were like a sprinkle of water on a duck's feather: They rolled right off of me. I had long since forgot, and let go of my resentment for prison guards Burns and Biesner for maliciously beating me, as well as the guard who'd killed those birds, and anyone else I could have held resentment for. I said a prayer for all of Marion, for all of the atrocities: Clutts and Hoffman getting killed by Clayton Fountain and Silverstein, as well as Ghetto, Doc Halliday, Bruce Pierce, Ritchie, people I'd met, and people I hadn't who'd been there and who would go there. Years later, and even today, I do not know how I was able to employ the technique of praying for someone, to let go of a resentment that I had for them.

After being out of prison for five or six years, my drinking and drug usage was affecting me spiritually, to the point of going into two separate and different drug rehabilitation centers, and eventually finding a non-profit 12 step self-help group with a 75-year-old road map for dealing with alcoholism. In all the personal work I've done, and continue to do to stay sober, what happened to me in prison has never been a subject in my writing, counseling, etc. All of it was left at Marion on that fateful morning until now.

The ride was bumpy and loud. Being alone I could sit anywhere and I sat on the flat stainless steel benches in the back of the armored van nearest the small windows. There were two tiny windows on either side of the van, but I didn't even bother looking out of them. I was too wrapped up thinking about my future; I had a real shot at freedom. I thought about all the people I had come into contact with while in prison. I thought about how long the prison sentences were for all the people in prison serving time for consensual crimes (drug trafficking) as opposed for non-consensual crimes (murder, sex trafficking, bank robbery). Why was I the lucky one?

I thought about all my lucky scrapes in prison with people, drugs, and staff. I had what they call "gambler's luck." My gambler's luck in life was far more than I'd ever had at a poker table. I was arrested at 23, now I was 28. I thought about my friend Tim Tyler, our travels with the Grateful Dead, and his double life federal prison sentence. Timmy was arrested for almost the same amount of LSD as myself, but had two minor prior felonies, and was serving a double life sentence in federal prison, and is going to die in prison. As the light grew stronger outside, my conversation with Gary looped in my head, like a record with a stuck handle: "I don't know if I am coming back. I am going to try not to."

I thought of the three people Gary shot execution-style on a beach in Florida. They were going to rat on him. How did he lure them down there? How did the government screw up his case in the state of Florida and release him from death row? Because of the main witness's testimony being tainted in another case. All these people's cases had stories. Suddenly I just said "Thank you," out loud, and had a feeling of gratefulness.

I finally arrived in Kentucky about three and a half weeks later. I had come from the new holdover facility in Oklahoma City where I'd had a cell all to myself. Because I'd come from Marion I was labeled as a super high-security risk. I met Brad, a Branch Davidian, there. He and I talked at great length about the whole Waco, Texas thing. He was a very down to earth person, and I could write a whole book just on our conversations. I got to recreate alone, but I still managed to interact with others. I had a different attitude. I tried to expect nothing; however, I had a real shot at freedom.

Once in Kentucky, I was ferried across the state and stayed in two county jails before I made it back to Covington County. Each sheriff that was in charge of me was always so intrigued by my story. They wanted to know how I survived Marion. What did I do to be sent there? What was Marion like? I was black-boxed the entire time. They were local sheriffs, rather than highly trained marshals, ferrying me from county to county, there were even two cars to transport me: one to carry me, and one to follow.

As we drove across the state, I noticed a lot of large billboards in Kentucky, put up by a local organizations to bring about support for the new proposed prison. They all advocated that it be put in "our county." I had only been in prison for five years and one month, but this seemed like a titanic turnabout from five years before. In 1992, there was massive public blowback against new prisons in Kentucky; people fighting not to have a prison built in their town or county, and now they were fighting to have them built. Apparently the realization of the prison business had hit the country.

CCA and now Wackenhut are the largest private prison contractors in the world. They have a large lobby today, and did in 1997 as well. The American Legislative Exchange Council or ALEC helped to lobby many three strikes laws throughout the entire country and keep these companies afloat under the guise of smaller government. Wackenhut is directly linked to Halliburton as far as getting government contracts, and money they spend on lobbying the U.S. government's war on drugs is a windfall for Wackenhut, who builds prisons and bills the state or federal government for each prisoner on a per day basis (on average $45,000-$55,000 per year per prisoner not counting cost to build the prison). They directly compete with the Bureau of Prisons and other state prisons for prisoners. It is now a business that Wall Street companies are involved in.

When I saw the sign, I thought it was an isolated incident, except when I got to that remote county jail that day in Kentucky. On the news was information on the lottery they held between two vying counties to see which one would "win" to get the new prison built in their county.

Once back in Covington, I had to be interviewed by the prosecutor, Laura Klein Voheers, her assistant, my lawyer, and J C, an undercover DEA Agent. When I came into the private room in the county jail, all they could talk about was Marion. Why was I there? What was it like there? The prosecutor was absolutely fascinated with Marion and the idea that me, a first-time, non-violent, smooth-skinned Grateful Deadhead defendant had ended up there. I had just cut my hair days before. I had it long very long. Over half the conversation was dominated by questions about Marion: me assaulting a guard in Marion, and how I got to Marion.

Under current law, now and then, any conduct that happens in prison can never be used with regards to issues on appeal in your criminal case. I took this to mean that I was going to have a favorable outcome.

Then there were a lot of questions about who I sold to, and who I bought from. I remembered Kurt telling me on the phone to stick to my guns, and I did. I did not give them any names. I kept reiterating that everyone I dealt with had names like Tree Limb, Daisy, Stone, Starlight, etc. I also said that after being brutalized in Marion, most of my memory was skewed at best.

Based on the previous 20 minutes of conversation with these people, and how intrigued they were with Marion, I didn't really think they were worried about me giving them information. At the end of the meeting, I got the feeling they were going to recommend the judge to apply the Safety Valve for my case. Ultimately, if they did not recommend it, the judge could still grant an application of the law, and since the Supreme Court still has not resolved the inter-circuit conflict regarding the application of the Safety Valve, it left some discretion as to interpretation.

My hearing was scheduled a few days later. I was on high-security status at the county jail they were holding me, which meant I had an interesting stay to say the least. They would not even give me a real toothbrush. Instead the "toothbrush" they supplied had a paper handle similar to a lollipop, and the brush was a perfectly cut round piece of semi-stiff sponge that barely brushed my teeth. The local sheriffs and jailers were treating me as if I was Hannibal Lecter because I came from Marion. One told me, "Blaeser! I can't let you buy commissary while you're here, you're still a high security risk." A county jail guard was stationed outside my cell for 24 hours a day, three shifts per day only leaving for bathroom breaks or to get a meal.

My mindset was a mixture of excitement, uncertainty, and annoyance. I walked at recreation, and started to embrace the fact that if I got a positive outcome at my hearing, I would be released that minute from court.

Prison was the furthest thing from my mind. The free world was knocking; however, that was a huge unknown—not something to be feared, but something to be cautious about. I would still have to find a job, and a place to live. As these thoughts crept in, I just continued to stay focused on whatever it was I was doing. Most of the time I would get into conversations with the other cell block prisoners. Most of them were going away for a long time, as they had just lost their trials or plead guilty, and were waiting for the bus to prison never-never land. They reveled with me in my shot at glory.

The day I left for court, I said goodbye and hoped not to return. County jails are very rough living conditions at best. The cells and recreation areas are smaller, they're dirtier, there is no standard for food (you usually get bologna for at least one meal a day), and they don't care what religion you are, so everyone eats the same.

The day before the hearing I had prepared a statement to say before the judge. I was in the holding cell at the federal courthouse in Covington, Kentucky with my appellate lawyer Kurt Phillips. As we were walking in Kurt smiled at me.

"Joel, you do not have to say anything Willy (Judge Bertelsman) and I went to law school together and I was his mentor," he remarked. It was an astonishing statement and I could still not comprehend what was really happening. I felt a ringing in my ears and dizziness in my body.

We all rose when Judge Bertelsman walked in and said hello to us.

"Hello, Judge Bertelsman," Laura Klein Voheers said.

"Hello, Judge Bertelsman," I said.

The judge addressed me as Mr. Blaeser, and the prosecutor as Mrs. Klein.

"Hello, Kurt," he said.

"How ya doin', Willy?" Kurt said.

The judge smiled and said "Just fine, thank you Kurt."

My brother Bradley and mother Rosemary were in the courtroom behind me. I looked back at my brother with an expression that read, did that just happen? "How you doing Willy?" My brother had this grin on his face. In all my years, I had never heard nor seen a lawyer address a judge by a nickname in such a friendly manner.

After the hearing, the prosecutor came into the holding area as I was signing all the release papers. I had not seen her since that night I was sentenced years before.

"You need to go drink a bottle and forget about this whole thing,"
As she said it, she motioned with her hand as if she was drinking from an upturned bottle. We both laughed and shared a mutual smile.

That evening, my brother, mother, and I stayed at a very nice hotel. The building was round, and on top of it was a restaurant that slowly spun around the city. Covington County Federal Courthouse was right across the river from Cincinnati. I ordered a Sam Adams and enjoyed a nice bison steak. After our meal, I decided to take a walk. My nose was overwhelmed with the smell of each car as it passed by. The smell of exhaust fumes was overwhelming. All the lighted signs up and down the street over stimulated my eyes. Then I turned down a boulevard lined with trees, just as the breeze picked up. The sound of the wind kissing the trees sounded like it never had before. My senses aroused as if I was hearing it all and smelling it all for the very first time. After that, I simply enjoyed the presence of all the people around me, walking around and talking to each other without a care in the world. It was almost surreal. I kissed the ground—it was great to have physical freedom again.

Within two weeks of me returning home back to Milwaukee, I received a package from Marion. It was my property—just some legal paperwork, and a book. Of all books I had purchased throughout the time I spent in Marion, most were given to some of my friends, but I kept a couple for myself. The rest were given away.

One week later, there was another package to arrive for me at 826 East Center, Milwaukee, Wisconsin. It was a very light package with no return address. All the paperwork and property I had in Marion that I had not given away was in the package I had received one week earlier. I found a scissors and started to cut open the tape holding the seams closed. I wondered who sent me something. Maybe someone was sending me something to help me get along now that I was back in the free world. What is it, I thought. Who sent it?

As I cut open the top and moved the flaps of the brown box open, I saw something dark. As I opened the other two flaps, I saw to my amazement and partial horror, the green duffel bag that Sparky made for me in the second prison I was at, FCI Englewood four years prior. My memory quickly ran through all six prisons I'd served time at. The face of the lieutenant who I'd had sworn at over the bag swam to the forefront of my mind. I was overcome with an immediate sense of gratefulness for being free. This sense and feeling dwarfed all initial feelings of horror and amazement. I could not help to feel a slight disgust for those who saved this green duffel bag for the last 25 months, only to send it to my new home. As quickly as I felt disgust, it turned to compassion. I said a prayer for all of those people working for the Bureau of Prisons and housed by them.

I was outside on my brother's deck at his art gallery One Nation at 826-east center street. It was around 11:00am on a warm October Day in 1997. The sun was shining in my face. I knew it was going to be another glorious day on East Center Street in the Riverwest neighborhood of Milwaukee.

God bless freedom I thought and said quietly to myself as I went about the day.

The End.
Peace and Love
Joel Blaeser

*(note, there is a link on my website, joelblaeser.com that leads to a intimate three part 27 minute video taking you deep into USP Marion, to see it, click on the red letters reading "Marion federal penitentiary" on the bottom of the aerial photo of Marion).

Author Statement

Most of the current federal and state drug laws by default and direct application act as a financial, spiritual, cultural and for 2.2 million inmates a physical hindrance of our god given human potential. Half of these 2.2 million American citizens are imprisoned because drugs are somehow related or tied to their crime, representing over 12% of the worlds prison population.

Our crime school prisons riddled with drugs do not rehabilitate and demonstrate the dire need for America to have the *legalize* discussion now.

When drugs are legalized, school kids in the inner city neighborhoods will become safer by not getting harassed at the bus stop on the way to school by the local crack dealer and suburban mothers will stop losing their sons and daughters to a over dose of intravenous heroin. Addicts seeking treatment or drugs will have safe access to them and not be the outcast current American society has them pegged to be. Billions will be saved from the annual 60-70 billion dollar American prison budget, (federal, state, and private prisons). Billions in new tax dollars will be created from the regulation of drug sales, and of course tens of thousands of long term jobs will materialize.

The recidivism rates for the American prison system inmate are high, state, federally and privately the system has averaged in some recent years as high as a 77% inmate return rate, (meaning that within 5 years of release there was a new felony charge, half of which on average were drug related). Since Pell grants have been restricted from prisoners in 1994, the U.S. prison population has risen over 100%.

When drugs are legalized like in other western countries such as Portugal, America will become safer, richer, more humane and less culturally oppressive to its own citizenry and hence all humans on planet Earth.

Visit and call your senators, congresswomen/men and like minded organizations, support them, help them until these unjust laws are changed forever........

I was released from court on 9-28-1997 and I have not been back to prison since, many speeding tickets but no felonies, and no alcohol since 12/29/03.